THE BEST PLACE TO BE

ALSO IN THE
History *of* Canada Series

THE BEST
PLACE TO BE

*Expo 67
and Its Time*

JOHN LOWNSBROUGH

General Editors:
MARGARET MacMILLAN
and ROBERT BOTHWELL

ALLEN LANE

ALLEN LANE
an imprint of Penguin Canada

Published by the Penguin Group
Penguin Group (Canada), 90 Eglinton Avenue East, Suite 700, Toronto, Ontario, Canada M4P 2Y3
(a division of Pearson Canada Inc.)
Penguin Group (USA) Inc., 375 Hudson Street, New York, New York 10014, U.S.A.
Penguin Books Ltd, 80 Strand, London WC2R 0RL, England
Penguin Ireland, 25 St Stephen's Green, Dublin 2, Ireland (a division of Penguin Books Ltd)
Penguin Group (Australia), 250 Camberwell Road, Camberwell, Victoria 3124, Australia
(a division of Pearson Australia Group Pty Ltd)
Penguin Books India Pvt Ltd, 11 Community Centre, Panchsheel Park, New Delhi – 110 017, India
Penguin Group (NZ), 67 Apollo Drive, Rosedale, Auckland 0632, New Zealand
(a division of Pearson New Zealand Ltd)
Penguin Books (South Africa) (Pty) Ltd, 24 Sturdee Avenue, Rosebank,
Johannesburg 2196, South Africa

Penguin Books Ltd, Registered Offices: 80 Strand, London WC2R 0RL, England

First published 2012

1 2 3 4 5 6 7 8 9 10 (RRD)

Copyright © John Lownsbrough, 2012

Excerpt from "It Sang What Was Hidden in Our Hearts," by Peter Desbarats,
published by *The Montreal Star*, October 30, 1967, used with permission.

All photos from the Library and Archives Canada/Canadian Corp. for the 1967 World
Exhibition are copyright © Government of Canaada and used with permission of the
Minister of Public Works and Government Services Canada (2012).

Manufactured in the U.S.A.

LIBRARY AND ARCHIVES CANADA CATALOGUING IN PUBLICATION

Lownsbrough, John
The best place to be : Expo 67 and its time / John Lownsbrough.

(The history of Canada)
Includes bibliographical references and index.
ISBN 978-0-670-06862-3

1. Expo 67 (Montréal, Québec)—History. 2. Québec (Province)—History—1960–.
3. Canada—History—20th century.
I. Title. II. Series: History of Canada (Toronto, Ont.)

T752 1967 B1.L69 2012   907.4'71428   C2012-900057-4

Visit the Penguin Canada website at **www.penguin.ca**

Special and corporate bulk purchase rates available; please see
www.penguin.ca/corporatesales or call 1-800-810-3104, ext. 2477.

ALWAYS LEARNING   PEARSON

For Margie and Bob

and

For Paul

and

To the memory of

Stewart and Gilbert Bagnani
June Callwood
Marnie de Kerckhove
Bob McDonald
Charles Oberdorf
Jay Scott
Eric Steiner
Penelope Waldie
Tordie and Jade Woods
and
Ethelwyn Zimmerman

CONTENTS

INTRODUCTION TO THE HISTORY OF CANADA SERIES

Canada, the world agrees, is a success story. We should never make the mistake, though, of thinking that it was easy or foreordained. At crucial moments during Canada's history, challenges had to be faced and choices made. Certain roads were taken and others were not. Imagine a Canada, indeed imagine a North America, where the French and not the British had won the Battle of the Plains of Abraham. Or imagine a world in which Canadians had decided to throw in their lot with the revolutionaries in the thirteen colonies.

This series looks at the making of Canada as an independent, self-governing nation. It includes works on key stages in the laying of the foundations as well as the crucial turning points between 1867 and the present that made the Canada we know today. It is about those defining moments when the course of Canadian history and the nature of Canada itself were oscillating. And it is about the human beings—heroic, flawed, wise, foolish, complex—who had to make decisions without knowing what the consequences might be.

We begin the series with the European presence in the eighteenth century—a presence that continues to shape our society today—and conclude it with an exploration of the strategic importance of the Canadian Arctic. We look at how the mass movements of peoples, whether Loyalists in the eighteenth century or Asians at the start of the twentieth, have profoundly influenced the nature of Canada. We also look at battles and their aftermaths: the Plains of Abraham, the 1866 Fenian raids, the German submarines in the St. Lawrence River during World War II. Political crises—the 1891 election that saw Sir John A. Macdonald battling Wilfrid Laurier; Pierre Trudeau's triumphant patriation of the Canadian Constitution—provide rich moments of storytelling. So, too, do the Expo 67 celebrations, which marked a time of soaring optimism and gave Canadians new confidence in themselves.

We have chosen these critical turning points partly because they are good stories in themselves but also because they show what Canada was like at particularly important junctures in its history. And to tell them, we have chosen Canada's best historians. Our authors are great storytellers who shine a spotlight on a different Canada, a Canada of the past, and illustrate links from then to now. We need to remember the roads that were taken—and the ones that were not. Our goal is to help our readers understand how we got from that past to this present.

Margaret MacMillan
Warden at St. Antony's College, Oxford

Robert Bothwell
May Gluskin Chair of Canadian History
University of Toronto

PROLOGUE:
ISLAND DAYS

Proud as peacocks
Ready to laugh
Quarrelsome as children
In this vast nursery
Even in anger
Loving each other—
And there wasn't a goddam thing in the whole country
That showed any of this.
Until we saw ourselves reflected
In the waters that ran like our own exuberance
In the river of our own excitement
That flowed like quicksilver
Under, around and throughout
The whole exhibition ...

—PETER DESBARATS, UPON THE CLOSING OF EXPO 67, OCTOBER 1967[1]

In the weeks and months that led up to the opening of the Universal and International World Exhibition in Montreal in April 1967, there was concern in certain quarters, if not consternation, that Canada had sorely overreached. That, Icarus-like, this costly and much touted exhibition would crash resoundingly to earth and, with it, the international reputation of its supremely eager-to-please host country.[2] One could only wonder what kind of magical thinking had contrived to situate a world's fair on specially created islands in the middle of the St. Lawrence River! Specially created islands, by the way, that as late as a week before the fair's April 28 opening still looked ragged and unfinished. The doubters and hand-wringers, well schooled in the lessons of colonial inferiority, could nod sadly among themselves and conclude it was a fine thing to dream big dreams. Ultimately, though, one ought to be reasonable and settle for the obtainable. Humanity's reach should definitely not exceed its grasp; to think otherwise seemed ... well, somehow almost un-Canadian. The Canadian way was about surviving, less so about prevailing. Such, at any rate, went a national stereotype and, over the decades and through many iterations of that theme, we Canadians tended to accept it as truth.

But then a funny thing happened.

Montreal's Universal and International World Exhibition—Expo 67, or just "Expo" as it became known—opened on the appointed day of April 28 and almost at once the mood of the country appeared to lift. This optimism was reflected in the country at large, yes—but especially among Montrealers, so thrilled for and proud of their city—the proudest, of course, being the city's irrepressible mayor, Jean Drapeau. And among other Quebecers, too, so recently in the thrall of the *grande noirceur* or "great darkness" of an era dominated by Quebec premier Maurice Duplessis, but now blooming with a newfound confidence in themselves and their future. Expo's arrival reminded us it was all right to dream big dreams.

Canada, Quebec, Montreal, all changed in their particular ways. Some changes proved transitory, but for those around at the time, and perhaps especially for those coming of age, Expo became a touchstone event. It was a metaphor for a myriad of hopes and aspirations that could dovetail into a collective pride at the success of the exhibition, the crown jewel of the celebrations marking Canada's hundredth birthday.

And clearly from even its early days, Expo *was* a success; it would not require a run of six months or 185 days for the world to reach that conclusion. It seemed that, early on, commentators started to refer to the "magic" islands of Expo 67—a description that, to an understating and skeptical Canadian sensibility, could have seemed a trifle cloying.[3] But not that year, I think.

That year, perhaps for the first time in many of our lives, we felt comfortable with hyperbole.

"HOW AFTER SPONSORING this World's Fair can we ever be the same again?" wondered author and columnist Peter C. Newman. "This is the greatest thing we have ever done as a nation (including the building of the CPR) and surely the modernization of Canada—of its skylines, of its tastes, its style, its institutions—will be dated from this occasion and from this fair ... It's a wow of a fair. It's fabulous. It's the sun and the moon and the stars ... And the more you see of it, the more you're overwhelmed by a feeling that if this is possible, that if this little sub-arctic, self-obsessed country of twenty million people can put on this kind of show, then it can do almost anything."[4] No less overcome was fellow Canadian author and journalist Pierre Berton. In a book he later wrote about the year 1967, Berton devoted one section to Expo: "When I covered Expo for *Maclean's*, I confessed in print that 'I feel captive to an unexpected emotion: a moistness in the eyes and a huskiness in the throat of the kind one usually experiences only in moments of national stress ... It was nationalism unabashed and I discovered later that others had felt it too.' ... Expo obsessed me. I made five trips to the fair, including a stay in Habitat and another memorable week parked in a boat at the marina with my family... At Expo we were all children, wide-eyed, titillated by the shock of the new, scampering from one outrageous pavilion to the next, our spirits lifted by the sense of gaiety, grace, and good humour that these memorable structures expressed."[5]

Novelist Mordecai Richler, a Montreal native who sought—and found—bigger opportunities in England but was then poised to make his return to Canada, thought otherwise. Perhaps his expatriate-soon-to-be-repatriated status kept Richler from being swept up in the general tide of huzzahs and hosanas. He cast a rather baleful eye on those people "demanding an alarmingly high emotional return from what is after all only a world's fair. A good one, maybe even the most enjoyable one ever. However, within it there lies merely the stuff of a future nostalgic musical, not the myth out of which a nation is forged. Unless it is to be a Good Taste Disneyland."[6]

The "Good Taste Disneyland" that was Expo 67 occupied roughly four hundred hectares that comprised two islands in the St. Lawrence as well as the Mackay Pier peninsula, renamed Cité du Havre, along Montreal's harbourfront. One of the islands, Île Ste. Hélène, had to be significantly enlarged; the other, Île Notre Dame, was an entirely new creation.

The islands signified a major technological and engineering feat, the product of millions of tonnes of fill dredged from both the river and the islands themselves, as well as from the tunnelling that accompanied the construction of Montreal's Métro, the new subway system, and from the flotsam thrown up in the building of new highways expected to bring American visitors to Quebec. Those who lived in Montreal at that time recall the low hum of the constant stream of trucks, loaded with fill, rumbling through the city streets en route to the bridges that would lead them to their island destinations. Back and forth, back and forth, for months. And this was only the preliminary work; the shaping and the building and the landscaping came afterwards.

Expo was what the International Bureau of Exhibitions, the world body formed in 1928 to regulate such exhibitions, termed a "Category One" exhibition. (The commonly used acronym for the bureau is BIE, from the French Bureau International des Expositions.) The Category One designation meant, among other things, that foreign nations who participated were expected to build their own pavilions. It was a matter of some prestige to be a Category One. There had not been many. The first was the Paris exhibition of 1937, but then a world war meant the next was not until the Brussels World's Fair of 1958. Then came Expo, the first Category One to be held in North America.[7] Its predecessor, the New York World's Fair of 1964–65 did not receive this BIE sanction, a fact that Expo movers and shakers were quick to note.[8]

Actually, Expo was intended as the anti–New York model, the latter deemed far too crass and commercial—a Bad Taste Disneyland. Moreover, the Expo movers and shakers did not appreciate this word "fair." To them, Expo would be different, not a commercial marketplace but rather an international exhibition dealing with ideals and values.

From the outset, Expo aimed to be a breed apart. Its title, Man and His World/*Terre des Hommes*, derived from the 1939 novel *Terre des hommes* by the French aviator and author Antoine de Saint-Exupéry, best known today for his whimsical fable *The Little Prince*. "To be a man," wrote Saint-Exupéry, "is to be responsible, to feel that by placing one's own stone, one contributes to building the world." In this vein, Expo would be a celebration of man and his endeavours and a reminder of the common ties among all men. "Unity through diversity" became its mantra. (Nowadays, this "man"-centric terminology can grate a little, but in 1967 we remained innocent of such concepts as feminism, identity politics and political correctness.) Expo's humanist emphasis mitigated the more traditional uses of a world's fair as excuses for nationalist flag-waving and showing off industrial and technological prowess. And while its field of vision certainly focused on a future more utopian than dystopic, Expo, in its sober-sided way, not infrequently invoked a critical spirit, posing questions about the moral responsibilities incumbent on this human creature it meant to celebrate. The future, in other words, might be rosy or bleak—the outcome depended on how man made use of his talents and resources.

Not that Expo managed to completely avoid the traditional trappings of nationalism or the tendency to brag about technological advances; these are, after all, an integral part of a world's fair. Their continued presence, though, scarcely diminishes the exhibition's actual achievement. In addition to the sixty-one nations participating with their own pavilions—a record number at that time—pavilion representation from Canadian provinces and American states, the private and corporate pavilions, and an amusement park called La Ronde, there were theme pavilions in which the Canadian Corporation for the 1967 World Exhibition (CCWE)—the federal government entity that ran Expo—had invested forty million dollars. And located at the easterly end of Cité du Havre stood Habitat 67, the innovative architectural experiment in urban design by twenty-nine-year-old Moshe Safdie, whose McGill University master's thesis provided its inspiration. A visitor would notice the Dominion Bridge crane poised beside Habitat, a testimonial to a work evidently still in progress. In fact, Habitat's history had been a particularly tortuous one. But in the initial weeks and months after Expo's opening, the talk not surprisingly tended to ignore the negative and accentuate the positive. Besides, Habitat immediately captured the public imagination. There seemed a growing consensus that Safdie's Habitat and the geodesic dome, or "Skybreak Bubble," that R. Buckminster Fuller designed as the United States of America Pavilion were Expo's two most iconic structures.

So many innovative examples of architecture, of all shapes and sizes, presented themselves: structures with flat roofs, curving roofs, roofs that resembled tents. So much of it avowedly, almost giddily, futuristic. "Expo 67 made you feel like you were strolling the streets of the capital city on Eminiar VII," one *Star Trek* fan recalled many years later on his blog site.[9] The French newspaper *Le Figaro* described Expo as "*la plus gigantesque Exposition de tout les temps*," while its counterpart *Le Monde* enthused about this "*Venise futuriste.*"[10]

The doyenne of architecture critics, Ada Louise Huxtable, declared in *The New York Times*, "Expo is a fun fair, the fairgoers fair, and the professionals fair. It has substance and style. Many of the details will be collected by architects, planners and designers the way wine fanciers

savor their vintages." She went on to praise the quality and sophistication of the exhibition, calling it "a six-month miracle [that] almost defies
description."[11]

FOR ALL THIS SOPHISTICATION on display, there was also, in the parlance
of an earlier time, something slightly "square" about the earnestness of
Expo and its message. That earnestness, though, jibed with a sensibility
that marked the changing and increasingly tumultuous period in history.
It came along just as many baby boomers—the Expo generation—came
of age. The generational shift was profound. In the Canada of 1967,
nearly half the population was under the age of twenty-five. The year
1967 also signified a crucial demographic dividing line: the baby boom
had formally ended and the birth rate in the centennial year was the
lowest that had ever been recorded. Many in the boomer cohort were
attending university, and the universities would function as a crucible
for the social upheavals about to take place in Canada.

In 1951, only one in twenty eighteen-year-olds continued on to
university; by the mid-sixties, the ratio had become one in ten. These
were the children of the affluent post–World War II years and many now
rejected what they regarded as the stifling and materialistic values of
their parents. "The twin evils of bureaucracy and technocracy were the
primary agents suppressing individuality, emotion, and humanity," noted
historian Doug Owram. "The opposites were thus established—the cold,
impersonal, exclusionist, and inhuman rationalism of the technocracy,
and the humanity, satisfaction, and inclusiveness of a reformed society."
Owram concluded this thought with a citation from a draft statement
of the aims and principles of the Company of Young Canadians, a 1967
initiative of the federal government designed to channel the energies of
youthful idealism in the manner of the Peace Corps in the United States:
"We yearn for a world in which man is at the centre of his man-made
universe"—a sentiment distinctly echoed in the language of Expo 67's
mission statement.[12]

A SNAPSHOT OF THE YEAR 1967 would include the ways the Cold War was exerting its alarming and brutal influences, not the least of which was the threat of nuclear annihilation. (The 1962 Cuban Missile Crisis offered a forceful reminder of this threat.) The rise of liberation theology signalled a newer phenomenon: national independence movements in developing countries. In the cauldron of Vietnam, the Cold War and liberation theology met, with spectacularly tragic results. That summer, America's cities ignited in race riots and the Middle East became a tinderbox, while in mainland (or what was then called "Red") China, Mao Zedong's Cultural Revolution continued its reign of terror.

Meanwhile, Indonesia decided to ban that trinity of decadent Western influences—the miniskirt, the Beatles, and James Bond.[13] Though even here, history, like a great river's relentless flow, demonstrated that nothing is as constant as change. There was already talk of the Beatles going their separate ways; the actor Sean Connery wanted out as agent 007; and the miniskirt—well, it went up and down and drove the prognosticators wild with anticipation. "Anything is in fashion as long as it's 12 inches above the knee," declared fashion guru Rudi Gernreich.[14]

Expo occurred as the "Age of Aquarius" dawned—the musical *Hair* opened in fall 1967 in New York—and even the politicians tried to demonstrate they were "with it." Prime Minister Lester B. Pearson, for instance, referred to "the psychedelic experience of Expo and other exciting Centennial achievements."[15] This was a time of "ins": sit-ins, love-ins, be-ins. A time when certain other phrases crept into the vernacular: "generation gap"; "do your own thing"; "participatory democracy." Not to mention the injunction to "never trust anyone over thirty." Sex, drugs and rock and roll fuelled the generational divide, but, as Doug Owram observed, "The infrastructure of the youth rebellion was in place long before the youth knew they wanted to rebel."[16]

For the most part, we in Canada came late to the party. We watched as our contemporaries in the United States marched in protest against their institutions of higher learning or the social injustices of racism or a war in South East Asia for which less-advantaged Americans always seemed the first to be drafted. The civil rights movement in the United States provided invaluable training in tactics and strategy for those opposing the war in Vietnam, as well as for those starting to challenge other aspects of an oppressive status quo.

On our side of the border, the nearest we came to some big idealistic cause was *la Révolution tranquille* or Quiet Revolution in Quebec. The death of the tyrannical premier Maurice Duplessis in September 1959 had opened the floodgates, and a Liberal government led by Jean Lesage ushered in a period of radical social transformation. Quebec's education system was revamped and removed from the exclusive control of the Roman Catholic Church; community colleges, or "CÉGEPs" (*Collèges d'enseignement général et professionel*/Colleges of General and Professional Education), opened doors for those hitherto deprived of the chance for higher learning and career advancement. The province's hydroelectric power was nationalized under then energy minister René Lévesque, a political figure for whom the year 1967 marked a turning point. *Maîtres chez nous,* Masters in our own house, Quebec for Quebecers, became the rallying cry. To achieve that goal meant an overhaul to drag the province into the modern age. It meant running to catch up.

The six years (1960–66) of Lesage's rule was a period of intense change—perhaps too intense for some, as Daniel Johnson's Union Nationale party defeated Lesage's Liberals late in 1966. Yet there was no returning to the so-called Dark Ages. Moreover, Johnson, like Lesage, was determined to assert a more autonomous role for Quebec within the framework of Confederation. "It is now clear to all of us, I think, that French-speaking Canadians are determined to become directors of their economic and cultural destiny in their own changed and changing society," then-Liberal opposition leader Lester B. Pearson declared in a speech to the House of Commons in December 1962.[17]

Certain Quebecers, however, did not believe in half-measures. They demanded independence. These separatists, still thought to be few, had become increasingly vocal. Rhetoric eventually gave way to violence, and in April 1963, a night watchman named William O'Neil was killed when a bomb went off in the army recruiting office where he worked in Montreal. A month later, seventeen bombs exploded in mailboxes in Westmount (a wealthy anglophone residential neighbour-hood in Montreal). The next year, a visit by Queen Elizabeth to Quebec City involved several tense moments, including an ugly confrontation between protesters and police. And as the date of Expo's opening approached, concerns mounted about the threat of terrorism. Yet, as the opening drew nearer, some saw reasons for at least a guarded optimism. "The death of night watchman O'Neil on April 20th 1963 was a turning point," wrote Wendy Michener in *Saturday Night* in January 1967. "Expo [is] providing an incentive to make things better in one hell of a hurry, and every improvement weaken[s] the case for violence."[18]

MARSHALL MCLUHAN, communications sage and newly minted Canadian celebrity, would famously observe in the early sixties that the world was becoming a "global village." As the host for Expo 67, Montreal, which politician and broadcaster René Lévesque called a "metropolis with the soul of a sunny village,[19] thus became the epicentre of this global village. And at the epicentre of that epicentre, one found Pierre Dupuy, ever the optimist, the believer in clear skies when everyone else concen-trated on the dark clouds. At nearly seventy-one years old, Dupuy was a distinguished diplomat now capping his career as the commis-sioner general of Expo 67, its highest official and his country's leading representative at this international event. (Each participating national pavilion boasted its own commissioner general.) Dupuy was cultivated, old school, a smoothie who had plied his smoothie ways in world capitals for years. His morning coat and striped pants seemed a second skin. His grey moustache was impeccable. His prodigious energy was matched by his prodigious network of international contacts. Pierre Dupuy thrived on pomp and circumstance, and his palpable enjoyment of the grand occasion could be infectious. Or not. Sometimes his manner got up people's noses. Even the naysayers, though, conceded him to be a dynamo. Fastidiousness certainly played a role in his insistence that, before the official public opening on April 28, Expo hold a preview opening for a select list of seven thousand dignitaries. For Dupuy, the preview ceremony seemed prudent; he had nightmare visions of too great a crowd thronging Place des Nations, the official greeting area situated on Île Ste. Hélène.[20]

So, following a luncheon for a select few of the select few held at the Pavillon d'Honneur (the island's Hélène de Champlain restaurant now become the hospitality centre for the visiting notables), Dupuy and company made their way over to Place des Nations. At the luncheon, Dupuy became reacquainted with Roland Michener, an old friend who, ten days earlier, had succeeded the recently deceased Georges Vanier as Canada's governor general. The new governor general and Mrs. Michener, along with Commissioner General Dupuy, arrived at Place des Nations in a horse-drawn carriage. One newspaper described the governor general and Dupuy as walking in slow step, "their faces solemn, their black hats firmly on their heads. They looked as if they were dressed for a formal state occasion rather than the opening of a gay, colourful world exhibition." The same reporter noted that Montreal mayor Jean Drapeau received warm applause on his arrival and "in true Drapeau fashion" raised his right hand, smiled broadly and waved at the crowd. Drapeau managed to upstage Quebec Premier Daniel Johnson, whose arrival occurred before the applause for the mayor died down.

Politicians, diplomats, judges, personalities from the arts and sciences and the professions, all were represented that day at Place des Nations. The widow of author-aviator Antoine de Saint-Exupéry was there, as was Paul-Émile Cardinal Léger, who occupied a front-row seat, as did federal opposition leader John Diefenbaker. (Lester Pearson's Liberals first bested Diefenbaker's Progressive Conservatives in April 1963 and now presided in somewhat precarious fashion over another Liberal minority government.) Former Liberal prime minister Louis St. Laurent received an escort to his seat, and when his neighbours in the stands realized who he was, they offered him a round of applause. Dupuy's optimism about the weather was generally borne out. Yet while it did not rain, wind off the St. Lawrence River made for a distinctly chilly afternoon. Some of the invited guests endured a three-hour wait before the ceremonies began. Several of the 235 Expo hostesses, the attractive and multilingual squadron of young women hired as official guides and greeters, donned their official white vinyl Michel Robichaud–designed coats to stay warm. Later, when they removed them, it was observed the vinyl on some of the coats had noticeably cracked.[21]

Dupuy led off the speeches. He was followed, in order, by Mayor Drapeau, Premier Johnson, Prime Minister Pearson, and Governor General Michener. Jean Drapeau spoke of Expo as one more instance of Montrealers rising to meet great challenges. "There were as many challenges as there were trees when our ancestors set foot in this country," he declared. The prime minister called it "a proud day for Montreal, for Quebec and above all, for Canada. By the time the gates of Expo are closed six months from now, its success will have made all Canadians prouder of our own country than ever before, and more conscious of the interdependence and the brotherhood of all men and all nations."[22] Following the speeches, a cadet carried the Expo torch to the front of the reviewing stand. Dupuy called out the names of the participating nations and, as each name was called, Boy Scouts unfurled that country's flag. Some flags unfurled better than others. Britain's Union Jack, for instance, emerged at the top of the pole upside down, an orientation that traditionally served as a distress signal! Then the moment arrived for Prime Minister Pearson to take the torch and light the Expo flame (after two attempts) that was to burn in Place des Nations until the exhibition's closing at the end of October.

The governor general declared, first in French and then in English, Expo to be officially open. Soon, nine Golden Centennaire RCAF jets were swooping low over the Expo islands and the city, while there erupted a cacophony of cannon fire and fireworks and sirens and church bells. "*C'est une explosion de bruits, de joie et d'émotion,*" Dupuy later wrote in his memoir of Expo. "*La cérémonie est terminée.*"

The preview ceremony may have ended, but Expo 67 had just begun, and with it a new chapter in the history of a country and a city. What follows is a chronicle of the event and the period in which it occurred. The hope is that those who remember Expo will become reacquainted with the excitement and, yes, magic of that period. And for those born later, perhaps they'll get a better idea of what all the fuss was about.

ONE

In at the Creation

By the time Expo opened, Montreal was a very changed place from what it had been only several years before. Looking across the St. Lawrence from the islands of Expo, the spectator surveyed a skyline where new skyscrapers designed by some of the foremost names in architecture now stood triumphant before the forests of Mount Royal. Place Ville Marie. Place des Arts. Montreal had undergone a profound physical metamorphosis and Expo 67 accelerated that phenomenon. It was a transformation much more than a facelift, a kind of rebirth. And it was altogether appropriate for what was then Canada's premier city, the "Paris of North America."

Established by de Maisonneuve in 1642 as the settlement of Ville Marie, Montreal owed its ascendancy primarily to its favoured geographical situation at the junction of the three major routes into the continent's interior: the St. Lawrence, Ottawa and Richelieu Rivers. As well, its location at the gateway of those rapids seemed to promise that one day further exploration would lead, so the wisdom of the time had it, to the Orient, the Grand Cathay. Which explains why the rapids and the canal later built to navigate through them came to be named "Lachine" or "China."[1]

Montreal is an island city, a river city, where the mighty St. Lawrence occupies its own special place in the popular imagination. Historian Donald Creighton spoke of "that instinct for grandeur, that vertigo of ambition, that was part of the enchantment of the St. Lawrence."[2]

"Where the Ottawa and the St. Lawrence meet, at Lac des Deux Montagnes and Lac Saint-Louis, they gradually invest and surround four islands, Île Perrot in the west, to the north small Île Bizard and big Île Jesus, in the centre and east the island of Montreal itself, a northern Venice," wrote author and native son Hugh Hood. "There are rivers and canals and bridges—my God, the dozens of bridges—all over the place. Though you may live in the centre of town and go to work for twenty years up and down the same bus line, without a glimpse of water, you can't help sensing it all around you. It's no accident that the big river has a saint's name; there's something godlike about the rivers ..."[3]

Montreal became the major shipping port of Canada and nexus of its business life, the mercantile spirit of the city intermixed with its religious and missionary roots. One year, the devout de Maisonneuve vowed to carry a wooden cross to the top of Mount Royal in supplication if God spared the settlement a likely flooding. When the waters of the St. Lawrence subsided, de Maisonneuve kept his promise and carried the wooden cross to the top of Mount Royal, where it remained until replaced by an illuminated cross donated in 1924 by the Saint-Jean-Baptiste Society.[4]

Montreal lore includes not just the Cartiers and Champlains, the Mances, Dollards and Le Moynes, but also the fur traders and merchant princes, entrepreneurs with names like Frobisher and McTavish, McGillivray and McGill. The Molsons seemed to be into everything: breweries, steamboats, railways, banks and hotels. That 1967 also happened to commemorate the 325th anniversary of the city's founding carried for many Montrealers greater resonance than any national centennial celebrations. They could be proud of their storied past and confident about their future. Never mind Toronto's growing importance as a financial centre and, thanks to the completion of the St. Lawrence Seaway, a rival port. Toronto was dull and lacked style (its new city hall excepted). Never mind that the Toronto Maple Leafs would somehow best the fabled Montreal Canadiens to win the Stanley Cup in May that year (though this proved not to be a harbinger of things to come). With Expo as its focal point, no one doubted that in the year 1967, Montreal was the best place to be.

Montreal's world exhibition was the second of its size and type since World War II, the first being the Brussels World's Fair held in 1958. There the emphasis had been on science—a brave new world as seen through the prism of the Cold War. The Soviets showed off their Sputnik space capsule. The Americans displayed the IBM electronic brain, RAMAC. The first public demonstration of the nuclear fission that brought the war in the Pacific to an end thirteen years earlier had occurred there. The iconic structure of the Brussels fair was the Atomium, a building that represented an iron molecule magnified 165 million times. A big success, Brussels attracted forty-two million visits. And it was at Brussels, on August 25, 1958, that Progressive Conservative senator Mark Drouin suggested publicly what a great idea it would be if Canada celebrated its hundredth birthday in 1967 as the host of such a world exhibition.

Drouin was in Brussels as part of a Canadian delegation that included Pierre Sévigny. Sévigny, a decorated war hero, was then associate defence minister in the Progressive Conservative government of John Diefenbaker, as well as Diefenbaker's Quebec lieutenant. Both Sévigny and Drouin were among the earliest advocates for the event that became Expo 67. Sévigny, in fact, was meant to hold the Brussels press conference and declare that ambition himself, but a case of the flu sidelined him and the honours fell to Drouin.[5]

In February 1957, Sévigny's cousin Louis Tassé had paid him a visit in the company of one Louis-Alphonse Barthe.[6] Barthe was a promoter and organizer whose area of expertise was circus-like fairs that he mounted across Canada. Barthe had previously discussed with former prime minister Louis St. Laurent the idea of government sponsorship of such a fair to celebrate the centennial, but had been turned down. He now tried again, but with the added pitch that such a fair could boost Tory hopes of electing Quebec MPs.

According to his widow, Sévigny was, at best, lukewarm on the idea and not all that keen on the concept of a world's fair in Montreal.[7] Corinne Sévigny took him to task. The idea intrigued her, though not the circus-like aspect; the fair she had in mind would be grander, "the greatest fair the world had ever seen." She recognized its political potential. The profile of the Progressive Conservative Party in Quebec was "zero," she admonished her husband; he should move on it. He did. "The next thing I know," she says, "he's taken it to Ottawa and Diefenbaker." Diefenbaker, according to Corinne Sévigny, was fine with the concept "as long as it doesn't cost us much." She says of Diefenbaker: "I was scared to death, because he could lose his temper ... He was tough. He was not thoughtful of people. I don't think he really liked people very much ... I don't know how Pierre stayed as long as he did—and Diefenbaker was very jealous of Pierre because he could speak so well."[8]

Barthe soon disappeared from the picture and Sévigny was deputed by Diefenbaker to line up the support of Quebec Premier Maurice Duplessis, the wily and controlling eminence in a province he treated as his fiefdom. Duplessis saw the plan's advantages, too, but counselled Sévigny that the latter needed the support of Montreal's mayor Jean Drapeau.[9] Drapeau, though, resisted the siren call. Anglophones would insist everything be in English, he thought, and having recently won the mayoralty after a highly publicized campaign against organized crime in Montreal, Drapeau expressed misgivings as well about Mafia infiltration of the project.

A dejected Sévigny relayed the news to a furious Premier Duplessis, who vowed to do all he could to defeat Drapeau in the next mayoralty election. He succeeded. Liberal senator Sarto Fournier, generally regarded as a yes-man of Duplessis, became Montreal's new mayor. The stars aligned. Diefenbaker, Duplessis and Fournier (also a good friend of Diefenbaker) all supported a fair. The next step was for Sévigny, Drouin and William Hamilton, the only Montreal MP in the federal government, to make a pilgrimage to Paris to consult International Bureau of Exhibitions president Léon Baréty on the procedures necessary to apply to hold a world exhibition. From there they moved on to the fair in Brussels, where Sévigny fell ill and the affable "Beau Mark" Drouin got to make the big announcement.

"A very good-looking boy," says Corinne Sévigny of Drouin, "and he knew it."[10] The widow of Pierre Sévigny is a formidable woman who, to this day, remains indignant that her late husband's pioneering efforts in the cause of Expo were overlooked later on. That they were probably had something to do with Sévigny's involvement with the East German–born prostitute (and possible spy) Gerda Munsinger, cynosure of what became known as the Munsinger Affair, a sex scandal raising questions about national security that broke in 1966.

By February 1960, intentions had become fact: Montreal would indeed seek to host the 1967 world exhibition. This was not its first attempt. World War I had doomed an earlier plan by Senator Rodolphe Lemieux for Montreal to celebrate its 275th birthday, as well as Canada's fiftieth, in 1917. In 1937, Montreal mayor Adhémar Raynaud suggested an international exhibition to commemorate the city's tercentenary. Bad timing again: another world war intervened.[11]

The world's fair format really began with the Crystal Palace Exhibition—symbolized by Joseph Paxton's iron-and-glass structure of that name—in London's Hyde Park in 1851. Canadian colonials saw to it that they were duly represented there, a flattering profile mandatory in light of the unpleasantness two years earlier, when irate citizens burned down the Parliament buildings in Montreal to protest a bill they viewed as compensating French-Canadian rebels in the troubles of 1837–38.

A trend had begun. World's fairs became a useful vehicle by which countries might trumpet their prowess in industry, manufacturing and science; eventually greater prominence was accorded artistic and cultural pursuits as well.[12] In essence, a world's fair offered the host nation the chance to billboard its own wonderfulness. And the great fairs left their mark. When New York hosted its fair in 1853, it, too, built a crystal palace. Even non-hosts sought to keep up with the latest fashion: though not hosting a fair, Montreal decided to build its own crystal palace in 1860, at the corner of Saint Catherine and Peel Streets.[13]

The Centennial Exposition of 1876 took place in Philadelphia, and among the new inventions introduced to its visitors were the typewriter, Alexander Graham Bell's earphones, Thomas Edison's telegraph and the sewing machine.[14] The 1889 Exposition Universelle in Paris marked the centenary of the French Revolution and, for the occasion, the French erected certain structures they intended as permanent, not least the 324-metre-high Eiffel Tower, whose symbolic and aesthetic impact haunted exhibition planners thereafter. There persisted, for want of a better term, a certain tower envy among planners. The backers of the 1901 Pan-American Exposition in Buffalo, for instance, employed as their main attraction the 119-metre-high Electric Tower, festooned with thirty-five thousand lightbulbs—though this fair is remembered not for any tower but for the unfortunate U.S. president William McKinley being assassinated during a reception at the Temple of Music there.

Earlier, the 1893 Chicago Columbian Exposition, the World's Fair marking the four hundredth anniversary of the discovery of the Americas by Christopher Columbus, eschewed this tower envy and managed to have an enormous cultural impact anyway, primarily because of its white plaster neo-classical architecture—the "White City" it was called—but in so many other ways as well. For some, the White City brought their initial encounter with electricity, particularly its uses on such a lavish scale. (They would see their first all-electric kitchen—and, for that matter, their first electric chair.) And they could visit a midway bigger and better than anything that had come before. They could watch moving pictures on Thomas Edison's Kinetoscope and taste for the first time the animal pleasures of Juicy Fruit gum and Cracker Jack–style popcorn.[15] (The introduction of the ice cream cone came later, at the Louisiana Purchase Exposition in St. Louis in 1904.[16]) There were even belly dancers! Not to mention George Ferris's astonishing wheel. Who needed an Eiffel Tower when you could go round and round on the Ferris wheel?

The major fairs continued to be in the vanguard of design. The 1900 Paris Exposition, for example, helped to popularize Art Nouveau, while the 1925 Paris Exposition did much the same for Art Deco. Scientific and technological innovation were showcased too. William Beebe displayed his deep-sea immersible bathysphere at the 1933–34 Chicago Century of Progress Exhibition, and an early television set was featured at New York's World of Tomorrow event in 1939.

Canada's presence at these exhibitions reflected a two-fold mission: on the one hand, to establish a profile of its own; on the other, to offer due deference to the mother country as a loyal member of the British Commonwealth. Such deference was illustrated tellingly at the British Empire Exhibition, held at Wembley Stadium in London in 1924–25. There, in the Canadian Pavilion, stood a life-size equestrian statue of the Prince of Wales, the exhibition's president and the future king of England, made entirely of … *butter*. From Canadian cows, of course.[17]

This earlier Canadian participation in exhibitions tended to emphasize natural resources and agriculture. Occasionally, the Canadians became caught up in the romantic images other nations presented—of a land of snowy vastness and daunting wildlife, an image that might as easily repel as entice the hard-working immigrants seeking a brighter future they hoped to attract. As recently as 1958 and the Brussels fair, many observers felt Canada's principal virtue at such events was its lack of ostentation, though this seemed in some ways a backhanded compliment. "'It's not that Canada is boring, melancholic or unimaginative,' observed one [such critic]. 'It is simply Serious.'"[18] The Montreal

Universal and International World Exhibition of 1967 meant to improve that dour image.

But first Montreal had to obtain the blessing of the International Bureau of Exhibitions (BIE), headquartered in Paris—and it had competition, primarily from the U.S.S.R, which sought the world exhibition for Moscow that year in order to celebrate the fiftieth anniversary of the Russian Revolution. Austria indicated its intentions, but subsequently withdrew from the race. While France assured Montreal of its support, the Montreal contingent viewed with alarm Russia's sponsorship of five of its satellite countries—Czechoslovakia, Hungary, Poland, Romania and Bulgaria—for BIE membership.[19] Assuredly, their rival was stacking the deck. Following four ballots, the vote deadlocked 15–15. A story later emerged that one of the delegates had a romantic assignation planned for that evening and objected to further voting; his recalcitrance prompted an impolitic Mayor Fournier to give him a piece of his mind, and the delegate, out of spite, then switched his vote from Montreal to Russia. Whatever Byzantine twists and turns the negotiations took, the Soviets won the day, 16 to 14.[20] Sévigny and Drouin, who had even paid their own travel expenses, were, according to Sévigny's widow, "terribly depressed and hurt."[21]

By early 1962, within two years of attaining the prize, the Russians had changed their minds—an eventuality foreseen by BIE president Léon Baréty. After the 16–14 vote, Baréty told a dejected Sévigny not to fret, the U.S.S.R would eventually pull out: "The Russians won't want the gaze of 20 million strangers and they won't want to show the whole world the misery of the socialist system. They're going to step aside."[22] Baréty's prophecy came to pass in April 1962. A recent exhibition of French goods, so one story goes, proved a little too enticing to the Moscow citizenry for the comfort of the powers that be in the Kremlin. A world's fair in their midst could only invite even more distracting examples of Western decadence and greater outside scrutiny.[23]

Baréty contacted Sévigny, and the Canadians prepared once more to enter the lists of the BIE, though with trepidation, as the words of the secretary general of the Brussels fair continued to ring in their ears: "The greatest problem is time. We started organizing five years ahead. It was our greatest mistake. We really needed seven!"[24] Montreal, assuming it secured its application, would not have even five years. Moreover, political changes had occurred. Maurice Duplessis died in the autumn of 1959. By 1962, the premier of Quebec was the Liberal Jean Lesage. Lesage, though, quickly came on side in support of the bid, as did Montreal's new mayor, Jean Drapeau, who returned to office in 1960 and who, in an earlier mayoral incarnation, had vehemently opposed any notions of a fair. "What changed your mind?" Sévigny asked Drapeau. Replied His Worship, with airy insouciance, "That was yesterday."[25]

What is that old saying about the passion of the convert? Jean Drapeau appeared on the scene to demonstrate this maxim's essential truth. Indeed no one could have shown himself as obsessively committed to an Expo for Montreal than Montreal's mayor. "Mayor Drapeau began his career as a fire-eater and seemed determined to culminate it as a dreamer," observed writer Raymond Grenier.[26] Drapeau followed the BIE machinations through an invaluable Paris contact, the French wine dealer (and former arms merchant) Georges Marchais (not to be confused with the French Communist Party leader of the same name).[27] Once involved in the chase, he exerted all his considerable energies. Prime Minister Diefenbaker, not wishing to alienate Toronto political supporters, decided to at least run the matter of the bid by Toronto's mayor Nathan Phillips. "No thanks," Phillips is said to have replied, "Give it to Drapeau. He'll go broke."[28]

The BIE told the Canadians their application had to be in by October 1, 1962. Drapeau was determination itself. "If Montreal doesn't get Expo this year," he reportedly said, "she'll miss the chance for the next twenty-five."[29] Diefenbaker, understandably, was a bit unnerved by the stringent timeline. But Drapeau prevailed. Ottawa submitted Montreal's application to the BIE in September 1962 and, by November, it became official: Montreal would host the 1967 world exhibition. This time, the vote in Paris was unanimous.

ON DECEMBER 20, 1962, the House of Commons adopted Bill C-103, the act that created the Canadian Corporation for the 1967 World Exhibition (CCWE). The initial grant to the CCWE was forty million dollars, a sum to be shared by the three levels of government, the federal government providing 50 percent, Quebec 37.5 percent, and Montreal 12.5 percent.

By January 1963 the Diefenbaker government named two prominent business figures, Paul Bienvenu and Cecil Carsley, respectively, to the positions of commissioner general and deputy commissioner general of the new corporation. By April of that year, the City of Montreal agreed to lend to the CCWE its distinguished and far-sighted director of urban planning, Claude Robillard. But, before Robillard could assume his duties as Expo's master planner, Mayor Drapeau held a press conference toward the end of March to announce the exhibition's site—an enlarged Île Ste. Hélène, a newly created Île Notre Dame, as well as the federally owned land along the Mackay Pier jetty that became known as Cité du Havre. The motives and timing behind Drapeau's decision became a source of some controversy. In certain quarters, the location invited consternation and unease. [30] Robillard's inclinations, for example, lay with the cause of urban renewal and the restoration and preservation of Old Montreal and not the sort of novelty gestures signified in the islands plan.

But Robillard dutifully pressed on and by May had pulled together an illustrious group of people from a range of professions to help flesh out Expo's theme. The group met at the Seigniory Club in Montebello, situated on property where Louis-Joseph Papineau, a leader of the 1837–38 rebellion, had once lived. The group, under the leadership of Dr. Davidson Dunton, vice-chair of Carleton University, included neurosurgeon Dr. Wilder Penfield; actor and director Jean-Louis Roux;

geophysicist Professor J. Tuzo Wilson, explicator of the theory of tectonic plates and continental drift; former National Gallery of Canada director Alan Jarvis; and author Gabrielle Roy, familiar not just in her native Quebec but to many anglo-Canadian high school students of a certain vintage for her homespun novel *La petite poule d'eau* (*The Little Water Hen*).

The Expo theme itself—and the connection to Saint-Exupéry and *Terre des hommes*—had already been established during a meeting in Montreal late the previous year.[31] Drapeau had attended, as had Pierre Sévigny and Claude Robillard. Sévigny would claim credit for the Saint-Exupéry reference and Corinne Sévigny maintains that her husband employed the phrase "*terre des hommes*" in speeches he made during the period when the Montreal delegation attended the BIE meeting in Paris in November 1962. She remembers clearly the allusion to Saint-Exupéry. "I tell you why I have knowledge of that," she says, "because I didn't know who Saint-Exupéry was." His name, and the occasion, accordingly lodged in her memory.[32]

On one specific point, the Montebello Group defied Mayor Drapeau—by giving an emphatic thumbs-down to his ardent desire that a tower symbolize the exhibition.[33] Drapeau could at least console himself with the knowledge that his islands scheme generated so much interest— a scheme, incidentally, that had historical precedent on its side. As early as 1895, a visionary by the name of A. S. Brodeur proposed joining Île Ste. Hélène—named in 1608 by Samuel de Champlain for his young bride—to the neighbouring Île Ronde as the site for an international exposition in Montreal. "The nights would be so gay and wonderful on this island," enthused *Le Monde Illustré*, "rising up from the waves like another Venise [*sic*] transplanted to the middle of the St. Lawrence ..."[34]

But Drapeau never rested on his laurels. Always, there was another angle to be played, another manoeuvre to be executed. Now, he had to work his wiles on a new government. Lester "Mike" Pearson's Liberals defeated John Diefenbaker's Progressive Conservatives in April 1963, sufficiently at any rate to ensure a Liberal minority government. Pearson, a distinguished diplomat awarded the Nobel Peace Prize for his efforts at the United Nations during the Suez Crisis of 1956, rode the coattails of that success to become the party's leader.

Pearson's leadership style might be termed aggressively diffident—in truth, he had little appetite for the blood sport of politics—but his policies indicated a determination to forge the bonds of unity within Canada, whether it was through the introduction of medicare or a national flag. He wanted to strengthen ties with French Canada (while loosening them with Mother England) and called his conciliatory overtures to Quebec "co-operative federalism." Others called it capitulation. When Pearson, with what his policy advisor Tom Kent describes as "typical Mike bravery,"[35] announced at the Royal Canadian Legion in Winnipeg in April 1964 that he would press for a distinctive national flag over the red ensign, all hell broke loose. Shouted one outraged listener, "You're selling Canada to the pea-soupers!"[36]

Pearson was not much of a fan of the bread-and-circuses showmanship that seemed to come so naturally to Jean Drapeau. "Mike's reservations were pretty much those of a man who has no great appetite for formal occasions of any kind," says Tom Kent. But Pearson recognized the enthusiasm for Expo on the part of his French-Canadian ministers and the role Expo might play in fostering national unity. Moreover, Mayor Drapeau could be persuasive. On July 8, 1963, Ottawa gave its blessing to the diking operations around Île Ste. Hélène and Île Ronde, which constituted the beginnings of what became the "magic" islands of Expo 67. "Drapeau manipulated Lester Pearson left, right, and centre," recalls journalist Alan Hustak. "Pearson kept mumbling, 'That sonofabitch, that sonofabitch.' [Drapeau] was a consummate politician. He knew whose balls to squeeze."[37]

That same day, July 8, Paul Bienvenu wrote his letter of resignation as Expo's commissioner general and sent it to the prime minister. Bienvenu had been troubled on a number of fronts, notably by what he regarded as a severe underestimation of Expo's ultimate cost and by a governance model that allowed too much power to Expo's board at the expense of its administrators. Both Bienvenu and his deputy, Cecil Carsley, had been shaken by a report speculating that Expo 67 could not in fact be completed until 1969, or even 1970. Pearson urged Bienvenu to stay the course, but by August 12, 1963, Bienvenu had reached the end of his tether and submitted his final resignation to the Expo board. The resignation became public knowledge ten days later.[38] August 12 was the same day two barges ferried out dignitaries to a site where the work could begin on the diking around Île Ronde and Île Ste. Hélène. During the accompanying ceremony, the young re-enactors representing the Compagnies Franches de la Marine (the defenders for many years of New France) fired off a blank from an eighteenth-century cannon that, because of its proximity to him, sent Bienvenu flying off his dais chair.[39] It was a moment that mixed slapstick and portent, guaranteed to churn the stomachs of management. This was a dark hour for Expo. Carsley subsequently resigned, and master planner Claude Robillard followed soon after. It was time to bring in a new team.

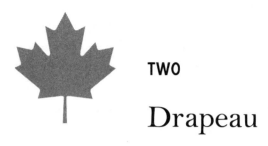

TWO

Drapeau

Expo might have happened without Jean Drapeau, though that notion seems difficult to entertain. Among the believers, he stood supreme, even if, initially, he had been cool on the idea. But once started on this course, nothing and no one could dissuade him. Informed that Moshe Safdie's Habitat 67 would not be completed by the April 28 public opening date, Drapeau didn't bat an eye, suggesting instead that a crane be left near the Habitat site bearing a sign that read, "Work in progress." "There are no problems," he became fond of saying, "only solutions."[1]

In his memoirs, Lester Pearson recalled an early Drapeau sales pitch when Pearson was still leader of the opposition. Pearson recalls how, after a dinner, the two spoke of their hopes for Expo: Pearson acknowledged that Drapeau most likely intuited that he, Pearson, was not as gung-ho on Expo as he might have liked. But nothing fazed the mayor. To Pearson's amazement, Drapeau pulled out his plans and got down on the floor to spread them out and show Pearson the concept for the artificial islands. Pearson thought this plan pure folly—artificial islands? when Canada already had four million square miles of land to offer?—and he had serious doubts about how, despite the mayor's positive reassurances, the Expo deadline could be met. Yet, it was, and as Pearson remarked, "the doves flew and the airplanes flew and the flags flew. It was a very moving and memorable opening day."[2]

Doggedness was always a Drapeau trait. Born in 1916, and raised in a lower-middle-class section of Montreal, the son of a Liberal Party functionary, he considered a business career before hedging his bets and studying law in night courses at the University of Montreal. Soon, he discovered his real love: politics. Drapeau had a natural aptitude for debate. "It wasn't a sympathetic voice," recalls a classmate. "It was a cold voice really, no warmth. His debating style was a combination of things. It wasn't Irish wit, French spirit or English humour. But it was some of all of these." Drapeau and his teenage friends formed a wing of the nationalist Association Canadienne de Jeunesse Catholique (ACJC), an association dedicated to the proposition that "the French Canadian race has a special mission to fulfil on this continent, and it must for that reason keep its character distinct from other races."[3] Drapeau christened their group after his intellectual mentor and one of the ACJC's principal founders, Abbé Lionel Groulx, godfather of Quebec nationalism. The disciple and mentor remained close through the years—Groulx offici-ated at Drapeau's marriage[4]—but, over time, Drapeau came to temper his nationalism.

Unsuccessful as a political candidate for federal and provincial office, Drapeau found his métier in the arcane world of Montreal civic politics and learned a lesson about accommodating *les anglais*. He continued to hold the vision of a special place for Quebec and, at one time, discussed with his friend René Lévesque the idea of a new political party dedicated to the premise of a sovereign Quebec in economic union with the rest of Canada.[5] But while Lévesque moved forward with that notion, Drapeau increasingly came to see the role of Quebec as remaining within the framework of Confederation. With Drapeau, pragmatism always seemed to balance, if not in fact outweigh, ideology. And it is probable his role as ambassador and toastmaster of Expo 67 played its part in softening any ideological edges.

With Expo, he had to be at the centre of the action. Nor was he shy about claiming credit. It is Drapeau who is credited with having actually come up with the phrase "Expo 67" as the name for the Montreal exposition—he said the idea came to him from a Maurice Chevalier song "La p'tite dame de l'Expo."[6] And of course it was Drapeau at his press conference on March 28, 1963, who presented to the world the idea of the specially created islands as a *fait accompli*. "Diefenbaker didn't know, Pierre didn't know, Bienvenu didn't know," says Pierre Sévigny's widow, Corinne. "I said to Pierre, 'What are you going to do about it?' And he said, 'I don't think there's anything I can do about it.' I've never seen him so discombobulated."[7]

But the islands soon ceased to be Pierre Sévigny's concern. The Liberals defeated the Progressive Conservatives in the April 1963 federal election, and now they were the ones who had to deal with the mayor and his islands. Drapeau, in fact, did not claim the credit for the islands idea. He bestowed that honour on Guy Beaudet, head of the port authority—though some saw this gesture as Drapeau's method of retaining control of the plan. The Montreal architect Bruno Bédard and his firm Bédard, Charbonneau and Langlois first presented the islands concept in January 1963, yet Drapeau, for his own reasons, preferred to ignore that particular initiative.[8] "Their plan included part of Longueuil and St. Lambert, and knowing Drapeau, I'm certain he would never have accepted to share the glory of Expo with the mayors of Longueuil and St. Lambert," says Yves Jasmin, who became head of publicity and public relations at Expo. Jasmin adds a further twist to the story. St. Lambert vigorously opposed the construction of Île Notre Dame, an objection traceable to 1944 when, in order to allow St. Lambert to benefit from the revenues of the Victoria Bridge, its land area was extended to the middle of the river. In other words, Drapeau would be building on St. Lambert land.[9] This would not do.

Drapeau acted expeditiously. He got a law passed to the effect that if Montreal was building an island, the island would become Montreal land and, for agreeing to this law, St. Lambert secured a concession: Île Notre Dame would remain a park, no high-rise apartments or industrial plants would be allowed. Principal fixer in this imbroglio was Pierre Laporte, the provincial member for Longueuil and St. Lambert and later labour minister in the Quebec Liberal government of Robert Bourassa.[10] In 1970, Laporte would die at the hands of members of the Front de libération du Québec (FLQ) and achieve instant martyrdom as a victim of separatist terror.

Expo officials sometimes had to rein in the dynamic mayor. Yves Jasmin remembers the time he sent a speakers' bureau employee to personnel for reassignment because she had badmouthed one of his hires. The employee complained to Drapeau, who phoned Jasmin and told him to rehire her. Then it became Jasmin's turn to complain, which he did, to Expo's deputy commissioner general, Robert Shaw. Shaw pointedly asked the mayor whether he wished to raise the personnel matter at the next meeting of the Expo board. Drapeau backed off, and for a time thereafter remained decidedly cool toward Jasmin.[11]

The most egregious form this mayoral interfering took occurred when Drapeau tried to impose a tower on the Expo site. Not just any tower either. Seized by the magnificence of the Eiffel Tower and its impact on the Paris Exposition of 1889, he proposed disassembling that splendid creation and reassembling it at Expo. A plan that, unsurprisingly, met resistance in Paris. Drapeau then suggested building a replica. That plan, too, received no support. Undaunted, Drapeau decided he would hire a French architect to design a new tower to stand at the tip of the La Ronde amusement park and rise to a height of 1,967 feet (note the symbolism of that number, please!). He duly contacted an architect and the architect duly submitted his designs—to groans from the architects and planners at Expo. Lucien Saulnier, for many years Drapeau's right-hand man at City Hall, and the one most able to control the mayor's flights of fancy, managed to route these drawings to the CCWE administration, where they received a thumbs down. "From the cost and revenue point of view it just didn't work," says Steven Staples, the chief planner. "The design of the tower was bent. We called it 'Drapeau's erection.'"[12] The Montebello Group had been emphatic on that point. As Montebello Group member Jean-Louis Roux noted, there had already been many vertical symbols for events of this kind. Enough was enough.[13] Instead, they insisted, "The unifying element must be sought in the Exhibition itself and its thematic development; the City skyline as a backdrop has all the identification necessary and no artificial symbol would be as original and magnificent."[14]

Actually, one building did show promise as an Expo symbol and that was Habitat. But Habitat proceeded in an agonizingly stop-start motion before eventually being cut back radically for cost reasons. Its architect, Moshe Safdie, suspects the federal government's tentativeness in support of Habitat had at least something to do with competition from Drapeau and his beloved tower. Safdie perceived Drapeau as seeking another Eiffel Tower or Seattle Space Needle as the exhibition's symbol, whatever the opinion of the Montebello Group. And while Safdie had the backing of Director of Installations Colonel Edward Churchill and Deputy Commissioner General Robert Shaw, even they could only do so much. Safdie knew there could not be two major symbols for Expo—the money simply was not there.[15] Jean Drapeau enjoyed repeating a joke the secretary of state of the Commonwealth told during his speech at Britain's national day at Expo. It was explained to him, said the secretary of state, that Mayor Drapeau had obtained sizeable majorities in the recent civic elections (94 percent in 1962, 96 percent in 1966) and had instructed voters how to indicate their ballot preference. "If for me," Drapeau supposedly said, "make a large cross beside my name. If against, then just make a very small cross beside my name."[16] So what if Drapeau himself probably fed that material to the visiting dignitary? No doubt about it, he was a popular figure. "I loved Drapeau," says Krystyne Griffin (formerly Romer), one of the capable twenty-somethings recruited for a key protocol role at Expo. "The most enlightened, charismatic mayor any city could have."[17] Though not everyone shared this love.

"Pushy, he took everything for himself," says Corinne Sévigny. "No matter what you said or did, it became his." Mme Sévigny still nurses her grudge. "We were never given our place. Never, ever. Pierre was not recognized. Until Yves Jasmin wrote the book [Jasmin's *La petite histoire d'Expo 67,* published in 1997], I don't think anyone knew he was in the organization." Insult was added to injury at the April 27, 1967, preview opening ceremony at Place des Nations. "At the opening ceremony, we were put on the seventeenth row or tier," says Corinne Sévigny. A considerable trek, especially as one remembers she had her husband, an amputee from war wounds, in tow. "We were never recognized, which broke my heart. That was mean. That was straight Drapeau."[18]

THREE

Les Durs

I remember the bus I used to take came along the boulevard in
Westmount and then went all the way down to St. James Street, which
is where all the head offices and businesses were. And I remember hearing these two men—English speaking—talking openly about how the
"frogs" were not going to be able to do it [Expo]. That they had no
experience in it. That it would only happen if anglos were in charge.
What was surprising to me was that they were so open about it. It was
the appalling lack of respect or courtesy.

—BROADCAST JOURNALIST GLORIA BISHOP[1]

While the mayor of Montreal worked tirelessly for the Expo cause both
behind the scenes and in the public eye, other presences emerged to take
up that cause as well. A new team was being assembled and one of its
key players was veteran diplomat Pierre Dupuy.

In a diary entry dated June 28, 1942, the Canadian diplomat and
belletrist Charles Ritchie noted: "Pierre Dupuy came to pay me a visit.
What an enjoyable war that little man is having! He exudes high politics

and dark diplomacy. He is intelligent—yes—but nine-tenths of it is his capacity to put himself across. From being a dim little diplomat he has become an international figure—the only Canadian except for the Prime Minister [Mackenzie King] whose name is known in Paris and Berlin political circles and in the inner circle in London."[2]

Putting himself across was evidently a Dupuy specialty. Born in Montreal in 1896, Dupuy received his Bachelor of Arts degree from the University of Montreal in 1917 and completed his law studies there in 1920. Upon receiving his L.Litt. degree from the University of Paris in 1922, he was appointed secretary to the Canadian commissioner general in Paris and held that post until 1927. First as second secretary and then as first secretary at the Canadian legation in Paris, Dupuy became one of the first Canadian representatives at the International Bureau of Exhibitions, an association that would make him a natural fit for the Expo duties he later assumed.

In 1940, Dupuy was appointed Canadian consul to Paris, but he withdrew to London that same year following the Nazi occupation of the French capital. He became chargé d'affaires to the governments of Belgium and the Netherlands in London, as well as to the French government in Vichy in 1940–41. Dupuy made several special missions to the French government in Vichy and was also entrusted with missions in North Africa in 1943. These duties led to a working relationship with British Prime Minister Winston Churchill, who later remarked Dupuy had been his "little window on the other side of the barricade."[3]

Post-war, Dupuy ascended the diplomatic ranks: ambassador to the Netherlands, then to Italy, then—in 1958—to France. He held this last posting until Prime Minister Pearson offered him the commissioner generalship of Expo in the first week of September 1963. Dupuy had flown to Ottawa for the meeting and Pearson, according to Dupuy, was apparently *"étonné et satisfait"* that he accepted the offer with such alacrity.[4]

Dupuy was shortly thereafter ensconced at the Ritz-Carlton on Sherbrooke Street in Montreal, home base until his suite at Habitat became available.[5] A cultivated man, Dupuy had a taste for the finer things. "You know, like the queen never carries any money, I suspect he just took [the perks] for granted," says Diana Thébaud Nicholson, who had roles at Expo in both protocol and operations and knew the main players. "I always resented the fact that he got so much ink—and the other people didn't."[6]

If Dupuy's energy and contacts provided undeniable assets, a deputy commissioner general would be required to balance out Dupuy's grand flourishes with down-to-earth managerial skills. Enter Robert Fletcher Shaw, born in 1910 and raised in Revelstoke, B.C., the son of a banker who earned an engineering degree and then set about learning the business, progressing over the years from labourer on a construction site onward and upward to the executive suite. Shaw joined The Foundation Company of Canada as an engineer in 1937 and worked his way through the ranks to become the company's president. He had won favour in the eyes of Minister of Trade and Commerce C. D. Howe, who hired The Foundation Company to amalgamate defence construction contracts, and on the basis of that performance, the company received several government contracts, including work on the Distant Early Warning (DEW) Line defence system. Shaw was tall, imposing, and possessed a deep commanding voice. He had a lengthy history of dealing with budgets and contracts, and he had a sense of humour. Told by a consultant when he first accepted the Expo job that the exhibition could not possibly be ready in three and a half years, Shaw later related, "I did the only thing sensible. I had the consultant fired."[7]

Observed one colleague: "Shaw was the solid guy with two feet on the ground; Dupuy was the dreamer. Expo would not have been the same without one or the other. Two Dupuys, it would have been a disaster; two Shaws, it would have been dull."[8] "He was someone you'd really like to get to sit beside at dinner," says the Montreal journalist and commentator Gretta Chambers. "There are some people who have both the intelligence of the head and of the heart and he had both."[9]

Shaw and his wife, Johann, daughter of a Toronto banker, were a devoted couple. Not so devoted were the Dupuys. Madame Dupuy refused to accompany her husband to Montreal, and as a consequence, the role of official Expo hostess went by default to Johann Shaw. Just months before Expo's opening, tragedy befell the Shaws. Their only child, a twenty-three-year-old airline pilot, disappeared with his light aircraft in the Charlevoix area. "They didn't find his body for almost a year," says Diana Thébaud Nicholson. "It was particularly tragic because he was not far from civilization."[10] Both Shaws courageously carried on in their respective Expo duties.

Robert Shaw helped bring in Colonel Edward Churchill as director of installations at Expo—meaning he had the responsibility for all the construction on the Expo site. Churchill had wide experience: he had set up Camp Gagetown and Fort Churchill after overseeing construction of airports and other installations for Field Marshal Viscount Montgomery's 21st Army Group headquarters in Brussels during World War II. The Department of National Defence lent him to Expo in late 1963.

The Winnipeg-born Churchill had organizational ability as well as the sheer bloody-mindedness required for what many onlookers considered an impossible task. Short and broad-shouldered, Churchill could be tough and abrasive. You did your job, or the colonel would be on your case. On one occasion, he pulled a construction worker off a bus transporting him to his work site because the worker refused to pay the fare. In the process, Churchill instigated what Expo's labour troubleshooter Jean Cournoyer called a "spontaneous strike." It so happened that a limousine bearing Pierre Dupuy and the French ambassador across Concordia Bridge to the Expo site met the striking workers moving in the opposite direction. The workers started to rock Dupuy's limousine. A rattled and livid Dupuy retreated to the administration building back at Cité du Havre to vent his spleen. It took several hours before the indispensable Cournoyer, with the backing of Robert Shaw, righted matters. No bus fare would be charged the workers, and the men returned to their jobs.[11]

What's amazing is that Churchill dealt as well as he did with the pressures of his job, though on at least a couple of occasions he had to be hospitalized due to overwork. "A hard guy, but fair enough," says Jerry Miller, an Expo planner.[12] "He just radiated energy," says Diana Thébaud Nicholson. "His staff loved him … He had an appreciation of the fine arts [too], but didn't have a lot of time for the fancy-pants people. He was a man's man, but women adored him."[13]

In the Expo hierarchy, the director of installations held rank over the exhibition's chief architect, an inversion of the norm in the traditional world exhibition arrangement of things. Given Churchill's pragmatism and tenacity, that switch may well have been a crucial factor in Expo's success. The man chosen as chief architect, Édouard Fiset, joined the Expo team at around the same time as Churchill. A Quebec architect whose father had been the province's lieutenant-governor, Fiset studied at the École des Beaux-Arts in Paris. Dupuy courted him avidly, but Fiset resisted. He had recently settled his family into a house in Quebec City and had a number of contracts with the provincial government. Eventually, however, Dupuy wore him down.[14]

Fiset's Beaux-Arts architectural training did not make him the immediately obvious candidate to oversee the type of cutting-edge architecture associated with contemporary exhibitions. Nonetheless, he earned admiration for his taste and reasoned equability in allowing others to do their jobs. Fiset had his hands full. It fell to him to explain diplomatically to the architects of the participating pavilions why their buildings had to look a certain way and be in a particular location, an often delicate assignment when national egos were on the line. To the surprise of some, Fiset and Churchill—the reticent aesthete and the blunt-spoken engineer—became great friends. And for that matter, they were part of a good team, some elements of which were already in place: accountant G. Dale Rediker for one, the gifted young lawyer

Jean-Claude Delorme for another. And other key positions were beginning to be filled.

Andrew Kniewasser, thirty-six years old at the time he accepted the position of general manager of Expo in October 1963, was already familiar with Pierre Dupuy; he had worked several years as a trade commissioner at the Canadian embassy in Paris. "Dupuy knew me very well," says Kniewasser. "Dupuy was on the first floor and I was on the third floor as a counsellor. Even before I got to Montreal I had a reputation as a nasty piece of work."[15] During those embassy days, Dupuy would be all charm to visitors, who then progressed to the third floor to hash out details with the hard-nosed Kniewasser, one of whose Expo nicknames was "the Teutonic Plague."[16] Kniewasser had been a delegate to the BIE after the Soviets withdrew their exhibition bid, his job at that time to obtain their support and that of other commission members for Montreal's application to succeed Moscow. The success of that mission did little to alter Kniewasser's jaundiced take on his superiors in Ottawa.

"The whole idea of it being a 'Montreal fair' was detested by the government," he says. "Mr. Diefenbaker reluctantly agreed to do it and his successor Mr. Pearson was dead against it." When Kniewasser presented his cost estimates to the Liberal government, the figures seemed so high that Finance Minister Walter Gordon turned positively gleeful. In Gordon's eyes, the numbers surely spelled *fini* to, in Gordon's words, the "fucking fair." Gordon apparently told Kniewasser, "Now go back to Paris and keep up the good work you're doing there."[17]

That the Liberal cabinet ended up voting in favour of Expo, Kniewasser attributes greatly to the suasions of Mayor Jean Drapeau: "Drapeau was a superb public relations persuader. He's the only politician who was always impeccable with me. He did something equally important and more difficult—he persuaded the citizens of Montreal to be hosts to the world. And the citizens of Montreal were one of the reasons the fair was such a success."

It was Kniewasser's job to ride herd on the three levels of government to ensure funding arrived on time and in the amount specified: "Every expenditure over $25,000 had to be approved by the three levels of government. How can you build a world's fair with that system? We did it." Former Expo protocol head Roger D. Landry describes Kniewasser as "the right guy for the job," noting that he was "tough, big, no bullshit."[18] Diana Thébaud Nicholson recalls his "prematurely grey hair and rugged good looks. He was scary to a lot of people, quite impatient. He had been a trade commissioner, for heaven's sake. And he had a lot to learn. Maybe, to cover his reticence, he acted like the tough guy."[19]

Another crucial member of the Expo team joined around this time. Shaw had approached Philippe de Gaspé Beaubien in mid-October 1963. Beaubien remembers that the call came on a Thursday and was out of the blue. "I said, 'How did you find me?' And he said, 'I spoke to three people and your name came up on two lists—and that's why I came to you first.'"[20] Not entirely clear at that time was where exactly Beaubien would fit into the organization. But Beaubien says Shaw told him he needed a "crazy French-speaking Canadian" to help balance out an administrative ticket of French and English. The "crazy" part came with the mandate: to accomplish in under four years what ordinarily would require seven. Beaubien had another business deal in the works— he was poised to purchase an aluminum fabricating business—but the Expo offer intrigued him.

Beaubien was a catch: thirty-five years old, handsome and person-able—and armed with a Harvard MBA. He was the scion of an old Montreal family. "It was a family that did a lot of inter-marrying," says Gretta Chambers, whose mother was a Beaubien. "In Outremont there was a saying, 'There are the English and the French—and those goddam Beaubiens who are into everything.'"[21] Beaubien himself offers an alternative version: "Outremont is made up of three kinds of people— the English, the Jews, and the Beaubiens."[22] His grandfather Beaubien was mayor of Outremont for forty-three years. To complete this image of total presentability, Beaubien had married a beautiful Boston socialite named Nan Bowles O'Connell.

Expo in fact had entered Beaubien's thoughts a week before Robert Shaw made his overtures. He and Nan-b (she added the "b" to retain her mother's maiden name) hosted a dinner party and one of the guests was a consulting engineer from MIT whom Colonel Churchill had hired to advise on the project. Beaubien recalls the engineer at their dinner table telling Nan-b, "This exhibition will *never* happen!" "I got upset," he says: "Who is this American who tells us we cannot do it?" His irritation might have had something to do with the consulting engineer being a former boyfriend of Nan-b. Still, their guest was hardly the only Cassandra. Nan-b, too, initially, voiced reservations. And Beaubien's father, also named Philippe, regarded the idea as preposterous. "The islands will float down to Sorel," declared Beaubien *père*.[23]

Beaubien, though, sensed promise and opportunity and signed on early in November 1963. He would become Expo's invaluable director of operations, meaning that after Edward Churchill built the exposition, Beaubien would take it over and run it. Soon after signing on, Beaubien became part of an Expo delegation to the BIE in Paris: their mission was to persuade the Bureau that, although Expo management had undergone changes, the project remained on track. Beaubien remembers the BIE meeting room being so packed with people, he had to stand on a staircase, which is where he overheard two Frenchmen in front of him dismissing the exhibition's prospects with the utmost condescension. *No way* the Canadians could pull this one off! "We came back with the feeling that this was what Europe was thinking of us," says Beaubien. "That was a great incentive."[24]

Other important members of the emerging Expo team were exhibitions director Pierre de Bellefeuille and public relations, advertising and information director Yves Jasmin, both of whom were in place by early 1964. De Bellefeuille was then editor-in-chief of *Le Magazine Maclean*, the French-language version of *Maclean's* he started in 1960. "Very attractive in an intellectually swashbuckling way," says Gretta Chambers of de Bellefeuille. While attending an annual meeting of the Federation of Quebec Journalists, a colleague informed de Bellefeuille that Andrew Kniewasser wished to speak with him. The two men knew each other slightly; Kniewasser's wife, Jacqueline, was a friend of de Bellefeuille's sister. "He told me he was recommending my appointment as director of exhibitions and asked me did I agree," says de Bellefeuille, adding "I agreed."[25] De Bellefeuille enjoyed his role at *Le Magazine Maclean*, but he sought greater challenges and Expo certainly appeared to offer them. (Incidentally, before he approached de Bellefeuille, Kniewasser had considered another journalist for the job—Pierre Elliott Trudeau.[26])

When Yves Jasmin entered the Expo ranks, it was as deputy director to Pierre de Bellefeuille in exhibitions; but soon de Bellefeuille helped engineer Jasmin's move into public relations, advertising and information. Jasmin was the sort of guy who rolled up his shirtsleeves and seated himself at the edge of a colleague's desk to talk up *"le brainstorming."*[27] Already an industry veteran—he had done public relations for Trans-Canada Airlines (later Air Canada) and Molson as well—Jasmin came recommended by Jean Drapeau himself.[28]

Part of the Expo mystique would be the way in which it blended both French- and English-speaking talents—a paradigm for Lester Pearson's vaunted ideal of a bilingual Canada. Yet the Expo administration was never truly bilingual. While he sees some validity in the oft-repeated comments about Expo as a model of French–English cooperation, Pierre de Bellefeuille offers this qualifier: "Bob Shaw, he used to say that everything was bilingual at Expo, that everybody spoke two languages ... [But] he himself had no knowledge of the French language at all. Rediker had no knowledge. Churchill had no knowledge. Just having these three heads of the organization would ensure that anything serious would be discussed in English."[29]

The Expo team department heads got their nickname from Andrew Kniewasser. He called them *"les durs"*—the tough guys, the strong ones.

In addition to their weekly meetings, *les durs* met informally on a regular basis for dinner and discussion at each other's houses. Jasmin recalls one such meal, *chez Beaubien*, where the group discussion centred on comments made by opposition leader John Diefenbaker in the House of Commons, to the effect that Expo officials were spending money as if they were at a Roman orgy. "You're right!" muttered an exasperated Jasmin, extending the metaphor. "And *we're* being fed to the lions!"[30]

They were a tight-knit group, *les durs*. When the Expo board considered firing the recently installed Jasmin because Expo publicity in those early times seemed either pessimistic or just plain scarce, *les durs* rallied round. Jasmin stayed put.[31] Though not a department head, Bob Shaw was an honorary *dur*. "Dupuy set the tone but Shaw did the job," says Jasmin. They were loyal to Bob Shaw because he was loyal to them. When Shaw's Foundation Company became entangled in a legal case that concerned overbilling, noises were made at the CCWE board about letting him go. "I think we'd better tell them, if they get rid of Shaw, they get rid of all of us," declared Kniewasser to his fellow *durs*. The storm passed. Shaw remained.

They also worked very hard. "We were possessed," says Kniewasser. The psychologist Hans Selye was hired to do a study on them and their work habits; in his report, Selye concluded their jobs were so stressful they'd all be dead within a year. Anyway, this is how Kniewasser describes it. He says he received the Selye report, read it, and then placed it in the wastebasket. "No one saw it," he says triumphantly, "and no one died."[32]

THE STORY GOES that Colonel Churchill used to survey the Expo construction site with binoculars from his office at Place Ville Marie. If work was progressing too slowly, Churchill would bark into the phone and deliver an earful to whomever was down there.[33] Chances were good, however, that Churchill himself would be down at the site, roaming about, leading the charge, urging on his troops. Churchill's plan of attack followed a scheduling process, then new, called the critical path method (CPM). The CPM offered a visual managerial tool, a kind of flow chart, that showed at a glance the interrelationships between all the various activities taking place on the Expo site. Planning for each project was divided into stages, and the stages stored in a computer that could monitor their progress. Workers and materials available at certain times could be allocated across the board to those areas where they were needed—that is, the builders were not locked into a serial step sequence. Invaluable as an engineering tool, the critical path method proved a boon to Kniewasser in his role as general manager. "It was critical for me to get the governments to do things," says Kniewasser, who could be a bulldozer when he needed to be one. "'Look fellas, if we don't get that done by such and such a time, the exhibition is not going to open!'"[34] ("Kniewasser had a difficult job because he was in a sense the main executive," maintains Pierre de Bellefeuille. "Pierre Dupuy and Robert Shaw, in their own ways, did not look after details. They were concerned with the high authority. The man who had all the details on his work table was Kniewasser."[35]) "Without Critical Path," Peter Kohl later declared—Kohl was in charge of an operation that included 70 restaurants, 72 snack bars and 600 other shops—"I wouldn't have known *when* I was going to be able to take over *any* building."[36]

For Churchill, day one of the CPM started on November 7, 1963—the day, not incidentally, that he started at Expo. His first order of business was erecting a dike wall behind which construction on the site could begin. One of the less fortunate environmental consequences of the plan was that it meant the eradication of certain nesting places for migratory birds. Birds, however, were not a top priority. While the initial thinking had been to dredge the bottom of the river in order to obtain fill that would create the islands, that approach came to seem particularly tortuous. "Shaw and Churchill said to hell with that, we'll dig it out of the islands themselves," says Andrew Kniewasser. "So they dug big quarries instead of trying to get it out of the river."[37]

This plan could not hope to provide sufficient fill, either, even with the addition of millions of tonnes of landfill provided by the truckload from excavations on Montreal's new subway system and the new highway that would bring in visitors from the United States. So the planners and builders created lakes, lagoons and canals on the islands to compensate for this lack of fill—new features that actually ended up greatly enhancing the Expo experience.

As Churchill and the building of Expo moved ahead, however, changes were taking place in the fair's planning department. When Claude Robillard walked away from his master planner's role, he bequeathed it to his deputy, the Dutch-born Daniel "Sandy" van Ginkel. Van Ginkel and his wife, Blanche Lemco van Ginkel, an architect-planner herself and her husband's professional partner, cared deeply about the preservation of Old Montreal. They had been working on a plan to save it since the early sixties and their ideas eventually found expression in what became known as the Old Port Study. In fact, the Old Port Study, says Blanche Lemco van Ginkel, "was not to do with the port at all. What it was was [a plan] to save Old Montreal." The most imminent threat appeared to be a proposed elevated expressway that would slice through the old part of town. But no one in Montreal approached them, so the van Ginkels looked to the port authority as a potential saviour. "If we couldn't get anybody interested in saving the Old City," she explains, "maybe the port should be concerned."[38]

Drapeau had recently been returned to the mayor's chair and, says Blanche Lemco van Ginkel, "we can't be sure whether it was really because of the Port Study or some other reason, but he nixed the elevated expressway." At one point, they feared Drapeau might seek an exhibition site down river from the city, along the lines of the New York World's Fair in Flushing Meadow. The van Ginkels pushed for the exhibition to be in the downtown area and produced a plan demonstrating how this aim could be achieved. "It was also based on helping Old Montreal to come back," she says.[39] But, in rather short order, Drapeau fastened on the idea of the islands as the main Expo site. The notion of incorporating the Mackay Pier into Expo did remain, though, and early on in the planning it was designated as the only part of the site for permanent buildings: these included the new administration building, an art gallery, the five-storey theatre housing the National Film Board's multi-screen Labyrinth, architect Arthur Erickson's Man in the Community theme pavilion and, most famously, Moshe Safdie's Habitat.

Safdie had been one of the bright young things van Ginkel corralled into Expo's planning department. Fresh out of McGill, Safdie once worked for van Ginkel's Montreal firm. He rejoined his former boss and mentor on condition the Expo work allow him to develop the Habitat housing plan that had grown out of his MA thesis at McGill. Safdie says it was he who first came up with the idea for "spines" of water on the islands to compensate for the lack of fill.[40]

Soon enough, Safdie separated himself from the Expo administration so he could devote his full attention to Habitat. His mentor, van Ginkel, separated himself even sooner. Van Ginkel had definite ideas and did not shy from expressing them. He found the Expo management structure untenable. While Churchill's role as director of installations meant he held rank over Édouard Fiset as chief architect, Fiset held rank over van Ginkel. "Sandy was the boss; he was in charge of preparing the master plan," says Steven Staples, another young talent in the planning department. "All of a sudden Churchill comes in, a chief architect is hired, and planning is supposed to be under the chief architect."[41] Exit Sandy van Ginkel as master planner in the fall of 1963; enter Steven Staples as his successor. Staples had been born in Dar es Salaam, and then lived in Southern Rhodesia (now Zimbabwe). He attended school in South Africa, including architecture school at the University of Capetown, before graduating from Harvard in 1960 with a master's degree in planning. Upon graduation, he worked for a while in the United States before deciding to return to Rhodesia. But white supremacist Ian Smith's re-emergence as that country's political leader put the skids to the self-help housing program Staples was working on and Staples returned to Cambridge, Massachusetts. At that point a former classmate named Frank Vigier came knocking with the Expo offer; Vigier also recruited two other gifted Harvard graduates, Jerry Miller and Adèle Naudé.

As they struggled to meet a pressing deadline, the young planners at Expo, already familiar with the elements of uncertainty, received a particular scare that autumn of 1963 when word circulated that Dupuy had approached a French architect to do a master plan. "Dupuy got a favourite French guy of his to do the master plan," says Steven Staples. The "favourite guy" was the Beaux Arts–style architect Eugene Beaudoin. "This is all secret, we didn't know about this," explains Staples. "Our design group wrote a letter. The upshot was that Dupuy and Fiset, booked on a plane to go to talk with him, [were] delayed. Beaudoin was given time to prepare some kind of plan and he would be invited to Montreal and he would present that plan to Churchill, planning and management. Which he did—and made a complete ass of himself. He didn't know anything about Montreal. That was the end of Beaudoin."[42]

Churchill referred to the Beaudoin uproar as the "palace revolt."[43] Sandy van Ginkel wrote a letter to Dupuy in support of his junior colleagues: "The affront of the appointment of M. Beaudoin is not only a blow for them all professionally—more serious than that—all the hope and all the good spirit is crushed because again they cannot count on the trust and security from their superiors that is required in order to create something worthwhile."[44] For his part, Dupuy attributed the controversy to a "misunderstanding," stating that "there was no question of commissioning a Foreign Agency to prepare our Master Plan. In any case, M. Beaudoin would not have accepted this task for the simple reason that he lacks time to assume such a heavy commitment."[45]

With the Beaudoin spectre lifted and the master plan locked in by the end of 1963, attentions turned to getting the islands in shape so they could be developed and built on when the City of Montreal formally ceded them to the CCWE. That ceremony took place on the new islands at the stroke of midnight on June 30/July 1, 1964. "Mr. Dupuy arrived in style to sign his lease," observed one onlooker. "He crossed the river in a boat done up like a Christmas tree."[46] At midnight, looking back across the St. Lawrence toward the city, the invited dignitaries watched as one Montreal landmark after another was illuminated with each stroke of the clock. The cross on Mount Royal. Place Victoria. Place Ville Marie ... On the twelfth stroke, the lease was signed and, with the signing, came the thunder of fireworks. For the period from June 30, 1964, to December 31, 1969, Montreal agreed to rent the islands to the CCWE for the sum of one dollar a year. They had another two years and ten months to realize their dream.

PRAYERS SEEMED in order for Edward Churchill and his critical path method. The Expo people were running to catch up—and they did not always appreciate the oversight of their political masters. For instance, according to Andrew Kniewasser, Hydro-Québec agreed to sponsor the Man the Producer theme pavilion but expressed reservations about how the development of that exhibit was proceeding and suggested Expo hire someone of its choice to put things right. Hydro-Québec fell under the purview of the province's Ministry of Natural Resources and the minister at the time was René Lévesque. At Lévesque's bidding, Kniewasser led an Expo delegation to Quebec City. The meeting took place in an amphitheatre. Following a discussion with Kniewasser and his colleagues, chief architect Édouard Fiset and chief estimator Edward Romer, Lévesque repaired to the audience section to sit with his entourage during a question-and-answer session. "We got savaged by Lévesque in the most undignified and humiliating way," says Kniewasser. Fiset, "very shy and timid," apparently at one point burst into tears. Lévesque, says Kniewasser "had a very nasty side to him."[47]

As a member of Quebec Liberal leader Jean Lesage's *équipe de tonnerre* and a standard-bearer for the province's Quiet Revolution,

René Lévesque had, along with his ministry, overseen the nationalization of hydroelectric power in the province. "I don't think there's another place in the world that has ever witnessed such a catching up touching so many domains in such a short time," Lévesque wrote in his memoir.[48]

For another—often more rural—section of the electorate, such a transformation came perhaps a little *too* fast and furious. Daniel Johnson's Union Nationale party would defeat the Liberals in December 1966 and consign Lévesque and his Liberal colleagues to the opposition benches in the National Assembly, though Johnson's government continued initiatives set in motion by Lesage. Johnson shared Lesage's general enthusiasm for Expo as an opportunity for French Canada.[49]

By then, Lévesque's situation was complicated. He had formulated a manifesto advocating a separate national status for Quebec, but with what he called "sovereignty association" between this new state and the rest of Canada. It was a position that isolated him from many in his party. Before Expo ended, he would be sitting in the assembly as an independent and, within a year, would establish the separatist Parti Québécois.

Tough guy Kniewasser became inured to being the target of criticism from the various levels of government, though he could not always shield his Expo colleagues. Beaubien, for example, travelled to Quebec City to defend his plans as director of operations and received, in his words, a "bawling out" from Lesage that was "close to insult."[50] Those early days of Expo were not especially happy ones. Politicians tended to reflect, or at any rate try to second-guess, the mood of their constituents on the subject of Expo 67. "The English saw it as a gift to the French and the French saw it as a gift to the English," says Beaubien, who received a number of letters accusing him of being a *vendu*, or sellout, to the anglos.

In those early days, Beaubien's situation appeared especially nebulous. "People didn't see my job as important," he says. The important job, the key position, belonged to Ed Churchill, racing against time to get Expo actually built. As a consequence, and ever mindful of Expo's expanding budget and the growing timorousness of the political masters controlling that budget, Deputy Commissioner General Robert Shaw attempted to persuade Beaubien to hold off on hiring staff until at least 1966. But Beaubien forcefully demurred. He felt that "you've got to have the user there"—that is, operations personnel in place who could assess the construction from the point of view of the potential visitor. To his credit, Shaw proved not unyielding. He studied each request on the basis of its reasonableness. He agreed to Beaubien's request that he be able to hire some top and middle management. Says Beaubien, "I'm sure I drove Ed Churchill crazy because my guys used to go to meetings with the designers and engineers and they'd come back to me and say, 'Philippe, it's not practical.' And I'd go back to Ed and say we'd have to do it in another way."

While tensions continued to ratchet up in anticipation of the April 28, 1967, opening to the public, some brighter news on the public relations front started to appear by the end of 1966. Earlier groundwork began at last to bear fruit. Studies indicated that, across Canada, Expo was now regarded as a *Canadian*—and not just a Montreal or Quebec—initiative and that national pride was somehow involved.[51] It had been a good idea, then, to send Beaubien and the Expo hostesses on those selling junkets. A good idea of Kniewasser's to move the Expo board meetings around to different cities and provinces. A good idea to persuade the Lumbermen's Association to build a tower on Île Ste. Hélène so visitors could watch the progress of construction. Cab drivers, restaurant owners, church and women's groups, hoteliers, not to mention the demimonde of "hospitality" workers, all were invited to come have a look and spread the word.[52] A good idea, too, to mount that extensive information blitz of schools in Canada and the United States.[53] When the New York department store Macy's devoted one floor to an Expo display, the floodgates opened. Other stores clamoured to participate. "They became our enabler to get into all those other places," says

Larry Schachter, one of the principal figures in advertising and promo-tion associated with the Macy's coup. After Macy's said yes, Canadian department stores like Eaton's and Ogilvy and Morgan's wanted to be part of the advertising bandwagon too.[54]

As he watched the Rose Bowl Parade on television in January 1966, Schachter had another brainwave; the following year, Expo had a float not only in the Rose Bowl Parade but in the Orange and Cotton Bowl Parades as well. The Expo logo—that distinctive circle of stick-like figures, each pair symbolic of friendship, created by the Quebec designer Julien Hébert—started to become ubiquitous.[55] Yves Jasmin persuaded Miss Universe of that year to model the outfit to be worn by the Expo hostesses.[56] A twelve-page full-colour pamphlet pullout appeared in *Reader's Digest*—the largest advertisement (at a cost of $450,000) ever placed in the United States version of that magazine by Canadian adver-tisers. The cost was borne equally by the CCWE, Canada's Centennial Commission, and the Canadian Government Travel Bureau.[57] Another coup: the performers Maurice Chevalier, James Mason, Olivia de Havilland, Victor Borge and the Soviet cosmonaut Yuri Gagarin all agreed to appear, without fee, in television ads promoting Expo 67. Then there was the coup that wasn't. Schachter was on the point of negoti-ating a photo op for Habitat in the "Playboy Pad" section of *Playboy* magazine when Pierre Dupuy nipped that idea in the bud. This was *not* part of the refined image he sought to project.[58]

Yet, even as Expo's image finally started to improve in the months leading up to the public opening, the skeptics remained. "We were in jeeps and big rubber boots because the whole thing was a sea of mud," Jane Pequegnat Burns, then an Expo press aide, says of those pre-opening weeks. "And we would say to people, 'Well, it looks like a sea of mud now, but just *wait.*'"[59] Trees were being planted in the frigid March soil. Sod would be laid over that sea of mud right up to the last minute. And the day before the opening, workmen painted portions of the grass green to make them more presentable to the eye.[60]

"I was a little angry about the daily media for bad-mouthing it stupidly," says Charles Oberdorf, then a recent arrival from the United States and working as an assistant producer at CBC Television. "It was weird to be there in January and know that it was going to be a hit—*and* it's going to be ready! I *knew*! I'd seen the scheduling. The sod was not due to arrive until two days before the opening—*because it's April!* That was what deceived so many reporters. It was all there. If you went to Churchill's department you could see the scheduling—and he was on target."[61] Just the same, you don't know until you know. Until then, the naysayers and skeptics have an edge. A bit of graffiti was spotted that tauntingly played on this apprehension. "Avoid the crowds," it said, "Come to Expo."[62] Expo, of course, had the last laugh.

FOUR

The Other Mayor

Officially the first person through the gate at Place d'Accueil on April 28, the public opening of Expo 67, was a bearded thirty-nine-year-old jazz drummer from Chicago named Al Carter. Al Carter held ticket number 00001. Al Carter had a particular hobby: he liked being first. He was the first to arrive at the 1964–65 New York World's Fair. The first passenger to pass through the St. Lawrence Seaway. First to visit the 1962 Seattle World's Fair. Expo was to be his swansong—an ending with a "first-class first." And so eager was he to arrive first, he appeared at the entry gates a day early. Asked how much this singular hobby had cost him over the years, Carter responded, "I was thinking about it on my way to Montreal and to be honest, I'd rather not think about it again." Right behind him through the turnstiles were two Sir George Williams University students, a McGill student, and two hitchhikers from British Columbia.[1]

At a 10 a.m. ceremony, Colonel Edward Churchill, the Canadian army engineer who was Expo's director of installations, the man most responsible for having the Expo site ready by the opening date, handed over the "keys" of Expo to Philippe de Gaspé Beaubien, the suave director of operations whose responsibility Expo now became.

For Churchill, there came an immense feeling of relief. For Beaubien—who became known as the "mayor of Expo"—there was an overwhelming sense of anxiety. At the preview the previous day, two hundred security guards had staged a wildcat strike.[2] The potential sources for his worry were everywhere. Overcrowded pavilions. Lost children. Stalling minirails. A host of calamities that are the special turf of world exhibitions.

As if to confirm him in his apprehension, at 11:30 a.m. on April 28, the three-million-dollar Gyrotron ride at La Ronde amusement park broke down, stranding eighty passengers high up in their seats for two hours. The ride operators blamed an "over-phrasing" between the Gyrotron's push and pull motors, a dry encapsulation offering cold comfort to those stuck, especially the ones parked in the giant silver pyramid portion of the ride, where one has the illusion of venturing through darkest space. The crowd total at the end of that opening day was 407,500, or about three times the official prediction. The next day, the number climbed to 423,000.[3] By Sunday, the third day, they had easily passed the millionth visit mark. While earlier estimates projected a total attendance of perhaps thirty million for the entire six-month run, those estimates, it became clear, needed to be revised upwards. Expo was a hit. Beaubien's worries could only increase exponentially.

That opening morning, Beaubien watched this sea of people pouring into the Expo grounds and felt his pulse quicken. "You're exhilarated," he remembers of that occasion, "but at the same time I had to say, 'How am I going to make this work?'"[4]

THEY LEARNED QUICKLY. In a matter of weeks after the April 28 opening, decisions were made to create a new autobus system between La Ronde and the Métro entrance; a bus service to tour the island park; greater frequency of Expo Express trains; an enhanced system of embarking and debarking from the Expo Express; and a method of controlling numbers on the station platforms. They also intended to add to the number of restaurants and cheap food vendors.[5] "We doubled the number of garbage cans in the first week," says Beaubien. "Because it was so clean, people kept it clean."[6] In a June poll asking people what they liked most about Expo, 30 percent said the architecture; 22 percent the layout and efficient operation; 17 percent the courtesy of Expo employees; 15 percent the cleanliness; 11 percent the enormous size; and 10 percent the pavilions.[7] Washrooms had to be added—at one desperate point, a supervisor informed Beaubien a man was urinating from a balcony at Place d'Accueil, right above a lineup of people waiting for the bus to Saint Laurent.[8] The sheer numbers kept them running as fast as they could. Lanes had to be redone, flowerbeds replanted. As of June 1, Beaubien banned most taxis and private cars from Île Ste. Hélène because of traffic congestion.[9] Imagine building a city, Beaubien said, and then opening it to the public but not knowing how your city plan is actually going to work. That was the case here.

From a two-storey below-ground operations centre on Île Ste. Hélène, about one hundred metres from the island's Métro station, Beaubien and his staff kept track of the goings-on on the Expo site. A network of eleven branch controls fed into the operations centre, which was dominated by a large map of the site, eight TV screens that monitored thirty-two closed-circuit cameras, mobile television units, and four rear-screen projectors that provided information on program details, enlargements of grids that indicated buildings, and electrical, gas and water channels. A row of coloured lights on this information nexus known as the "action board" relayed the status of efforts to handle emergencies. A red light indicated emergency; a white light indicated that the branch concerned had been notified and steps were being taken; a green light gave the all-clear.[10] In addition, a daily "OPS," or operations control centre, record was kept of items mundane and otherwise, such as these selections from May 24:

1203 hrs PR reported no one to escort or lead Cardinal Léger from CANA [Canadian Pavilion]

1247 hrs La Ronde reported small fire under roller coaster—all under control

1835 hrs PS Busby reported that driver of Bottling Boy truck parked at Cey[lon Pavilion], who initially was believed to have been inebriated, actually had a heart attack. He had been taken to a hospital and his firm informed.[11]

One bizarre incident involved a frantic phone call to the "action room" from the mass transit controller's office. The transit official at the other end of the line claimed he was under cannon fire. At OPS control, the thought did cross their minds this individual was having some sort of nervous breakdown. But then Beaubien and team arrived to discover that a cannonball actually had come crashing through the mass transit controller's roof.

Piecing the story together, Beaubien discovered that two cadets from the Compagnies Franches de la Marine, hired for the summer to add a touch of pageantry, were responsible. Their job was to walk the Expo grounds and fire off hourly the miniature cannon they towed behind them. But then they had come upon the cannons at the Old Fort on Île Ste. Hélène and decided to have some fun with a *real* cannon. (It is more than likely they had also enjoyed a few beers.) They stuffed the cannon with some old shirts and powder and lit the assemblage, not realizing an ancient cannonball was also inside. The cannonball shot off in the direction of La Ronde and tore through the roof of the mass transit controller. Miraculously, no one got hurt.[12]

When Beaubien was not at the control centre, he was generally out on the site, accompanied always by his Bellboy pager; since the Bellboy afforded no two-way communication, whenever it beeped, Beaubien headed to the nearest phone.

The issue of crowd control concerned Beaubien from earliest days. He had visited Robert Moses's 1964–65 New York World's Fair and come back to Montreal unimpressed: "It was a disaster. Line-ups of up to four hours to get into pavilions. And I was disillusioned when I got back. 'How am I going to level the crowds?'"[13] One answer would be found in what became an Expo 67 signature element and one of its most innovative marketing tools: the twenty-five-dollar passport. "As soon as people start spending that much money," says Beaubien, "they had an investment."[14] As a means of levelling crowds, this passport, or multi-use ticket, offered alternatives, if at first one could not get into the more popular pavilions. Too big a lineup at the Czech Pavilion? Then try the Thai Pavilion and get your passport stamped there. This seemed good psychology, even if the visitor at some point probably had to brave another lineup at that popular pavilion.

Beaubien's efforts ensured the passport idea won over certain national commissioners general who objected to it on grounds that it impinged on their sovereignty. The impingement, in this case, being the necessity of added staff to stamp the passports. With help from the American and British commissioners general, Beaubien carried the day.[15] Expo, however, never completely licked the problem of lengthy lineup times at some of the more popular attractions.

At the heart of the visitor issue was the matter of transportation, and here Expo planners played an important role. "Time was the biggest challenge for the whole enterprise," says Steven Staples, who took over from Sandy van Ginkel before the master plan was completed. They had to run just to stay in place, there was so little lead time. Staples supervised the conceptual design of the transportation systems; the engineers under chief engineer Gilles Sarault supervised the structural aspects. His task was complicated by the fact that Staples had little dealing with chief architect Édouard Fiset: "Basically I talked directly to Churchill and basically I was in charge of attendance and interpreting that information to people in the operations department. Different countries wanted to know how many people would be going by their buildings, how many wash basins and how many fountains should be placed. The most important thing was the transportation."[16]

Moving sidewalks running at different speeds had been a feature at the Paris 1900 exposition. They would not be at Expo 67. "Moving sidewalks would never have had the capacity to serve what we later found out was required," explains Staples. By the end of 1963, the idea of a computerized train system was being discussed (at the eleventh hour, the planners added conductors as window dressing, on the assumption riders might grow alarmed at not seeing them), a train that would extend in a five-and-a-half-kilometre trajectory from Place d'Accueil on Cité du Havre all the way around to the La Ronde amusement park. "But exactly what form it would take was not decided until sometime in 1964," says Staples. "Because between 1963 and early 1964 there was a call for proposals for the major and minor transportation systems."[17]

For the major transit system, Expo Express, the decision was made to go with a version of the type used by the Toronto Transit Commission. The minor systems took longer to sew up. But in the summer of 1964, Churchill and Beaubien visited the fair in Lausanne, Switzerland; they also paid visits to Disneyland and the Canadian National Exhibition in Toronto. "Lausanne was very important," says Staples. "It was a very well designed and operated national exhibition … They had a minirail there which partially went through some of the buildings. It was designed by the Swiss firm, Habegger. The elevated minirail became the idea for the secondary transportation systems."

Negotiations began with Habegger to bring the Lausanne minirail to Expo, to become the Yellow Minirail; eventually they sited it on Île Ste. Hélène and La Ronde. Then negotiations continued with the same manufacturer to provide a large high-capacity system—the Blue Minirail—that would cross the Cosmos Walk connecting Îles Ste. Hélène and Notre Dame. It would first pass through the U.S. Pavilion, R. Buckminster Fuller's twenty-storey geodesic dome, and then under the roofs of the Ontario Pavilion and under the bridge next to the pedestrian path adjacent to the Quebec Pavilion. That it did not pass through more pavilions had to do with time and money. "The minirail is controlled by a signal system, it's not operated by people," says Staples. "So it's a very complex control system that has to be put in place. Besides, it was impossible to negotiate agreements with all the pavilions ... There were a lot of serendipitous situations. For example, the Blue Minirail went past the Atlantic Provinces Pavilion, which ... had a restaurant on the second floor. The Blue Minirail route came right past the restaurant windows so people on the minirail could see the people in the restaurant eating their lobsters. That became a very popular restaurant."[18]

Expo Express was free of charge and covered the circumference of the Expo site, and the two elevated minirail systems covered at closer but more limited range the site's interior. There was also a trailer train called the Balade, which hauled a group of cars on wheels around designated pathways. Pedicabs, helicopters, gondolas and hovercraft rounded out the transportation options.

Staples and his colleagues paid special attention to traffic flow since Expo had only two main entrances, the Métro stops at Île Ste. Hélène and Place d'Accueil, and a minor entrance at La Ronde off Jacques Cartier Bridge. In April 1965, KCS (Quebec) Ltd delivered a report on projected traffic flow. KCS was founded by Josef Kates, an Austrian immigrant whose resumé included the design of an automated traffic signalling system—said to be the first of its kind anywhere—for Metropolitan Toronto.[19] The report guided the planners as they projected the capacity for Expo Express (thirty thousand persons an hour, one way), the minor transportation systems and the public pathways.

These pedestrian pathways were key to the overall Expo concept. Strolling about and taking in the sights and sounds at one's own speed— here was the principal mode of Expo transportation. Ample expanses of lawn enhanced the sense of space and openness; indeed, a minimum of 40 percent of a building's site was allocated for green space.[20] Moreover, suppliers and their trucks could come onto the site only at night when the crowds had gone. Expo was a total environment. The landscape, the transport, the signage—all of it was of a piece with Expo's futurist conception. Rhona Richman Kenneally and Johanne Sloan note in the recently published *Expo 67: Not Just a Souvenir,* "Expo 67 can be seen as a kind of utopic urban satellite in opposition to the wider municipality that fed and sustained it—a municipality that, despite the intentions of Mayor Jean Drapeau to sanitize Montreal's street scene by sweeping its detritus (human and otherwise) under the rug for the visitors, maintained a seamy side commensurate with its reputation for hedonistic activities." Kenneally and Sloan point out that this was not the first time such an exhibition served as a glorified alter ego for the city hosting the event and cited the Chicago World's Fair of 1893, known as the "White City" because everything—buildings, streets, sculptures—had been covered in white paint, and thus created a prettified and marked contrast to the real-life "grey city" of Chicago.[21]

The sense of futurism was everywhere. In the sophisticated modes of transportation, certainly, and in the overwhelming architecture of all shapes and sizes. But also in more subtle ways. In the elegant and modern drinking fountains and street lamps and wastebaskets and benches created by Luis Villa.[22] And in the signage, much of it the work of Toronto designer Paul Arthur, considered a crucial link between the Canadian design community and the modernist design school of Europe.[23] It was "a laboratory for art and design," says William Thorsell, then the twenty-one-year-old manager of the Western Provinces Pavilion, who would later go on to become editor of *The Globe and Mail* and CEO of the Royal Ontario Museum.[24]

Paul Arthur's company provided directional signs, site maps, area maps and directories for Expo. Arthur used words when necessary, but preferred images. Of the two dozen pictographs Arthur developed for Expo, one of the more notable instances featured male and female images for washroom signage. This was novel for the time (and customary today), though the initial execution left something to be desired. The trousered man and skirted woman lacked sufficient definition. The upshot was that men occasionally entered the women's washrooms. Sometimes they held parties there. Security had to be called in to roust them. "The pants were not long enough," says Beaubien. The images were corrected, the pants adjusted.

Another notable instance of the use of images was Paul Arthur's animal silhouettes that denoted parking areas. Though here, too, unforeseen communication problems could occur. One American visitor grew angry after asking an Expo employee to explain her animal symbol to her. As it happened, the symbol denoted a seal, and *seal* in French is *phoque*. The employee obliged but evidently forgot to translate. "*Madame*," he said, "*c'est un phoque*." The visitor gave him a hard slap across the face.[25]

Certain language problems seemed inevitable. Arlene Perly had a job at the Russian Pavilion and was bemused so many American visitors appeared innocent of the French presence in Canada. They kept asking her questions like "Why are the bridges called *pont* bridge?" Perly (who would become Perly Rae after marriage to the lawyer-politician Bob Rae), seventeen going on eighteen and in her final year of high school in Toronto, says, "We took great pride in being bilingual." One couple approached her for help in finding their way back to their hotel. "They had carefully written down the name they remembered from the subway stop," she says, "and it was '*Sortie Seulement*.'" She wonders what happened to that couple.[26]

Following "ten years of incarceration" at Collège Regina Assumpta run by the Sisters of the Congregation of Notre Dame in the north end of the city, Louise Arbour stood poised to enter law school at the University of Montreal in the fall of 1967; Arbour would go on to become chief prosecutor at the Hague tribunal on war crimes as well as a justice of the Supreme Court of Canada (1999–2004). But at that time she was just one of the many newly liberated students looking to the future and a summer job at Expo. They all wanted jobs at Expo, she says, because the pay was "grossly, disproportionately superior to anything any one of us had made in the previous summer." She applied to be an Expo hostess but was "summarily rejected" because she did not meet the five-foot two-inches height minimum. "I didn't really speak English either," she says, "but I thought I could bluff." Expo guides were required to be bilingual. So, for that matter, were the telephone operators at Expovox, or La Voie d'Expo, the switchboard where she did manage to get a job. There were fifty phone operators at the St. James Street headquarters of Expovox when she started and "they just kept increasing the number—they grossly underestimated the number they would need." The Bell Canada operators were supplemented by students like herself. Operators sat in rows and wore headsets; one never actually picked up the phone. There was a supervisor for every ten operators and the supervisor could listen in to see how they conducted themselves.

"My supervisor, I think we understood each other implicitly," says Arbour. "I don't think she spoke any French. And I looked at her: 'Don't go there.' I'd had no exposure to English except what you learned in school. But the discipline of learning a language on the phone is you can't lip-read. So you don't have that crutch. You have to be hugely concentrated. On the other hand, you have no self-consciousness because the other person can't see you. By the time I was finished I thought I was good.

"One night I got a call, 'Miss, there's gonna be a bomb at Expo tonight.' I thought he said 'bum.' We were trained to be very apologetic. 'Oh, yes, I'm really sorry. Occasionally there are some of them at night …' He hung up. A few seconds later I saw another operator practically jump out of her chair. She must have gotten the same guy."

Then there was the caller who asked Arbour to provide the number of a whorehouse. "I'd never heard that word before," she says. "I thought he had said 'warehouse.' So I said, 'Well, we have several. Would you like the main one on the Expo site or would you prefer one of the ones downtown?' There was a lot of heavy breathing—him, and I think my supervisor, who was listening in."[27]

When it came to written signage, Robert Shaw notes, "We put the French first and English second because it was obvious more Francos would be reading the signs than Anglos. It didn't take a royal commission to figure that one out. We just went ahead and did it. And no one complained."[28] A few did, however, find fault in a way that was distinctly political. The separatist magazine *Parti pris* labelled Expo an "*immonde mystification,*" which, loosely translated, means something along the lines of "rotten con game." The magazine mocked Expo's efforts to fabricate a bilingual idiom—"Centre bilingual centre," "Centre validation centre," "Visit-Visitez Expo," such terms, as Eva-Marie Kröller notes "all derided as the colonizer's new game."[29]

Sometimes one had to marvel at the manner in which possible complications could be finessed. "When a waiter came to your table at a restaurant at Expo," says Graham Fraser, who would in time become Canada's commissioner of official languages, "he would come to the table and smile. And he would wait for you to initiate the conversation—and pick the language. That stuck with me. I thought, 'Boy, that's smart.'" For Graham Fraser, Montreal took on a kind of glow because of Expo. Expo seemed to attach to itself so many positive qualities: achievement, efficiency, the whole incredible style of it all. "Whether it was English and French working together, various technological breakthroughs, in terms of movies (which often turned out to be a flash in the pan), you had the sense of 'Oh my God! This is the way we will live!'"[30]

"In a lot of ways it was like the Olympics," says educator and former Olympic champion runner Bruce Kidd, "in that there was an international crowd and even though you spent a lot of time outside pavilions in lineups—the Czech pavilion was an hour long wait—there were great conversations, people from different countries and different parts of Canada."[31]

"I'd never been outside North America," says Ann Malcolmson, a Toronto social worker who came to Expo with her husband. "To be able to see these pavilions that were so different and serving food that was so different and the mode of dress so different—that was a real eye-opener for me, a sense of the world I'd never seen before."[32]

Not that all fair-goers succumbed entirely to Expo's enchantments. "I remember the confusion inherent in the fairgrounds in Montreal," wrote Alfred Heller in his *World's Fairs and the End of Progress: An Insider's View*. "Where was north, where south? I was never sure. Where was up, where down? The buildings, taken together, were architecture without grounding, as in the inverted pyramid that was the host country's pavilion. But the architecture journals were enthusiastic. An article about Expo 67 in *Architectural Record* celebrated a 'brilliantly ordered visual world.' The Montreal expo was in the 'universal' style in the tradition of fairs that took place in Paris during the last half of the nineteenth century: I mean outsize, often pretentious buildings, spacious grounds, and a feeling that no matter how long you stayed you could never comprehend this sprawling monster."[33]

For six months, director of operations and "mayor of Expo" Philippe de Gaspé Beaubien was the man in charge of this "sprawling monster." This was his city, his responsibility, his headache. "He never got the good news," his wife Nan-b would say, "he always got the bad news."[34]

One thing was for sure: wherever he went, Beaubien cut a dashing figure. "He was our Clark Gable," says Deirdre McIlwraith, who worked first as an Expo hostess and later at the Pavillon d'Honneur. "[He was a] French-Canadian *seigneur* with a beautiful wife from Boston. He spoke to everybody, from the cleaner on up. He was director of operations, so he had to know what was going on in every little nook and cranny."[35] Keeping abreast of every little nook and cranny inevitably took its toll on any recreation time. "I went to shows with my wife," Beaubien muses, "but I never finished a show."[36] ("He was there," says Nan-b, "for *three seconds*!"[37]) Nan-b, as wife of the "mayor," had her share of social duties as well. "You had to have the right height of glove for the different time of day," she remembers—the whole experience cooled her on the formal social scene. "I knew I never wanted to be a society lady," she says. "I realized what an empty life that was." Says Gretta Chambers about Nan-b de Gaspé Beaubien: "She was gracious and grand and really his partner. He always treated her as if she were the queen and he her consort."[38]

Even after the opening of Expo, the dinner meetings continued among the department heads, *les durs*. "It wasn't a fun meeting for me," says Beaubien, especially after Expo opened the gates and the central role shifted from Ed Churchill to him. "Like Churchill, I had no time." Moreover, his colleagues often arrived with "helpful" suggestions, about, say, the hostess uniforms or the parking facilities. "When we opened," says Beaubien, "most of them said, 'Jesus, it's done!' And for me it was just starting."[39]

Perhaps this attitude partly explains Director of Exhibitions Pierre de Bellefeuille's later criticism of Beaubien. "He was too superficial," says de Bellefeuille. "At *les durs*, Beaubien was not a major contributor. We had very deep concerns philosophically and Beaubien had no interest in these issues. Because Man and His World is an open door to philosophy and some of our discussions went fairly deeply into philosophy. Beaubien had little interest in these issues. Churchill did."[40] Beaubien, however, had his definite strengths. He was a "brilliant salesman," says Diana Thébaud Nicholson, who worked with him at Expo. "You stick him on the stage and let him talk about Expo and everybody wanted to buy in."[41]

"Kind heart, very warm," says Gretta Chambers. "He's basically warm and sympathetic—he doesn't put on the warmth, he really feels. He is not intellectual and Nan-b is, but he is very bright and *entregent*. Whatever he does, he enjoys. That again is very attractive."[42] Beaubien brought energy and pragmatism to the party and if, as some suggested, he was an "operator," always alert for the next important person or big opportunity to appear on the horizon, then surely such qualities well befitted a "mayor of Expo."

The job demanded long hours. Many nights Beaubien would sleep over in a guest suite at the Pavillon d'Honneur, only to be turfed from his room at dawn by the Pavillon's twenty-seven-year-old *maîtresse de maison*, Krystyne Romer, who, with her staff in tow, would be arriving to install fresh flowers and tidy the room for the next visiting dignitary. The long hours meant Beaubien did not see as much of his three young children as he would have liked. But every evening, he phoned home to tell them a bedtime story. "He never missed," says Diana Thébaud Nicholson. "An incredibly devoted father."

AS A DEVOTED FATHER, Beaubien understood that children as well as adults would want to visit Man and His World. It was Beaubien who favoured an amusement park at Expo. Pierre Dupuy, with his fastidiously cultivated tastes, was disinclined. But Beaubien prevailed. He was more of a showman, who understood that families with kids needed diversions beyond the elevating dimensions of an art gallery or pavilion. "To me," says Beaubien, "it was not a noble intellectual pursuit—it was a *fun* thing!"[43] He envisioned a "high-level amusement park" and set about his research, early on securing an audience with Walt Disney, the reigning maestro of the amusement/theme park business. The Disney ties to world's fairs went way back, from the time Disney's father Elias Disney laboured as one of the thousands of workmen on the Columbian Exposition of 1893[44] up to the more recent New York World's Fair of 1964–65, at which Disney 3D displays could be found everywhere.[45] Introductions with Disney were helped by the fact that Nan-b de Gaspé Beaubien and Sharon Disney, Walt's daughter, as children, had attended the same New Hampshire summer camp.

Another model for Beaubien was Tivoli Gardens in Copenhagen. But he needed to convince a doubter, Lucien Saulnier, Mayor Drapeau's indispensable lieutenant at City Hall and chair of its executive committee.

Beaubien proposed to Saulnier they take a trip to Copenhagen so the latter might then understand the wisdom of having an amusement park. Beaubien had the good salesman's gift of knowing you strike while the iron is hot. He proposed to Saulnier they go that very day and, to Saulnier's credit, he accepted the sudden invitation. Saulnier, known as a leavening influence on the impetuous Drapeau, was regarded as generally conservative on spending matters. Convincing him would be the charm. They went, they saw, and Saulnier returned convinced. Expo would have its amusement park, a fifty-five-hectare piece of land at the easterly end of Île Ste. Hélène to be called La Ronde. It would temper the tone of high culture suffusing so many of those early Expo plans.

It also meant a steep learning curve for Andrew Hoffman, one of the young planners hired to execute the Expo master plan. Where other planning colleagues were given responsibility for the realization of Îles Ste. Hélène or Notre Dame or of Cité du Havre, Hoffman, at least in his own eyes, drew the short straw. "The least attractive bit of the pie was the amusement park," he says.[46] But he got into gear and flew to Copenhagen in autumn 1964 to learn firsthand from the chief designer of Tivoli Gardens. Further travels took him to Disneyland in California, the Six Flags amusement park in Texas and the New York fair site. He began trying "to learn the trade of what makes people tick in an amusement park."

Hoffman hired Californian Herb Rosenthal to design the master plan for La Ronde. Taking his cue from the overall Expo master plan, Rosenthal designed La Ronde thematically—Creation, Discovery, etc.— and, in Hoffman's words, did "the most futuristic show on earth." Maybe Rosenthal's design seemed too brilliantly futuristic. Faced with tight deadlines, Colonel Churchill and his engineers could leave nothing to chance. Churchill mothballed Rosenthal's scheme and Hoffman then turned to the Toronto design consulting firm of Sasaki and Strong. "Dick Strong," says Hoffman, "was not so much an idea man as an application man." "Application" was a word dear to the practical Churchill's heart.

Elements of the Rosenthal plan remained as inspiration, though. Above all, says Hoffman, what they wanted was a "fun fair Expo." Hence, the Discovery of the West area with its fort, flume and saloon. Hence, other key components of La Ronde, like the four-million-dollar permanent aquarium and dolphin pool, a joint venture of the City of Montreal and the Aluminum Company of Canada; Children's World, an amusement park within an amusement park, constructed specifically for children in the four to nine age range; the Ride Centre; an Old Quebec Village; and the Garden of Stars theatre, which featured popular entertainments. Perhaps the most popular area was the Carrefour International, where one found many of Expo's best boutiques as well as restaurants ranging from the British Bulldog Pub to the Bavarian restaurant with its oompah band to the Hawaiian Theatre-Restaurant. The Czechs, whose pavilion proved a big draw, made their presence felt at La Ronde, too, with the Koliba Chalet restaurant at the Carrefour International and their film-with-live-action *Laterna Magika* show.

Hoffman says he received "absolute and full support from Colonel Churchill," though this hardly prevented Churchill from regularly chewing him out at the Friday afternoon critical path meetings. Churchill demanded action, action, action. When Hoffman had difficulty reaching a decision on the colour of certain buildings at Children's World, Churchill told him to stop thinking and decide. "And if you don't," Churchill warned him, "I will—and I have *terrible* taste!"

The decision to go with La Ronde represented a concession of sorts to cotton-candy populism, though the Expo people continued to display a degree of snobbery where Toronto's Canadian National Exhibition was concerned. Their amusement park, they contended, would definitely be a sizeable cut above the CNE, which belonged to the world of carnival barkers, not high-toned exhibits. Evidently, one tense moment did occur in 1965, when Robert Shaw called Hoffman and his colleagues into his office to introduce them to Paddy Conklin, the CNE's general manager. "'You people are farting around here a lot and Paddy Conklin is ready to take over La Ronde for a few million dollars, but you keep out of it,'" Hoffman says Shaw told them. "And of course we all had a collective heart attack and we presented the 'cons' against the idea, why a Canadian exhibition could not be undersold for a few million dollars and a few less grey hairs. And Paddy Conklin was outside the office and Shaw went out and said something like 'Sorry, old boy.' He just let Paddy Conklin go and he walked away. He could have applied political pressure and he didn't." Told later of this account, Beaubien downplays the actual threat: "By that time the die was cast. It was too late for Paddy's type of show."[47]

One of the more colourful people with whom Hoffman worked was Sean Kenny, designer of the Gyrotron. The triodetic-structured ride began in space and ended deep down in Earth's core with an encounter with a mechanical monster rising from molten lava. The Gyrotron did not impress the irreverent young editors of *Expo Inside Out!*, who deemed it a "fizzle."[48] Indeed, the Gyrotron had its problems—it got stuck opening day, temporarily stranding scores of passengers—and some of the Expo brass considered it a white elephant.[49] But the Gyrotron fooled the pessimists, becoming the most successful ride at the fair.

Nor could anyone deny the inventiveness and charisma of its young creator. "Ireland's mad, baby-faced maniac, made up of blarney and genuine magic," is the way actor Christopher Plummer describes Sean Kenny.[50] "He was a genius as a designer, but he was one of those people who started living at 11 p.m. in the evening and by 3 A.M. would say, 'I have to get into a fight with somebody!'" recalls Andrew Hoffman. "And I would say to him, 'Not with *me.*'"[51] Kenny's contract with Expo enabled him to stay six months at the exclusive Ritz-Carlton, where, presumably, he enjoyed the high life, which would have included such visitors as the British starlet Judy Huxtable. "When Judy Huxtable walked out of the Ritz-Carlton in her light purple pantsuit that was all the rage at the time," says Hoffman, "there wasn't a man on Sherbrooke Street who didn't melt." Here it was, "Swinging London," in the heart of Montreal. Sean Kenny died several years later, at the age of thirty-six, from, in Hoffman's words, "an overdose of drugs, sex, and alcohol."

La Ronde had a twenty-five-million-dollar budget and Hoffman estimates they ran seven million dollars over. After Expo opened, Hoffman's job was to keep it running smoothly. Thoughts that La Ronde might live on after Expo existed in the minds of management but remained quietly nugatory; to have articulated them at that stage, says Beaubien, would have caused other Canadian cities to cry favouritism.[52] As for Andrew Hoffman, of the time he spent at La Ronde, he says, "Twelve hour days, I lost my hair, practically divorced ... It was a *tre-men-dous* experience!"

FIVE

At the Pavillon

While the fun fair at La Ronde provided amusements on a mass level, diversions of a more rarified order could be found across Île Ste. Hélène at the Hélène de Champlain restaurant. Drapeau had allocated it to Expo 67 for use as its Pavillon d'Honneur, the place where visiting dignitaries from far and near could be wined and dined and allowed to take a breather in one of the upstairs guest suites. Twenty-seven-year-old Krystyne Romer (later Krystyne Griffin by marriage) became its *maîtresse de maison*—a role that normally might have gone to someone more senior, though even then her imposing six-foot height and aristocratic features lent her a natural hauteur perfect for the job.

"He chose me," she says of Commissioner General Pierre Dupuy, "because he said, 'She'll know when to appear and disappear—and she's a workhorse.'"[1] She has fond memories of Dupuy. "I think of him: how did he have that freshness? I loved him so much. He was an older man ... He thought I was sort of in love with him—I loved him but I was not *in* love with him—so he was always giving me information about life and love. He liked spending time. He was like an old squirrel,

a chipmunk. Round face, physically small. Charming. He was a flirt, he
was very French. He knew how to notice everything. He would notice
the smallest things about you and tell you what pleasure you gave with
them."

Deputy Commissioner General Robert Shaw worked with Krystyne
Romer's father, R. Edward ("Red") Romer, at The Foundation Company
engineering firm and had hired him as the chief estimator for Expo—
the person whose job is to calculate the likely cost of carrying out the
work. Trained as an architect but active mainly as a civil engineer, Romer
would, according to his daughter, walk the Expo site with a Pentax
camera around his neck and a pipe in his mouth. Krystyne describes her
father as "one of the quiet geniuses" and "very noble looking." Before
Expo, she was organizing conferences for IBM International in Paris, and
her father's connection may have been one of the reasons the Expo team
turned to her when searching for a person to head up visitor services.
Pierre Dupuy also knew of her family through her uncle, Tadeus, a distinguished diplomat, but the Expo official who approached her was Philippe
de Gaspé Beaubien, who was, as she puts it, "more my generation, the
other ones were venerable." She accepted his offer even though it meant
a lower salary than her current job. But like others of her generation who
signed on at Expo—and at Expo, she says, "you took young people"—
Romer saw the opportunities in running her own show. Many of the
younger hires, the ambitious ones, perceived the advantages in taking
an Expo job. "One thing that built Expo at the time was the youth of
the people who were doing it," says Roger D. Landry, who ended up
a protocol head. "When you're thirty [he was thirty-one], you're not
afraid of it. When you're forty, you're not afraid of it. I can tell you I
would never have had the career I had if I had not had that experience."[2]
Landry eventually became publisher of the major Quebec newspaper *La
Presse*.

By 1966, Krystyne Romer had, in her words, "veered strictly into
protocol" and become the *maîtresse de maison*. Protocol was a sensitive

area because, as she says, "you can give offence with a wink." It was understood you never wore red around royalty because that was their colour and theirs alone. It was understood you never wore black because black was the colour of mourning. A visit by the emperor of Japan's brother meant she had to ensure no chrysanthemums were in evidence because these were reserved solely for floral displays for the emperor. A visiting head of state might be offered three principal meals: dinner in Ottawa with the prime minister and governor general; luncheon at the Pavillon d'Honneur; and perhaps a dinner reception with the mayor at City Hall. At the Pavillon, luncheons averaged forty to forty-eight guests and each person was seated according to rank, fanning out from the guest of honour at the centre of the table; seated across the table directly opposite the guest of honour would be Pierre Dupuy.

Romer wrote out each menu herself and planned the flower arrangements. For the crown prince of Norway, a bachelor, she arranged the table with blue cornflowers. The prince got the joke. "I believe this is what is called a 'bachelor's button,'" he said to her with a grin.[3] When her Polish grandmother urged her to boycott a luncheon for a Russian dignitary—her grandmother had twice been exiled to Siberia—she felt conflicted, but her father told her to carry on and do her job. She did, though not without the tiniest touch of subversion. When that luncheon ended, Dupuy approached her. "Mademoiselle Romer," he inquired, "did I detect the bleeding heart of Poland [flower] in that arrangement?" She confessed that he did.

One of Romer's more challenging menu assignments was for a visiting dignitary who had one paralyzed arm and the other half-paralyzed. Eating meant using a spoon and she decided on calves' brains. "I almost got fired by Kniewasser," she says. "Someone said I'd served 'innards.'" The calves' brains caused her trouble with G. Dale Rediker, Expo's director of finance and administration whose turf included security. The problem: the calves had to be slaughtered five to six hours before the meal, but no one could gain access to Expo before eight in the morning. "I came into my office at 8:00 to 8:30 A.M. and all the security phones were flashing," she says. "If it's a double red flash, it's straight to Rediker's office." A truck filled with calves' brains had sought access to the site from the Jacques Cartier Bridge entrance and Rediker demanded an explanation. Ultimately, the truck was cleared and the luncheon went off, though later Romer had to report to Kniewasser and receive her dressing-down for serving "innards."

Today Kniewasser speaks of Romer affectionately and mentions how he once interceded after she kicked a security guard in the groin.[4] Not so, says she. That story, she says, is "allegorical." She, too, speaks fondly, though. "He was young and good-looking," she says of Kniewasser. "When he was very pleased, he'd stand up and stretch his chest and pop the buttons on his pale blue shirt."[5]

The shah of Iran preferred asparagus consommé and cheese at the start of a meal. He also required long-stemmed roses strewn before his path as he walked across carpets specially delivered from Iran. Only two notable Expo visitors rated the bow termed in protocol "*la grande révérence.*" The shah was one, Emperor Haile Selassie of Ethiopia the other. (Queen Elizabeth II, who bypassed the Pavillon during her visit to Expo, received only a half-reverence.) "I did the Grand Reverence and he picked me up and said, 'No, you are the queen here,'" she says of the shah's visit, information imparted with a sly smile. "I had some moments," she says.

Queen Juliana of the Netherlands, who, with her husband Prince Bernhardt, spent the war years in Ottawa after the Germans invaded the Netherlands, had a less ceremonious attitude. Arriving at Dorval, and determined to stretch her legs after the flight, she ignored the ten-limousine cortège waiting by the plane and proceeded across the tarmac to the terminal. A somewhat aghast Lionel Chevrier, commissioner general for state visits to Expo 67, watched her as she made her way. "Planes were taking off and landing all over the place," he recalled, "but she walked right across the whole business."[6]

For Romer, the most beautiful woman to arrive at Expo was Queen Sirikit of Thailand, and among the most reluctant guests, Newfoundland premier Joey Smallwood. Smallwood attended the public opening of Expo and was expected to join his fellow premiers for a luncheon at the Pavillon d'Honneur. But he did not show up. When Romer tracked him down in a nearby parking lot, "Sweetheart," he told her, "I want to see the show, I don't need to go to any luncheon. Bring me some food here." She persuaded him to at least put in an appearance.[7] Among the non–heads of state who turned up during the run of Expo was Broadway musical comedy star Carol Channing, heading a production of *Hello Dolly*, who arrived with a red bag full of her own food and was "noisy and fun."

The first head of state to arrive at Expo also proved among the most memorable. Haile Selassie, emperor of Ethiopia and (among his many titles) Lion of Judah, arrived in his own Rolls-Royce with his beloved chihuahua Lulu at his side. The Expo team had been warned about Lulu, who was "never to be addressed as a dog."[8] Lulu was always with the emperor—in fact had dashed up the airport escalator ahead of him and received, by mistake, a royal salute.[9] The rule about dogs not being allowed on Expo grounds was suddenly unimportant. Romer knew the drill. No notice was to be taken of little Lulu's ... problems: As she instructed her staff, "She's incontinent. If she pees, you leave it. You don't run out with a mop!" Moreover, Lulu would eat what the emperor ate, but dipped in milk and fed by him. Upon arrival, Lulu quickly lived down to expectations. "Lulu jumped out of the Rolls-Royce with the emperor," she remembers, "and immediately puddled at the entrance of the stone floor pavilion. I saw one of my men with a cloth and I warned him away." At least one Expo official preferred to see the upside. "This guy normally travels with elephants," Andrew Kniewasser told his team. "Count your blessings."[10]

Following the luncheon in his honour, the emperor announced himself in need of a rest and, as protocol required, Romer (who, at six feet, towered over him) walked backwards in front (you do not turn your back on an emperor) and led him upstairs to his suite. "Haile Selassie is a little man," she says, "five-foot-two or something. He lies down, and he says to me, 'Of course, you will stay with me.' And I am saying to myself, 'What am I supposed to do? Does he expect me to lie down on the bed with him?' Then I had a brainwave! I picked up Lulu and moved backwards from the bed and said, 'I will not be very far.' And I stood in the doorway for forty minutes while he rested."

Awaking refreshed, the emperor told Romer "an angel" brought him a very good dream and he handed her a gold coin. Descending the stairs to rejoin the other guests, he took her hand and they walked down hand-in-hand. "And I could just see the consternation on the faces of the Canadians," she says. "I didn't know what to do—*he* took *my* hand!" Things were put right, however, when Haile Selassie took Dupuy's hand and the three of them, still holding hands, exited the Pavillon d'Honneur. The emperor of Ethiopia enjoyed his time at Expo so much, he stayed on two extra days. Other dignitaries also extended their visits, a compliment to Expo that nonetheless created bottlenecks and security headaches for Philippe de Gaspé Beaubien. While the emperor of Ethiopia, the oldest head of state, enjoyed his three-day visit to Expo, the world's most powerful head of state was in and out in roughly ninety minutes. But then, U.S. president Lyndon Johnson had much on his mind, and Expo 67 never ranked high on his list of priorities.

SIX

Wonders of the World: Part One

Pierre Dupuy had his notions. He envisaged an Expo 67 where the "noble nations" participating—that is to say, Canada, the United States, Britain and France—would occupy a place of honour on Île Ste. Hélène, while the other nations could be placed on Île Notre Dame. Expo planners, on the other hand, had their own ideas. For instance, according to Moshe Safdie, the planners felt that the Canadian Pavilion, the pavilion of the host country, should not be at the entrance but at the end of the circulation path. "In the same way, more or less as if we were designing a shopping centre," said Safdie, "we said the U.S. and Russian Pavilions ought to be at opposite ends of the circulation pattern, like two big department stores, with all the small pavilions in between like small shops."[1] But if Dupuy could not always have his way on matters such as placement—Canada, Britain and France, for example, ended up on Île Notre Dame—no one could deny his persuasive powers in reeling in the participating nations. There were sixty-one national pavilions in all, plus certain U.S. state pavilions and the Canadian federal and provincial presences.

Dupuy's signal contribution to Expo had been in the months and years he spent employing his formidable arsenal of diplomatic contacts to bring the countries in. Now he could exult in the results of his efforts, commemorated, with the requisite pomp and circumstance, in a national day for each participating nation at Place des Nations. The national days were celebrated on Tuesdays, Wednesdays and Thursdays of each week, and protocol demanded twenty-two cannon bursts for heads of state, nineteen for representatives.[2] Some journalists found the ceremonies tedious—too much protocol, too many speeches, too much counting out of the cannon bursts. Pierre Dupuy loved every minute.

A particular coup for Dupuy had been securing the participation of twenty-one African countries, of which twenty were independent. But since many of these countries had only recently achieved their independence, they lacked the necessary means to underwrite a proper pavilion. Undeterred, Dupuy helped engineer a cooperative effort among the three levels of Canadian government to create Africa Place, a series of interlocking hut-like buildings with brick walls and white plastic roofs designed by Australian-born, then-Toronto-based architect John Andrews. The majority of the African countries elected to assemble under the Africa Place umbrella, with Ethiopia and Mauritius electing to have their own pavilions. Fifteen of these African countries were francophone.

With a sense of celebration at being able to welcome new members into the "club" of nations, Expo officials also had to be aware of heightened sensitivities on the issue of race. Before Expo opened, the New York Urban League, a black advocacy group, accused Expo of discrimination in hiring and suggested in a letter to U.S. president Lyndon Johnson that the United States withdraw from the exhibition. The Urban League's critique never gained much traction, and the charges were rejected by the participating commissioners general.[3] But in July, eight of the fifteen francophone African pavilions closed their doors to protest what they deemed failures on the part of Expo management. (The anglophone African pavilions did not join in because their complaints had already been addressed.) The sources of complaint included lax security and maintenance, in reference to several robberies at the Congo, Ivory Coast, Gabon and Togo pavilions; Expo's choice of American black dancers to perform at Africa Place in traditional African costume; and the allegation that Expo had not received African dignitaries with proper regard for their rank. The offended pavilions soon reopened. A joint communiqué stated, "The Corporation will take all the necessary measures to ensure a prompt and permanent solution."[4] Within a week of that kerfuffle, the Uganda Pavilion shut down temporarily, but for reasons relating to hygiene and aesthetics rather than affronted sensibilities. The rotting meat used to feed the alligators there had created a foul odour.[5]

The idea of a shared pavilion approach was repeated, at their own initiative, by the Scandinavian nations, and Dupuy invited Arab countries to consider the sharing arrangement as well. The United Arab Republic (UAR), the temporary union of Egypt and Syria (after Prime Minister Pearson personally contacted Egyptian president Gamal Abdel Nasser),[6] entered Expo on this basis, together with Algeria and Kuwait. Tunisia and Morocco decided to have their own pavilions. About a month after Expo's opening, though, Kuwait pulled out because of Canada's "hostile attitude" during the crisis in the Middle East. (This was the summer of the "Six-Day War" between Israel and its Arab neighbours.) The Kuwait portion of the Arab countries pavilion remained unused and in limbo, though later there was talk of converting it into a restaurant.[7] Protesters twice disrupted the UAR Pavilion, both incidents occurring before Egypt had agreed to a ceasefire with Israel. Pavilion officials were tight-lipped about the disturbances. "Nothing at all happened here today," declared an official after one such disturbance. "The police were here simply as visitors."[8]

Dupuy nursed his special disappointments. The chronological proximity to the New York World's Fair of 1964–65 hurt Expo to an extent. Certain nations that had participated in that earlier event ended up paying far more than they had bargained for. These countries feared similar overruns in any Expo 67 commitment. Not a few decided to pass. "The main example of this was Spain, which had one of the most popular pavilions at the New York World's Fair, but the cost was horrendous," explains Pierre de Bellefeuille, Expo's director of exhibitions and the person who, with Dupuy, shouldered a major part of the load in wooing nations to participate. "So Spain was particularly reluctant to join Expo 67."[9] In fact, Spain never did sign on, a blow to Dupuy, who resorted to all manner of stratagems, including pressuring Lester Pearson to write a personal message to the Spanish head of state Generalissimo Francisco Franco. Dupuy says he consoled himself with the knowledge that Spain's presence would be felt in the magnificent art works by Velázquez, Goya and El Greco, on display at the Expo art gallery as part of the Man the Creator theme.[10]

But Spain was not the only letdown. Venezuela joined Expo, and three months later temporarily shuttered its pavilion out of respect for the hundreds killed in a devastating earthquake in Caracas. In the main, however, non-participation by South and Central American countries proved discouraging for Dupuy.[11] Meanwhile, Mexico blamed its late opening on the time it took to ship its exhibits to Montreal.[12] Another late starter—and quick finisher—was the exhibition's smallest pavilion: St. Kitts, Nevis and Anguilla set up an umbrella and a table and Miss Statehood stamped passports for twelve hours and then that was it—they were gone.[13] Ireland announced its intention to participate but eventually decided against.[14] Three young New Zealanders erected an ad hoc New Zealand "pavilion" near the Australian Pavilion's kangaroo pit, the pavilion in this instance a pup tent assembled in the pelting rain. The youths toasted the pup tent with champagne, then offered an "authentic" Maori war dance before security officers hustled them away.[15]

Certain rejections Dupuy took personally. Luxembourg decided to pass, even though Canada had provided a refuge for the ruling family during World War II.[16] Perhaps Dupuy's greatest disappointment resulted from the failure to induce mainland People's Republic of China (often known as Red China in those days) to take part. "He had a dream that did not materialize, of China participating," says Pierre de Bellefeuille. "He spent a lot of time trying to convince the board of Expo and convince people who might have some influence on China that China should participate."[17] The excuse for this non-participation was that, because Canada did not officially recognize Peking (now Beijing), the mainland Chinese could not be invited through the ordinary diplomatic channels. On the other hand, a lack of diplomatic channels had not prevented Canada from selling the Chinese several hundred million dollars' worth of wheat.[18] As it was, China was represented at Expo by the nationalist Republic of China (Taiwan), in a pavilion described by one critic as "a heavy box surmounted by a garish San Francisco Chinatown roof."[19] Early into the run of Expo, the Chinese Pavilion suffered extensive fire damage, though careless smoking and not skullduggery was thought to be the culprit.[20] The pavilion reopened its doors a month later.

Dupuy nevertheless assembled an impressive list of participants. The dependables, like Britain and France, agreed early, as did Belgium, host of the previous international exposition. The Netherlands, Austria and West Germany came in, as did Israel, Iran, Italy, Czechoslovakia, Switzerland and Japan. Jamaica and Cuba agreed to participate, and so did Haiti, whose minister of commerce and industry blamed its tenuous tourist trade on "hell on earth" press reports—as if the press could have invented the ghastly François "Papa Doc" Duvalier, the tiny island country's despotic ruler.[21]

Dupuy understood well that two indispensables in the mix had to be the Cold War superpowers, the United States and the Soviet Union. He reminded the Soviets that by pulling out of holding their own exhibition in 1967, they had forfeited millions of visitors, but that all was not lost because they could come to Montreal for their celebrations and find all the advantages, several times multiplied, there. Besides, they would be only eighty kilometres from the U.S. border and—Dupuy was a pro at playing on their Cold War competitiveness—how better to demonstrate the superiority of their civilization?[22]

Getting the Americans onside required its own careful handling. The New York World's Fair of 1964–65 disappointed many and, according to Dupuy, U.S. officials expressed an attitude that the time for the great fairs had passed. When he'd mention the Montreal exhibition, their reaction would be, "If New York couldn't make a go of it, how do you see Montreal succeeding?" It was, as he conceded, *"un fort courant à remonter"*—a tough current to swim against. Yet to Dupuy the argument was simple. Montreal's Expo would not be a "fair." It would be a Category One Universal and International World Exhibition under the auspices of the International Bureau of Exhibitions in Paris. The New York fair's commissioner, Robert Moses, had proceeded without BIE sanction and had thereby failed to attract many high-profile foreign participants. Still, if Dupuy felt confident about American involvement because of the two countries' close historical ties and associations, he realized he could stoke that determination by stressing the Russian plans for Expo: in the face of such plans, how could the Americans *not* mount a full-court press of their own?[23]

Expo planners situated the two superpowers across from each other, the U.S. Pavilion on Île Ste. Hélène and the Russian Pavilion on Île Notre Dame, separated by the Le Moyne Channel but linked by a bridge named Cosmos Walk—an apt title since both pavilions featured significant space science exhibits. "Whereas the Brussels fair represented the atomic age (despite the Sputnik orbiting of the previous year), the Montreal exhibition depicts the space age," wrote John M. Lee in *The New York Times*. "Thanks to the East–West rivalry, Expo visitors can inspect the biggest group of Gemini capsules, Vostoks, Surveyors, Luniks, Apollo command modules and Molnia communications satellites ever assembled."[24]

While both nations boasted about their space know-how, the aesthetic divergence between the two pavilions could not have been more pronounced. The Russians were generally all business and heavy on the technological prowess. The Americans went lighter and offered a more playful attitude toward their culture's offerings: pop art and photographs of movie stars and movie memorabilia, Raggedy Ann dolls and Elvis Presley's guitar. A similar contrast between the Soviet and U.S. exhibits occurred in Brussels in 1958, but the 1967 juxtaposition prompted greater controversy.[25]

The U.S. exhibit, courtesy of the cutting-edge Cambridge Seven Associates design team, bore the brunt of that controversy; more often than not, those most critical were the Americans themselves. They decried the choices—*movie stars? pop art?*—and the absence of solemnity. Republican governor George Romney, father of Mitt and regarded as a leading contender for the following year's Republican Party presidential nomination, declared himself "bitterly disappointed" with his country's showing.[26] Indeed, a survey later revealed the Russians to have been the bigger crowd pleaser,[27] an indication perhaps of a public liking for hardware over frivolity, though Cold War politics and the natural curiosities it engendered obviously played their part. Nonetheless, the American exhibits had their ardent partisans, who admired them precisely because of this lighter touch, admired the sophistication and sense of confidence it betokened. "It's been done with a sense of humour," said the Canadian-born Hollywood director Mark Robson (whose pop-trash *Valley of the Dolls* was destined to be one of the box office hits of Christmas 1967). "If I wanted to see hardware, I would go to a hardware store."[28] Many others echoed that theme. "I found the U.S.S.R. Pavilion a bore," says Charles Oberdorf. "The only thing interesting was the live sturgeon tank producing caviar."[29] On the other hand, even the dissidents had to admit a certain admiring fascination. "Earnest and plodding and awful—but *amazing*," remembers one of them.[30]

The Russian Pavilion had a curved roof that swept down from a forty-two-metre height and then swept back up again. It resembled a ski jump and was supported by two enormous V-shaped trusses. The pavilion walls were of glass. To one viewer, it seemed "a rip-off (but airy and inviting nonetheless) of Eero Saarinen's Dulles airport."[31] It was designed by Mikhail V. Posokhin and built by the Italian company Feal of Milan, and some noticed a resemblance between its roof and that of the Italian Pavilion, both with their long, curving slopes.

For sheer beauty and audacious simplicity, though, nothing matched Buckminster Fuller's twenty-storey geodesic dome housing the U.S. Pavilion. Designed in association with architect Shoji Sadao and sponsored by the United States Information Agency, the "Skybreak Bubble," as Fuller called it, was a hemispheric structure made up of 1,900 interlocking and moulded acrylic panels held together by a steel pipe frame. The blinds on the panels could be adjusted to shield the interior from sunlight during the day and then retracted to allow in the natural light from outside in the evening. The bubble stood 60 metres high, was 75 metres in diameter, and contained 190,000 cubic metres of space. "Our life consists of rectangular spaces," says the lawyer and art critic Harry Malcolmson, "and the dome was a fresh and unique spatial experience. It was important because Fuller intended people to live in the biosphere—for the Americans to select him was so radical."[32] Perhaps not unexpectedly, the Russian press refused to be impressed, *Pravda* dismissing Fuller's dome as a "soap bubble."[33]

Fuller's bubble had its occasional problems. Rain sometimes leaked through the dome, and the silvered plastic sun blinds controlled by solar-activated motors sometimes malfunctioned. In the words of an observer, "the effect, especially from the outside, was really very decorative—like lots of flowers in varying sizes of opening—but presumably Buckminster Fuller was not amused!"[34] The general consensus, however, was that Fuller's dome was sublime.

"I loved that feeling of standing on that top deck in the U.S.

Pavilion," says Charles Oberdorf. "As Buckminster Fuller pointed out, you could see your path there from downtown Montreal and never lose sight of it. The only other place that has ever affected me like that was the Cologne Cathedral. You can't believe you're in an envelope that big with a membrane around it." Transport to these lofty reaches came via what was billed as the world's longest free-span escalator. "The joke going around," says Oberdorf, "was to compare it to the escalating war in Vietnam." (If he had one reservation about pavilion management, Oberdorf cited the use of young American marines as pavilion security. In addition to security personnel offered by Expo, nations often provided their own, and often played to colourful stereotype—the British, for example, using bobbies; the French, caped gendarmes. The growing unpopularity of U.S. involvement in Vietnam at times made the young marines targets. "They took a lot of heat from the kids," says Oberdorf. "It was a stupid decision to use them. They—the Americans—should have gotten some great New York cops."[35])

The binary relationship of the U.S. and Russian Pavilions found a modified echo in the placement of the British and French Pavilions. "Two of the largest and most bombastic of Expo's guests," in the words of architecture critic Ada Louise Huxtable, had their pavilions in near proximity to each other on Île Notre Dame.[36] Sir Basil Spence, architect of the British Pavilion, had created an exterior with a block-like Union Jack adorning the truncated-looking tower. It was likened by one critic to a "mausoleum,"[37] while in *artscanada* James Acland noted witheringly, "Sir Basil Spence has single-handedly created the most wildly inappropriate building at the fair. Every cliché and trick of the 1920s and 1930s has been used in this plaster-box 'modernistic' mish-mash. Not a touch of fantasy or of delight in the new worlds of man and technology enliven this torpid exercise in symbolic theatre."[38]

The exhibits inside, though, frequently spiked with irreverent humour, won plenty of fans. The Beatles were represented, of course, since they had become avatars of the mid-sixties "Swinging London" phenomenon, not to say one of their nation's major new revenue streams. Pre-opening controversy attended the decision to move the "Fab Four" from the "Genius of Britain" section to the "Britain Today" section. No longer pictured alongside Bacon, Newton and Darwin on giant billboards suspended from the forty-five-metre tower chamber, the Beatles had been relegated to four head-and-shoulder shots measuring about six inches and displayed on a table in the corner of the room. "They are not topical anymore," one of the pavilion hostesses blithely explained to a reporter. "Any music of theirs that we are playing was not recorded very recently. They shouldn't be in the 'genius' section."[39] Another popular feature of the pavilion was in fact the pavilion hostesses themselves in their specially designed red-white-and-blue Mary Quant miniskirts; miniskirts adorned other pavilion hostesses, but the British hostesses wore the shortest ones.[40] Miniskirts (*les minijupes*) were the moment's fashion fixation and cause of the occasional scandal, as when Italian film actress Claudia Cardinale decided to wear a mini on a visit to St. Peter's Basilica in Rome.[41]

The French Pavilion, designed by Jean Faugeron, oppressed in a different way than did the exterior of the British Pavilion. James Acland pushed back: "An immense bastion of concrete and steel, an over-inflated Guggenheim Museum with cylindrical decks facing into a light well, the French Pavilion by Faugeron perhaps works very well inside; but outside, presumably overcome with remorse at its gargantuan scale, someone has tacked on loosely a mess of aluminum fins unrelated to the structure, the theme or the intent of the whole. The result is a thoroughly untidy building."[42] Opinion was definitely mixed, but few critics appeared to flat-out love it. It had "a kind of dazzling super liner luxe," commented Ada Louise Huxtable,[43] but, for the reviewer from *France-Soir*, it resembled nothing so much as "a henhouse put together by a Sunday handyman."[44] The exhibitions inside the French Pavilion, however, including a splendid display of art, captivated many visitors. The pavilion was "overflowing with exhibits like a gigantic warehouse,"[45] commented one reviewer—though another visitor describes it as a calming place and remembers "the music and the dark light," noting "it was very textured and veiled."[46] The music was by the innovative composer Iannis Xenakis, whose multidisciplinary credits included the design of the Philips Pavilion at Brussels in 1958. At one point early in the run of Expo 67, the French Pavilion's commissioner general, Robert Bordaz, evidently felt his pavilion was altogether a little too low-key, perhaps a little too "veiled." English–French rivalry being what it was, Bordaz and his colleagues chafed at the long lineups at the nearby British Pavilion. What was their secret in attracting the crowds? Only after they realized the rival pavilion had fewer entrances did they readjust their sights, or rather their entrances. Closing some of their doors, they got the longer lineups desired. *"C'est la politique de la porte étroite"*—the politics of the narrow doorway—was the wry comment of Expo's Yves Jasmin.[47]

WHILE THE U.S.S.R. outspent the United States on pavilions by $12.3 million to $9 million, their host country outspent them both. Canada laid out $21 million for its own pavilion, whose central feature was an inverted pyramid of a building that bore the Inuktitut name "Katimavik," or "gathering place." That $21 million broke down into one-third for installation, one-third for exhibition, and one-third for operations. The upstart firm that won the commission to design the pavilion was Ashworth, Robbie, Vaughan and Williams, three of whose partners were based in Toronto, with Rod Robbie based in Ottawa. Having come to Canada from England in 1956, Robbie shared an office in Ottawa with the architectural firm of Matthew Stankiewicz, the latter well connected to the Canadian government's Exhibitions Commission. In 1963 the commission's creative director Tom Woods deputed Robbie and Stankiewicz, along with Paul Schoeller (whose firm had amalgamated with the other two), to prepare a study recommending what Canada's level of participation in Expo 67 ought to be. The trio came back with three levels of participation according to budget: $21 million, $18 million, and $15 million.

"The government picked the $21 million," says Robbie. "There were sixty firms that were after it from across the country. We had a little bit of an edge because we knew the people at the commission. We put our heart and soul into it ... This crowd were all landed immigrants. I didn't speak posh English—and I was the spokesperson."[48]

Their main competitors, according to Robbie, both big organizations, were the John C. Parkin firm from Toronto and Arcop (Affleck, Desbarats, Dimakopoulos, Lebensold and Sise) from Montreal. Arcop had already won the contract to design the Man the Explorer and Man the Producer theme pavilions. All of them showed up that fateful day to make their pitches to Deputy Minister of Finance Robert Bryce. "Ahead of me was John C. Parkin," says Robbie. "This guy was like oiled silk. I forget who represented Arcop." He entered the massive committee room, in the centre of which was a long table at whose head was the deputy minister of finance. Bryce told him his firm had been short-listed and to get on with his presentation. Robbie then launched into an impassioned speech about how Canadians always sold themselves short: "'You've done more than grow half the wheat in the world! What about the scientists? What about the artists?' I got so worked up, I burst into tears. 'This pavilion,' I said, 'has got to put Canada ahead of the U.S. and the Russians.' Bryce said, 'Pull yourself together!' And I thought: I've really screwed this. Then Bryce said, 'We are here as the representatives of the government of Canada and we have to be told by someone who is clearly a landed immigrant how we should present our country to the world.' Then he said, 'Oh, by the way, you've got the job!' I was stunned." Rod Robbie went out and got pleasantly smashed.

Expo's chief architect Édouard Fiset wanted the Canadian Pavilion to be confined to one acre and he could be stubborn. "I said, 'No bloody way,'" remembers Robbie, "'we ought to be the apex of the triangle opposite the U.S. and the Russians and facing right across at Montreal.

We want eleven and a half acres!' He had a fit over this. We got the minister [Mitchell Sharp, at that time federal minister of trade and commerce, responsible for Expo 67] to put the squeeze on and there was a very tough [Canadian Pavilion] commissioner general, H. Leslie Brown, and he supported us one hundred percent." Canada's ended up the largest pavilion at the exhibition. Surrounding it on another eleven acres on Île Notre Dame were the provincial pavilions for Ontario, the Western Provinces, and the Atlantic Provinces, as well as the Indians of Canada Pavilion, with the Quebec Pavilion somewhat apart, anchoring a row of European pavilions and positioned next door to France.

Placement was no small matter. Some still remembered the disaster of Brussels in 1958, when the Canadian Pavilion had been completely dominated by the high blank wall of the Russian cinema building next door. Canadian planners discovered this infelicity too late—as opposed, say, to Hitler's architect Albert Speer who, in preparing for the 1937 Paris exposition, happened accidentally upon the plans for the Russian Pavilion that would stand directly facing the German Pavilion across the Champs de Mars and thus had time to make the necessary (and fittingly grandiose) alterations so Germany would not be outshone.[49]

The inverted pyramid shape for Katimavik came about by chance. The team had been experimenting with geometric solids using cardboard boxes. The men all smoked, and they placed a large, green, upside-down, pyramid-shaped ashtray in the middle of the boxes they were playing around with. Something clicked. "It was not the right shape because it had a flat bottom but we decided that we could make thirty-degree pyramids," says Robbie. The idea of pyramids harked back to Robbie's time in the British army in Egypt during World War II. As he saw it, one of the central narratives of Expo 67 was about how Canada was an evolving country, assimilating many new people unto itself. And, as he explained, "The pyramids ... are a symbol of stability. Those legs that hold it up are almost like a pair of hands. It was an audacious statement. This is a country that everybody put in its second rank and we wanted something that made a strong statement." A portion of Katimavik was covered by a translucent plastic; Robbie noticed the material on a building at the 1964 Lausanne fair in Switzerland and admired the effect.

The mosaic nature of Canada's population was represented by a large globe, the "People Tree," located outside Katimavik, bearing colour photographs of the country's diverse ethnic populations—a "multi-coloured, illuminated magazine cover tree," in the more cynical (certainly funnier) estimation of Mordecai Richler.[50]

At one point, the Front de libération du Québec (FLQ) threatened to blow up one of the Katimavik legs. RCMP officers in civilian mufti swarmed the site, while right under their noses, two men dressed in workers' overalls drove away with a stash of copper pipe. Robbie remembers the biggest challenge as not the separatist FLQ but the weather, specifically the strong gusts off the St. Lawrence River. "The wind!" he says. "It just came up the river at full speed."

For Rod Robbie, his work on the Canadian Pavilion represented the highlight of his career, larger than subsequent big undertakings such as the Toronto SkyDome (now called the Rogers Centre) and the Frobisher Bay project. "It got almost no credit from the architectural profession," he notes. "I think there was a certain amount of jealousy that this obscure group of guys managed to land this monstrous job."[51] But for Robbie, the proof of success lay in mingling with the crowds of spectators who came to give his creation a look, and observing their pleasure. What mattered was that he had pulled off the big job and broken through—with his un-posh British accent no less.

One person who did speak posh English was Sir Basil Spence, architect of the British Pavilion. Robbie had phoned Sir Basil early on to inquire whether his firm might secure a joint partnership on that prestigious pavilion, as foreign architectural firms needed Canadian partners when building on Canadian soil. Reaching Sir Basil at his Montreal hotel, Robbie started into his pitch and at once realized his cause was doomed. Sir Basil quickly cut him off. "I'm quite shocked!" Sir Basil declared in a tone of icy hauteur. "We don't *hustle* work!" Rod Robbie felt himself bristle. "Well, this is Canada and we *do* hustle work!" he replied indignantly, knowing full well that here was a match destined never to be consummated, and recognizing again that wall of resistance, that entrenched classism, that helped drive him from his homeland in the first place—to Canada, a place where people seemed less inclined to hold your un-posh accent against you, where you were *expected* to hustle work. A place, Rod Robbie realized, where he felt right at home.

The experience of the Lausanne fair had proved to be an inspiration to Rod Robbie when it came to Expo. Lausanne, specifically a tent-like pavilion there designed by the West German architect Frei Otto, had also inspired Macy DuBois when DuBois came to design the Ontario Pavilion at Expo. A series of open-ended tent-like shapes attached to steel poles and arrayed over six-foot granite blocks, the Ontario Pavilion had an easy and casual quality many found appealing. James Ramsay—who, as head of the Special Projects branch of Economic Development for Ontario, was placed in charge of the province's Expo participation—wanted a show-stopping finale for the pavilion and was dissatisfied with the exhibition space he then had. So he asked DuBois if that section of the pavilion could be transformed into a movie theatre. In the space of a weekend, DuBois roughed out a plan for a 570-seat theatre. The movie that would go into this theatre—Christopher Chapman's *A Place to Stand*—provided the show stopper.[52]

"The Ontario Pavilion punched way above its weight at Expo," says William Thorsell.[53] It certainly inspired Toronto's Ontario Place, which opened in 1971. The pavilion also helped to liberalize Ontario's puritanical liquor laws because wine and beer could be served there on Sundays, which was not the case at that time in the province the pavilion represented. Certain Ontarians, however, at least initially, before the laudatory reviews came in, loathed the $8.5-million pavilion. "It looks vaguely like a bat strangling under a white sheet," wrote a Queen's Park columnist. "It may be the bat was trying to fly away."[54]

The Quebec Pavilion, by the architects Papineau, Gérin-Lajoie, Leblanc & Durand, moved in a different direction. It, too, had borrowed from Lausanne, acquiring the services of the thirty-nine-year-old Swiss designer Gustave Maeder, who created 4,200 half-metre wooden cubes in primary colours to adorn its austere interior. "The severe spirit of Mondrian fills the Quebec Pavilion," noted Robert Fulford. "Rarely can there ever have been a large exhibition so pure, so rarified, as this one."[55] But as in the case of Ontario, in a different way and for its own reasons, Quebec sought to present a particular image of itself to the world.

As one observer noted, "In stark contrast to historical concepts of the Quebecois as drawers of water and hewers of wood, as the inhabitants of folklore and painting, Quebec here emerged as a modern technological society with its gaze fixed firmly on the future, a future secured primarily through advancements in hydro-electric energy, mining and forestry. Virtually no reference to history was seen in the Quebec Pavilion; for this, one would have to visit the Quebecois village at La Ronde."[56] The Quebec Pavilion reflected the changes wrought by the Quiet Revolution. This was the new Quebec. Not folkloric, but business-minded and canny enough to enclose that message within its own sophisticated aesthetic. The Quebec Pavilion figuratively—and literally—was carving out its own special place: when Macy DuBois approached that pavilion's management about a bridge link over the small expanse of water separating the Ontario Pavilion from Quebec's, he was turned down.[57]

"There they stand, side by side at Expo 67, the two pavilions of the two richest Canadian provinces, Ontario and Quebec, separated by only a few yards of water," wrote Robert Fulford in the *Toronto Star*. "Individually, they are interesting. Together they make a fascinating study in the motivations of provincial image-building. Ontario, you see, comes on robust and creative and maybe rather messy. Not neat at all. Quebec, by contrast, comes on cool and restrained and sophisticated. At Expo 67, Ontario's pavilion is a bottle of beer and Quebec's is the driest martini in sight." Not a few thought these images had it all backwards—that Quebec was really the robust beer drinker and Ontario the aficionado of dry martinis. The point was that their respective pavilions represented projections of how they wanted to be seen in 1967.[58] Fulford's *Toronto Star* colleague Ray Timson offered a more partisan take: "Ontario has clobbered the bejabbers out of Quebec on the site of Expo 67. To contrast the pavilions of the nation's two leading provinces is simply no contest. Ontario wins it hands down, as decisively as Wolfe took Montcalm."[59]

This compare-and-contrast media fascination with Ontario and Quebec tended to overshadow the other provinces—a fascination that, more than forty years later and after the economic rise of Alberta and British Columbia, can nowadays seem almost quaint. Not that the other provinces were ignored. A critic for *Canadian Architect* credited the Western Provinces Pavilion as having, in its realistic logging exhibit, one of the best single displays at Expo.[60] And spectators at the Atlantic Provinces Pavilion admired that building so much they kept stealing the attractive beach stones surrounding it as keepsakes.[61]

Expo 67 and its variety of architectural styles proved a revelation. It made people more aware of their physical surroundings and what those surroundings—outside the utopian setting of Expo—might become if more thought were devoted to planning and stylistic niceties. Home-grown architects, designers and artists started to receive the kind of notice new to them, and not just locally, but on an international level as well. In *The New York Times*, Ada Louise Huxtable praised the Quebec Pavilion, calling it "the sleeper of the show" and "the Barcelona Pavilion of 1967." Huxtable's reference is to the Barcelona Pavilion designed by Mies van der Rohe for the Barcelona Fair of 1929, a building—not to say its accessories, including the Barcelona chair also designed by Mies— that continues to exert an influence on contemporary architecture and design. For Huxtable, the Quebec structure combined "an exceptionally refined and sensitively detailed work of contemporary architecture with an exhibition design that is a three-dimensional sensory abstraction of sight and electronic sound that says, suddenly and stunningly, what a 1967 exhibit should be."[62]

For Moshe Safdie, Expo 67 still represents a high-water mark among world exhibitions. "I don't think anything's come close to it since," he says of Expo 67, adding that it had a major impact on architecture "particularly in Canada, because it opened up people's imaginations not just to architecture but to urbanism and landscape design."[63] Toronto landscape architect John Hillier was fourteen years old when he and his family, who then lived in Port Colborne, Ontario, visited the exhibition. "Anything big I knew of was smokestacks, so seeing these buildings was just remarkable," he says. Habitat. The American geodesic dome. Arthur Erickson's luminous Man in the Community Pavilion. The Métro. They positively flabbergasted this small-town boy. But there occurred no sudden epiphany. Hillier went off to the University of Western Ontario with thoughts of becoming a dentist. Still, images of what he had seen at Expo played and replayed in his mind. "How can I combine science and art?" he asked himself—a question that rather quickly led him to the conclusion that landscape architecture might offer a more satisfying future than gums and teeth. The next year, he moved over to the University of Toronto and enrolled in landscape architecture. He'd found his calling.[64]

SEVEN

Neighbours

Would he or wouldn't he? Lyndon Baines Johnson, thirty-sixth president of the United States, kept them guessing. Until the night before his designated May 25 visit, LBJ kept Expo officials in the dark about whether or not he would show up; originally scheduled for a July 4 visit, that plan was scrubbed when it conflicted with the visit of England's Queen Elizabeth.[1] For Expo officials, some consolation existed in the knowledge that John V. Lindsay, the charismatic mayor of New York City, was to arrive the same day. Meanwhile, another American luminary arrived around this time—Clare Boothe Luce, a playwright (*The Women*) and occasional diplomat, of whom the great wit Dorothy Parker, when informed that the imperious Luce was invariably kind to her inferiors, shot back, "And *where* does she find them?"[2] Luce was the very recent widow of media titan Henry Luce, whose flagship magazines *Time* and *Life* devoted lavish praise and ample coverage to Montreal's world exhibition. Clare Boothe Luce and Pierre Dupuy had been ambassadors together in Rome, so it was old home week again for the well-connected Expo commissioner general. Dupuy accompanied Luce on a tour of the exhibition, which took in the U.S. Pavilion as well as lunch at the Italian Pavilion, where a reporter noticed that Luce appeared fascinated by "a robot man that could perform all sorts of feats with a human instructor pushing the buttons. It unscrewed a screw, it poured liquid from one bottle to another and picked up a box of matches to light Mrs. Luce's cigarette." The reporter described Luce as "an obviously highly-strung but gracious woman, simply but smartly dressed in a grey outfit with off-white trimmings." Not as highly strung, perhaps, as Expo organizers waiting to see if the U.S. president would arrive.

Arrive he did, however, landing at 11 a.m. at Montreal International Airport and being helicoptered at once to a spot near Place des Nations. Johnson had a lot on his mind, not least the deepening horror of the Vietnam War and the growing tensions between Israel and its Arab neighbours that were to lead to the start of the Six-Day War on June 5. The decision to come to Expo was last minute and essentially an excuse to visit Prime Minister Pearson to discuss high politics at the prime minister's country place in the Gatineau Hills just outside Ottawa. For Johnson, it was a way of killing two unpleasant ceremonial pigeons with one stone—visiting Expo, in which he took almost no interest, and calling on Prime Minister Pearson, whom he disliked. The two duties could be run together in such a way as to minimize the time spent on either one. Lyndon Johnson would be in Canada roughly five hours and Expo 67 would account for ninety-six minutes of that stay.

AS SOON AS HIS HELICOPTER landed on the Expo site, the president encountered his first protester. Barry Lord, editor of *artscanada* and curator of the painting exhibit at Expo's Canadian Pavilion was a self-described "working-class lad from Hamilton," far to the political left.[3] Some years earlier, while assistant curator at the Vancouver Art Gallery, Lord joined a Communist Party offshoot called the Progressive Workers Movement. Spurred on to protest against the war in Vietnam, Lord had, by 1967, already taken up cudgels against the most powerful man in the world. A couple of years earlier, Lord was working at the art museum in St. John, New Brunswick, and had formed the St. John Committee to End the War in Vietnam. Learning that President Johnson and Prime Minister Pearson planned to meet in the province at a small village resort near St. Andrew's, Lord, armed with a protest sign, hopped on a bus and set off for a confrontation. Johnson arrived by helicopter and, as he exited, his eyes momentarily glanced in Lord's direction. "Our eyes met," claims Lord. "I shouted something like 'Get out of Vietnam!'" Lord was still in position a few hours later when the U.S. president made his departure. The helicopter's liftoff whipped his sign around and sent it flying out of his hands.

Now it was two years later and this second encounter, at Expo, according to Lord, happened by chance and not design. Lord happened to be flying into Montreal from Boston, where he had organized an exhibit of Canadian painting, and while in a cab from the airport, suddenly became aware of a voice on the radio stating that Lyndon Johnson would be visiting Expo that day. "And the cabbie says, 'Listen to that, they know the students are in school and the workers are at work and that's why he's coming today.' But I didn't think anything about it. I got out of the taxi—the taxi left me at the end of the [Expo] site and I had to make my way through these huge grounds." Somehow, he found himself at the front of a surging crowd at just the spot where Johnson's helicopter was meant to land. Lord swears he tried to move away, but the police at that moment erected barricades in front of him. "It began to dawn on me," he says: "Somebody up there was conspiring to put me in the right place at the right time. God has spoken clearly. I am predestined to be here."

Just before the president's helicopter landed, a marine band struck up "The Marines' Hymn (Halls of Montezuma)." The crowd remained quiet, says Lord. He, on the other hand, was not the quiet type. "*Boooo!*" he shouted. "Marines are murderers in Vietnam!" Within minutes, four plainclothes security personnel approached him. According to Lord, they spoke Spanish to each other and "wore suits with the mandatory white handkerchief just showing a quarter-inch above the lapel pocket. And all four guys looked the same. They came through the crowd very quickly." They hauled him off, two grasping his arms, two of them on his legs. He called out for help: "I was so vociferous in fact that they smashed me in the mouth." (They later claimed he fell and split his lip.) Sighting a Mountie, Lord yelled out *"Je suis Canadien!"* and that the men carting him away were not. But the Mountie seemed more intent on preventing the supporters following Lord from proceeding any further. One of these was a woman with whom Lord had chatted earlier, who had attended a large anti-war demonstration in New York City the week before. The plainclothes officers handed Lord over to two Canadian police who informed him about the civic ordinance allowing no political statements to be made at Expo and advised him that it was illegal to protest. He spent the afternoon and evening in a Montreal jail—where he had company.

Another protester thrown into jail that afternoon was Donna Mergler; she and her boyfriend caused a minor disruption during Lyndon Johnson's appearance at Place des Nations. Johnson was their target that day, but their protest was never just about him. It was also about the civil rights movement in the U.S., about liberation movements in Quebec and the rest of the world. "It wasn't Lyndon Johnson the person," says Mergler. "It was what he represented."[4]

Mergler belonged to a group of eight who were meant to protest that day of Johnson's visit to Place des Nations, but apparently, the others never showed up. She and her boyfriend, who worked for a newspaper, found seats near the stage. She had dressed conservatively for the occasion—suede coat, white gloves ("because everybody wore gloves at that time"). As Johnson began his speech, Mergler and her boyfriend stood up and shouted "Johnson *assassin*"—applying French pronunciation to *assassin* because, "Saying it in French was important to us."

"Our voices were picked up by the mic and we sounded like a hundred voices," she recalled. "And he stopped for a moment ... and two Montreal police came to get us. There is this lovely picture that went out around the world of this policeman with his hand over my mouth. I'm not very tall and a year later I remember meeting this tall black guy from the States who said to me that when he saw the picture he said to himself, 'I'll never go up to that country—the police are so large.'" Mergler and her boyfriend spent fourteen hours in jail and were charged with disturbing the peace. Her father, prominent civil rights lawyer Bernard Mergler, got them released, paying $150 bail for the two of them and $100 for Barry Lord. "My father was very proud of me," she says. "Worried that we would be accused of all sorts of things, as a father is. But also very proud."

Bernard Mergler represented the interests of Cuba in Montreal, and his daughter spent a summer in that country planting trees. When the day arrived to honour Cuba at Place des Nations, Donna Mergler— who went on to become a university professor—savoured the irony of finding herself among the invited guests on the dais when, not long before, she had been hustled away from the same arena by the police. Three years after Expo 67, Bernard Mergler was asked to negotiate for FLQ members seeking passage to Cuba, part of an episode in Canada's history known as the October Crisis. This was a dark time that, in those sunny days, seemed impossible to contemplate. "It was really odd," says William Thorsell about that period at Expo. "There was this big war going on and we were living in this bubble of optimism in Montreal."[5] Yes, but bubbles tend to burst.

LYNDON JOHNSON MOVED through the protocol paces in decisive fashion. First up was the twenty-one-gun salute at Place des Nations, accompanying the raising of the American flag as Johnson stood standing beside, and towering above, the diminutive Pierre Dupuy. When the Stars and Stripes reached the top of the flagpole, a large rip was revealed and the flag had to be immediately lowered. "Your presence here today is all the more appreciated because we know the heavy burden you have to carry like an Atlas," declared Dupuy in his welcoming remarks.[6] Before Johnson could reply, the cries of "Johnson *assassin*" from Donna Mergler and her boyfriend could be heard coming from the Place des Nations audience. A bylaw had been passed making political demonstrations at Expo illegal. Expo general manager Andrew Kniewasser says he received criticism from Americans when he barred protesters who gathered to picket LBJ. They told him it was their tradition. Kniewasser replied that it was not the tradition of Expo 67.

Anyway, Johnson paid little attention to the brief ruckus; on this visit and at this place, he heard mainly welcoming voices. Following the ceremony at Place des Nations, he did a quick tour of the U.S. Pavilion, though the only exhibit that appeared to capture his interest was a cattle branding iron. In his Expo memoir, Dupuy recorded how impressed he had been by the tall Texan: "*L'Homme moderne a visité la 'Terre des Hommes.'*"[7] At 12:34 p.m., a presidential helicopter whisked "*l'Homme moderne*" to his rendezvous with Lester Pearson in the Gatineau Hills.

Pearson understood well the delicacy required in any relationship between elephant and mouse. He was a diplomat by training and inclination. Even so, Lyndon Johnson tried his patience. This presidential visit rankled him greatly. Pearson had wanted a more formal visit at the prime minister's residence at 24 Sussex Drive, not this sort of rush-in, rush-out business. But Johnson's security people did not want him to visit Ottawa, and Pearson had instead arranged for a meeting at his cottage in the Gatineau Hills. He was especially displeased to arrive and find the presidential security people already there. As far as Pearson was concerned "a couple of Mounties could have done the job." Particularly galling was the security man who accosted him as he entered the cottage, and asked him who he was and where he was going. "I live here," replied a livid Pearson, "and I'm going to the bathroom."

It is a pity Maryon Pearson never kept a diary or, if she did, that it has never seen the light of day. From most accounts, she possessed a view of the political life one might charitably describe as astringent. If this life imposed a strain on her husband, it evidently posed a greater challenge for her. "I don't know how he ever lasted in that awful job," Gretta Chambers says of Lester Pearson. "Very principled. *Terrifying* wife."[8] One regrets not having Maryon Pearson's impressions of the high and the mighty with whom her husband came in contact. That afternoon's luncheon, by the way prepared by her, consisted of sweetbreads with fresh strawberries for dessert—a change of pace from the hominy grits offered the Pearsons two years earlier on their visit to the LBJ Ranch to mark the signing of the Canada–United States Auto Pact.[9]

The U.S. president was a figure of great political cunning and skill who crafted landmark legislation (the Civil Rights Act of 1964, Medicare in 1965) on the foundations of his youthful predecessor's martyrdom. At times crude and vindictive, possessed of a rococo vulgarity, Johnson was also a visionary who dreamed of America becoming a "Great Society." Though grateful to Pearson for supplying a Canadian peace-keeping force in Cyprus in 1964, LBJ and the Canadian prime minister were never close. Tom Kent, Pearson's principal policy advisor, was with the Canadian delegation when Johnson first entertained Pearson in Washington. Knowing the president was a horseman, the Canadians took along an RCMP saddle as a gift. "It was given to him and he sort of dismissed it," Kent remembers. "He was very ungracious about it. It was very clear that the personalities did not mesh. There wasn't a feeling of warmth between Mike and Johnson."[10]

Their relationship grew increasingly frayed as the sixties unfolded, and Pearson's call for a ceasefire in the U.S. bombing of North Vietnam in a speech he delivered at Philadelphia's Temple University in April 1965 hastened the unravelling. Vietnam became a wedge between the two leaders, though Pearson attempted to walk a fine line and not be drawn into outright condemnation of this important ally. "Pulling the eagle's tail feathers is an easy, but a dangerous, way to get a certain temporary popularity, as well as a feeling of self-satisfaction at having annoyed the big bird," he would declare in a speech. But more and more, Pearson's efforts to get along with the Americans suggested to some a form of capitulation. George Grant, a professor of philosophy at Hamilton's McMaster University, considered Pearson a sellout and the drift toward continentalism as robbing Canada of its heart and soul. Grant's outpouring on the subject, *Lament for a Nation*, became a surprise best-seller and spoke to the emergence of a more demonstrative Canadian nationalism. Walter Gordon, Pearson's one-time minister of finance and great friend (they had a famous falling out), began to hammer away on the matter of what he saw as the country's loss of autonomy in its business affairs, in the process becoming the godfather of Canadian economic nationalism.

If Pearson's critics in Canada became more vociferous, U.S. officials grew increasingly exasperated. U.S. Ambassador to Canada Walton Butterworth became particularly scornful of the Pearson government for stirring the pot of what he considered anti-Americanism.[11] Of Pearson, Graham Fraser notes, "He was comfortable with ambiguity and nuance, and that was his weakness as a politician. His comfort with ambiguity and nuance was also perceived as a weakness, as dithering."[12]

At their brief Harrington Lake meeting in late May 1967, the subject of Vietnam inevitably arose and Pearson advised Johnson he should stop the bombing unconditionally—should "put the Communists on the spot and remove their last proclaimed excuse for refusing to begin negotiations."[13] Pearson remarked on what he perceived to be Johnson's fear of appearing weak. Pearson thought Johnson more concerned about opinion polls than about diplomatic strategy. In Johnson, he saw a man in torment. And within the year, Johnson conceded the political battle, announcing in March 1968 that bombing of North Vietnam would cease unconditionally and he would not seek re-election as president. Race—the summer of 1967 witnessed fierce race riots in the U.S.—and a terrible war had shredded his dreams for a "Great Society."

Johnson's wife, Lady Bird, did not accompany him on that trip in late May. Their younger daughter, Luci, was about to deliver a baby and her mother's schedule was put on hold until the happy event had transpired.[14] It was late August when Lady Bird Johnson arrived at Expo and, unlike her husband, she actually stayed a while. A downpour did nothing to deter her as she made her way through eight pavilions on the first day of her visit. She had, as Nan-b de Gaspé Beaubien put it, "an agenda in her mind"—specifically her role in planning the Lyndon Baines Johnson Library in Austin, Texas. A dervish in a green silk dress and matching coat, she came to study Expo's architecture, as well as its gardens and methods of moving people about. She greatly enjoyed the Czech Pavilion, and the British Pavilion's mod fashion show received her seal of approval, though as her sixteen-person entourage left the British Pavilion, one of her secret service officers was heard to grumble, "Whoever designed that pavilion should be shot." She loved the mariachi greeting from the band at the Mexico Pavilion (the five musicians had once performed at the Johnson ranch in Texas) and the Man the Creator art exhibition.

Lady Bird Johnson also became a fan of the colourful fences Mayor Drapeau erected to hide from the tourist's eye certain of the less inviting Montreal sights; at one point on the second day of her stay, she halted her motorcade in order to get out and take pictures of the fences, an interest stemming from her own involvement in a highway and roadside beautification plan back in the United States.[15] But, informed that architect Moshe Safdie had recently been in Washington, D.C., to discuss the prospect of Habitat as a possible solution to U.S. inner-city housing problems, the First Lady of the United States grew circumspect. A radical departure from the standard block-like apartment towers that quickly became a blight of urban development, Habitat promised something new. But it marked a real departure from convention. Asked if she would enjoy living in a place like Habitat, she replied, "No, I'm too old fashioned in my taste, I suppose."[16] She also seemed bemused by the seven holes in the wall at the Man the Provider Pavilion, meant to represent, she was told, the Carnation Milk Company cow. The "transparent cow" was a 4-metre-long, 2.5-metre-high section of white plywood with seven holes that stood for the mouth, rumen, reticulum, omasum, abomasum, intestines and udder of a cow; the holes were marked by rings of flashing lights. "It's rather abstract," explained her guide. Lady Bird Johnson surveyed this creation from a number of vantage points before giving up and walking away. "It certainly is," she replied.[17]

Lady Bird Johnson admired the rose garden at the Pavillon d'Honneur, but she did not in turn overly impress Krystyne Romer, the Pavillon's young *maîtresse*. Lady Bird was fine, says Krystyne Griffin—*except* she forgot to toast the queen, which was part of the luncheon drill. As the time for the toast arrived, the First Lady pulled out her compact and began to apply blush to her cheeks, then placed the compact back in her purse. By that point, Mrs. Johnson had forgotten the toast to the queen. "She didn't know protocol," declares Griffin with finality. Earlier, one of Lady Bird Johnson's aides had remonstrated about the lunch. Could it be quick? wondered the aide. After all, and as Premier Joey Smallwood had also noted, the whole point was to see the exhibition, right? In fact, ventured the aide, now treading on decidedly dangerous ground, why not just serve hot dogs? This did not impress. "You don't *ask* what people are serving for lunch," sniffs Griffin. "They just had no know-how."[18]

EIGHT

Wonders of the
World: Part Two

Lady Bird Johnson's handler had a point, though. There were so many things to see and so little time in which to accomplish this goal—a common refrain at Expo 67.

Each pavilion had its partisans, its particular ways to entice and delight. A major surprise was the Czech Pavilion, which combined elements appealing to both connoisseurs and masses, a blend making it one of Expo's hottest tickets. There was, for one thing, its impressive collection of crystal, ceramics and glass. Another attraction was the pavilion's use of film and live performance, as well as audience participation, in its Kinoautomat, which created a sensation. Likewise, its innovative use of photographs printed onto textiles and cubes was a major art story of the exhibition according to Barry Lord, who described it as "critical" because it featured "the application of photography to any surface, the whole blowing open of the image, moving it into three dimensions and not just two."[1] Art, technology and industry had been seamlessly interwoven into an arresting series of exhibits in this pavilion. "Like the opposition of the American and Soviet Pavilions, the message of the Czech exhibit was eminently political," remarked Eva-Marie Kröller. "In the midst of the Cold War, stylish Western humanism triumphed not only over cloutish Eastern communism, but an earlier Eastern variant of humanism as well."[2] Such a display of sophistication and vitality spoke to the ferment and optimism of what would be called the Prague Spring, a period of political awakening brutally terminated by the Kremlin and its Warsaw Pact allies later the following year. In hindsight, the Czech Pavilion acquired an even greater lustre.

However, at least one person found this pavilion "the most overrated" of all those at Expo. Writing in *Canadian Architect*, Audrey Stankiewicz faulted the Czech Pavilion for its winding corridors and static displays and "non-existent" route, so that spectators became log-jammed along the way. Still, people appeared prepared to accept these inconveniences for the sake of what was on offer inside.

More intriguing, perhaps, as a structure was the Netherlands Pavilion, assembled from fifty-three kilometres of aluminum tubing and illustrating a form of architecture known as a triodetic system. Even more intriguing—it was a more significant structure—was Frei Otto's West German Pavilion, an immense tent of steel cables and plastic roof suspended from steel pylons reaching thirty-six metres at their peak. At night, its tent-like roof glowed. Otto's pavilion enchanted and inspired.

The West German Pavilion was, hands down, the single best building in the entire exhibition, pronounced architecture critic James Acland.[3] A mini-tempest erupted after a reporter claimed the tent's structure, in outline and from an aerial vantage point, delineated what appeared to be the territorial boundaries of the Third Reich. That controversy dissipated quickly enough, though it underscored how tender sensitivities remained two decades after the end of World War II.[4] While Otto's creation mostly charmed, its contents left a few nonplussed. "The interior gave me the feeling that, after the pavilion was erected, somebody peeked inside,

snapped his fingers and exclaimed, 'Mein Gott! We forgot the exhibits!'"
gibed one writer.[5] A lovely envelope with meagre substance—one heard
this knock on more than a few pavilions. "Superb, ornate shells," sniffed
British theatre critic Kenneth Tynan, "with rather hollow interiors."[6]

Courting lots of attention was the Cuba Pavilion, a small white structure built from interlocking and protruding cubes. Charles Oberdorf
recalls dropping by the pavilion on April 27, the day of the VIP opening
preview of Expo. "It was finished way before everyone else," he says.
"But on the VIP day I noticed it wasn't open. A little later I ran into
a CBC sound man who was walking around with the architect of the
Cuba Pavilion, and I said, 'What's going on?' And the Cuban architect replied, 'The government of Cuba doesn't believe in Very Important
Persons. We are having a reception for the construction workers, ushers,
electricians—the workers.' An hour later I ran into the PR guy from the
Russian Pavilion and I told him this story and I could see him turning
ashen. He had been trumped."[7]

It had been six years since the abortive Bay of Pigs invasion under-
written by the United States and four years since the Cuban Missile Crisis.
Feelings still ran high in both countries: the United States restricted visits
and dealings with Cuba, whose leader, Fidel Castro, would remain a
U.S. bogeyman for decades, and the Castro regime painted America
as the source of all evil in the world. "Cuba exhibits a lot of harsh
newspaper headlines with stress on words like 'AGGRESSION' and
'ATOMIC BLACKMAIL,' and there are pictures of Vietcong soldiers
in chains, not to mention Fidel Castro at liberty," wrote E. J. Kahn, Jr.,
in *The New Yorker*. "The United States gets slapped around pretty hard
in that pavilion, and maybe the best thing for an American to do after
inspecting it is to step into an adjacent Cuban bar ... and have a first-
rate Cuban rum drink."[8] The bar at the Cuba Pavilion, according to
one reporter who was a regular, became a watering hole for the press.[9]
And the steel drums, the rum, and the dancing all added to the pavilion's allure. The Cuba Pavilion also became a magnet in another sense,

attracting bomb threats from anti-Castro exiles. Before Expo opened, there had been portents. A bomb exploded outside the Cuban Embassy in Ottawa, and a Cuban exile leader in Miami took credit for the March 1967 bombing of a Montreal auction house selling furniture said to have been confiscated in Cuba by the Communists.[10]

The Japanese received criticism for a pavilion deemed too—well, too New York. An alley that led to the Japan Pavilion had Japanese motorcycles lined up on both sides, and Expo management had not been told this would happen. As director of exhibitions, Pierre de Bellefeuille decided to have a word. "Too commercial." This criticism harkened back to New York in 1964–65—also considered "too commercial." De Bellefeuille spoke with the Japanese commissioner general and the offending motorcycles were removed from the alleyway. The rules of Expo carried a lot of weight, notes de Bellefeuille. In fact, the Japanese themselves proved highly critical of their own pavilion, part of a soul-searching that anticipated their own hosting duties three years later at Expo 70 in Osaka.[11] Expo 67 impressed them. Dupuy enjoyed telling of the time Osaka planners asked him where he found his foreign advisors and he told them Canada's Expo had had none. His listeners were incredulous: "You mean this is an *amateur* exhibition?" Dupuy said he then responded—one imagines here the proud puffing out of that chest—"We began as amateurs, but now we're experts—and at your disposal!"[12]

Israel was not then twenty years old as a nation. Its exhibition space included a portion of the Dead Sea Scrolls. It also featured a period photograph of a Nazi soldier aiming a rifle at a Jewish boy, who was about to be executed. Beside that photograph stood a pedestal bearing a young boy's pair of scuffed shoes. This juxtaposition created a profound impression. "Nobody spoke one word," recalled an observer. "But many wept."[13]

Everywhere, people discovered their favourite hangouts. Alan Hustak, a twenty-one-year-old reporter for Radio-Canada armed with a press pass, discovered a taste for caviar at the Iran Pavilion and the pleasures—less elegant than caviar, maybe, but potent nonetheless—of a special rum drink at the Jamaica Pavilion. Barry Lord found solace at the Algerian Pavilion. "They did it all in beautiful tile and there were carpets on the tile, all beautiful warm colours," he says. "You could lean against the wall, it was all coved corners."[14]

Many found a refuge at the Australia Pavilion, with its large, wool-carpeted upstairs room that featured lounge chairs equipped with French and English speaker sets offering commentary on that country's history; green cushions signified English-language speakers, orange cushions French. The information was transmitted at such a low level, noted E. J. Kahn, Jr., that one could get pleasantly lulled into sleep. The Australian pavilion could seem very attractive after a long day's sight-seeing and there was often competition for those comfortable chairs: "'You're English in a French chair,' a woman said to me accusingly, but I disposed of her with a casual '*Je ne comprends pas*,' which is about the extent of my French."[15]

THE NATIONAL PAVILIONS contributed greatly to the flavour and fascination of Expo; but in the earlier stages of planning, thinking moved in a different direction, meaning that the national aspects should be de-emphasized in favour of the broader theme of Man and His World. (In fact, the Montebello Group preferred the less hubristic "Man *in* His World" [italics mine] to the eventual "Man and His World.") "THE NATIONAL PAVILION AS SUCH HAS NO PLACE IN A TRUE INTERNATIONAL EXHIBITION," urban planner and architect Blanche Lemco van Ginkel had typed, in capital letters, for a speech she delivered to the Province of Quebec Association of Architects Convention in January 1963.[16] Several months later, the Montebello Group echoed these sentiments in recommendations of its own. But, as Pierre Dupuy might have said, this was to swim against a strong current, and national pride inexorably asserted itself, though the issue of time and the BIE's own rules also weighed against any thematic dominance of this nature. Still, Expo committed forty million dollars to theme pavilions at an exhibition where these theme pavilions now shared centre stage with the national and private or corporate pavilions. There were originally four themes. Man the Explorer covered a number of areas, including Man and Life; Man, His Planet and Space; Man and the Oceans; Man and the Polar Regions; and Man and His Health. Man the Producer covered Progress, Man in Control, and Resources for Man. Man the Creator covered Fine Arts, Photography, Contemporary Sculpture, and Industrial Design. Man the Provider covered Agriculture.

When the decision was made to radically cut back Moshe Safdie's conception for Habitat, space was created at Cité du Havre for a fifth theme pavilion, Man in the Community, designed by Vancouver architect Arthur Erickson and generally considered the most beautiful of the theme buildings. A pyramid of wood and plastic, with the tip of the pyramid forty-two metres high and open to the sky, its exhibits regarded human experience from a variety of perspectives, including the effect on humanity of a more hectic and at times alienating modern urban culture. "From a distance it looks rather like an oriental pagoda, a geometric, cone-shaped fretwork, exuding that tonal warmth that only an all-wood construction can possess," commented one writer. "The overall impression is one of elegance and serenity. The pavilion would, one feels, look quite at home in Bangkok."[17]

Two of the major theme pavilions, Man the Explorer on Île Ste. Hélène and Man the Producer on Île Notre Dame, were designed in the four-sided triangular—or truncated tetrahedron—shape that became another singular feature of the Expo 67 "look." In their case, however, execution undid conception. There were not enough welders in Canada to create all the truncated tetrahedrons required by the architects Affleck, Desbarats, Dimakopoulos, Lebensold and Sise. The component parts had to be bolted together, and the effect was unlovely.

A number of exhibits in the national pavilions had their own take on the Man and His World theme. Greece had Man the Measure of All; Scandinavia, Man in Unity; South Korea, The Hand of Man; and the Soviets, the earnestly inelegant Everything in the Name of Man for the Good of Man.[18] Such man-centricity had a way at times of overshadowing the humbler aspirations of the Montebello planners in their efforts to resist hubris and vainglory. "It is in the nature of world's fairs to be proud and optimistic," noted Robert Fulford, "and Expo was no exception."[19]

EARLY ON, SOME WONDERED whether Expo planners had set themselves too lofty a standard. Andrew Kniewasser says he received a study commissioned from the Stanford Research Institute in the United States, concluding that the exhibition would attract sixteen million visitors and ought to be designed in accordance with the mental age of the projected average visitor—that is to say, a twelve year old.[20] As in the case of Hans Selye's report on management stress, Kniewasser says he pitched this report into his wastebasket. Reacting in opposition, they "over-designed" the exhibition in order to challenge as well as entertain the visitor. "In addition to having countries come and build pavilions, we decided to have theme pavilions and so take the theme seriously," says Kniewasser. "Tricky—we had our mitts full just running an exhibition, but to put themes on top of that was bloody courageous." Courage and altruism, though, were not the only motivators. Marketing surveys discovered that potential American visitors indicated the more pedagogical aspects of the fair would be a strong selling point for them.[21] At Expo, they were determined to raise the bar and they were most keen not to become another New York. Too commercial.

Of two pavilions dear to the heart of Pierre Dupuy, one emerged not in the form at first envisaged and one nearly did not emerge at all. The day after his appointment as Expo's commissioner general, Dupuy called on Paul-Émile Cardinal Léger of Montreal to talk up a pavilion that would gather all the world's religions under one roof. Unity was always Dupuy's major theme. Unity of man. Unity of religions. He approached the Vatican to outline this ecumenical approach and, while it shortly became clear that Dupuy's ecumenicism was still not shared by a sizeable number of his fellow Christians in Canada, there was always Plan B: a unified *Christian* Pavilion.[22]

An unassuming structure of wood and white stucco, with a roof "shaped like a gigantic checkmark," the Christian Pavilion stood next to the United Nations Pavilion on the path to the Canadian Pavilion. Eight Christian denominations spent over one million dollars toward its construction and the exhibits within; it marked the first time Catholics and Protestants worked together on a project of this kind. The pavilion's designer, Charles Gagnon, a Montreal artist, was quoted as saying, "This is what Marshall McLuhan talks about—total communication."[23]

Inside, no guide or voice-over narration was offered; nor was there any mention of Jesus or God. Instead, visitors proceeded through three chambers, or zones, of which the second featured a fourteen-minute film entitled *The Eighth Day*, consisting of found newsreel footage that started with tranquil images and ultimately gave way to harrowing shots of the Holocaust and the mushroom cloud of a nuclear bomb. The third zone offered photographs of everyday life, accompanied by questions from a Biblical text.[24] One reviewer called it a "trip to hell and back," another an "Ecumenical Shock Pagoda."[25] Many appreciated the pavilion's ambiguity and the soft-sell approach used to reach a more secular "modern" visitor, but not a few loathed it. In a number of respects, the pavilion's theme dovetailed with the Expo philosophy, but in at least one respect, as historian Gary Miedema points out, it chose to go off-message—in its emphasis that human efforts and technology would not be enough to ensure progress without divine assistance. "In the end, an evangelical component remained a part of the pavilion's message," observed Miedema. "It boldly challenged Expo 67's grand story of the past, future, and present, and trumped it with its own."[26]

Yet, as Miedema also points out, in at least one instance Expo managers used the Christian Pavilion to willingly subvert their own message of inclusiveness. They did not want the more blatant forms of Christian evangelism in their exhibition and, accordingly, when approached by representatives for American evangelist Billy Graham, they directed the Graham people's inquiries to the Christian Pavilion management to whom they had given control of such matters. This was a cunning strategy as it worked to drive off the Billy Graham people, who wanted managerial autonomy. Expo had earlier allowed in a group called Sermons from Science, whose evangelism was just as blatant as Billy Graham's, but the proselytizing came paired with science films and a patina of the educational. Sermons from Science seemed somewhat anomalous amid Expo's vaunted rainbow of inclusiveness and Miedema concludes its approval probably had to do with its early pavilion application and the circumstance that businessmen, not a religious organization, advanced its cause.[27]

Meanwhile, concerns were being expressed about the representation of other, non-Christian, religions. Dupuy consulted the Sultan of Morocco in an attempt to have him build an Islamic mosque in addition to the national pavilion, but the Sultan chose instead to erect a minaret at his pavilion's entrance. The Thai government agreed to erect an eighteenth-century Buddhist temple outside its pavilion, and Montreal businessman Sam Steinberg spearheaded a group from the city's Jewish community to finance the Pavilion of Judaism. This pavilion housed a Jewish chapel, a collection of Judaica, and featured lectures and art exhibits. In Steinberg's words, the pavilion "represented a kind of coming of age of Judaism in Canada." The Pavilion of Judaism, noted Gary Miedema, "offered beauty and rest, not shock and provocation" and, unlike the Christian Pavilion and Sermons from Science, it featured an inclusive message that fitted nicely with the Expo theme. (On the other hand, Expo had no luck at all in obtaining Hindu representation.)[28]

Dupuy also pushed for a Youth Pavilion. Initially, he met resistance from Robert Shaw and Colonel Churchill.[29] Such a pavilion did not figure in the original plan and would have to be pulled together very quickly. Pierre de Bellefeuille stepped in, though, and agreed to take the project on. Thus, the Youth Pavilion took shape, and Dupuy saw his wish come true. Located at La Ronde, the Youth Pavilion had a dance café and a film theatre, as well as an agora with a four-hundred-person seating capacity and a roster of guest speakers that included Marshall McLuhan, René Lévesque, Raymond Aron and Paul Goodman. Leonard Cohen came and read from his poetry there.

"Michael Snow used to do sculptures in the backyard," remembers Monique Simard, a hostess there. "Every day we would have five to ten activities. It was daring, experimental, modern there. The intensity every day of having fun! Every day you would discover something."[30] Simard went on to head the French section of the National Film Board. In her capacity as a Youth Pavilion hostess, her duties included escorting around distinguished visitors such as Marshall McLuhan. I asked her: what was he like, McLuhan? How did he seem to her? "Old!" she replied. "I was twenty-four!"

In a lot of ways, Expo 67 was all about youth and youthful aspiration. One of its most prominent alumni was a young man whose university thesis became the basis for an Expo *cause célèbre*. This was Moshe Safdie. We meet him next.

NINE

Icons

Two generations, two iconic structures: for many, the U.S. Pavilion's geodesic dome of R. Buckminster Fuller and the Habitat 67 of Moshe Safdie conjured Expo 67. Fuller was then in his seventies and Safdie his late twenties, yet both shared a youthful vigour in their desire to apply technology in the service of humankind's betterment. By then, Fuller had become an almost mythic figure, a visionary and one of the leading inter-disciplinary thinkers of his age—an "evolutionary strategist" he called himself—and in him and his vision the younger man could find much to admire and draw inspiration from.

Safdie well remembers their first meeting. The Habitat design drawings had just been completed and made public, and an Expo public relations person brought Fuller around to Safdie's office to view the model and drawings of the work. It was, in its way, an historic encounter. The Expo PR man felt it necessary to explain Fuller's achievements, but of these Safdie was already well aware. Indeed, the entire Safdie office was at once in a state of excitement about the visit. Safdie led Fuller to the area where the plans for Habitat were laid out. Safdie began to describe the plan's intent but, after several minutes, Fuller stopped him, told him an explanation was not necessary, he could see what Habitat was all about. A year passed before they were in contact again. By this time, Expo had opened and the Fuller dome had been recognized for the sensation it was. Fuller had written Safdie a letter in response to a newspaper report suggesting Fuller did not think highly of Habitat. Fuller heatedly denied that claim, and in fact lent Safdie encouragement on the latter's controversial project. For Safdie, Fuller's letter offered a great morale boost.[1]

Fuller wore many hats—inventor, philosopher, architect, mathematician, poet, among them—and has been described as "a quintessential American mix of hard-bitten pragmatism and dewy-eyed optimism."[2] Born into an old Yankee family in Milton, Massachusetts, in 1895, Fuller's journey toward eminence began inauspiciously. He dropped out of Harvard, failed at his father-in-law's construction business, drank too much and spent too much. According to Fuller lore, matters became so grim that, in 1927, at age thirty-two, he ventured to the Chicago lakefront and contemplated suicide. Then came an epiphany. He made a bargain with himself, he said, that he'd discover the principles operating in the universe and apply them for the benefit of humanity. Recent studies suggest the lakefront scene and epiphany are part of a deliberate myth to gloss over a far more turbulent formative period than the great man himself would ever reveal. One scholar found evidence of depression and anxiety dating back to the time Fuller's eldest daughter died in 1922, and through financial setbacks and the collapse of an extramarital affair with eighteen-year-old Evelyn Schwartz, who was half his age.[3]

In any event, from this fecund "strategizing" came ideas for the Dymaxion three-wheeled electric car and the Dymaxion House, the latter a six-sided shelter suspended from a central steel mast whose parts could be carried by helicopter, lowered onto the construction site and assembled in a matter of days. Fuller, wrote the architectural critic Nicolai Ouroussoff, was "not about creating a radical aesthetic for a

new age. [The Dymaxion House] was conceived as a purely technological solution to a fundamental human problem: the need for affordable shelter."[4] From his studies, Fuller found his signature shape, the
tetrahedron, a four-sided pyramid that became the structural basis for
the dome.[5]

Fuller had developed his first dome prototype by 1948, and by 1954
had perfected the structure and taken out a patent. The dome was useful
in a number of situations: on the DEW Line defence system, as portable
housing for U.S. marines, and as exhibit buildings and homes. Fuller
went on to envision, but never execute, a dome that could encase part
of Manhattan. The Fuller dome's apotheosis, however, was the U.S.
Pavilion at Expo 67, from its very beginnings "an international symbol
of America's enchantment with the future, the architectural equivalent
of the Apollo spacecraft."[6] The dome became the foremost example of
why Expo came to be called the "space-frame" fair. And it was not
just the Buckminster Fuller "Bubble" encompassed by that phrase.
There were the two major theme pavilions, Man the Producer and Man
the Explorer. The West German Pavilion offered another example, as
did the Netherlands Pavilion. And what they all had in common was
the achievement of being able to cover large spaces economically and
flexibly through the distribution of the building's weight over the widest
area possible, using various methods that employed materials such as
aluminum and plastic. Expo 67 offered a notable showcase for this
"space-frame" school of architecture.[7]

Bucky, as his friends called him, was a godfather to the ecological
movement in his goal to find ways of doing more with less. An early
prophet of sustainability, his message that solutions must be considered globally in order to meet humanity's needs fit squarely with Expo's
thematic message of global interdependence. He inspired the *Whole
Earth Catalog*, which, with his own book *Operating Manual for
Spaceship Earth*, made him a hero of the counterculture. Hippies and
more conservative clients alike favoured Fuller's dome structures, and

Disney, in homage, would build the geodesic structure Spaceship Earth at its Epcot Center in 1982.

The British chemist Harold Kroto visited the dome in 1967 and, years later, with his American colleagues Robert Curl and Richard Smalley, discovered the C_{60} carbon molecule, whose precise structure eluded them until he and Smalley, who also paid a visit to the Fuller dome, recognized that it mimicked Fuller's Skybreak Bubble. They came to the conclusion, says Kroto, that the C_{60} molecule, a molecule with sixty carbon atoms arranged on the surface of a sphere, had a similar topological geodesic configuration to the Expo 67 dome. Kroto later named the C_{60} molecule the "C_{60} buckminsterfullerene" after Fuller. Their discovery earned the three chemists the 1996 Nobel Prize in chemistry and created a new branch in the field known as "fullerene chemistry," which in turn helped give rise to nanoscience and nanotechnology, the manipulation of matter on an atomic scale.

Fuller was a gadfly who exulted in ideas and plans and visions— and loved nothing better than speaking about them to the enraptured audiences who came to listen. Canadian architect Peter Hamilton remembers attending a Fuller lecture held in a Paris park in the mid-sixties and how the star attraction talked for over eight hours; Hamilton and his friends took a meal break and returned to find Fuller still going strong.[8] Long before she became Canada's governor general, Adrienne Clarkson interviewed Fuller for her CBC television program *Take 30*. She recalls, "At a certain point in the interview I stopped listening, which is very rare for me. With him I suddenly went into a kind of sphere of my own and realized when I came out of it, he was still in the same sentence. It was like floating on words with him. It was fabulous."[9]

One day, while lunching at the Windsor Hotel during Expo year, author and broadcast journalist Patrick Watson spotted Fuller, whom he had first met a decade earlier and become good friends with following a 1965 interview. He was shocked. The stocky, exuberant little man he remembered appeared drawn and thin and on his last legs. But no,

Expo Commissioner General Pierre Dupuy surveys progress on the construction of the Canada Pavilion, though a morning coat rather than a hard hat was more this man's polished style. *(LAC/Canadian Corp. for the 1967 World Exhibition fonds/ e00099756918)*

In the bleakness of winter, Montrealers were reminded by signs such as this one on Île Verte that they had something to look forward to. *(LAC/Canadian Corp. for the 1967 World Exhibition fonds/e001096679)*

Gathered for the opening ceremonies of Expo 67 are (from left) Expo Commissioner General Pierre Dupuy, Governor General Roland Michener, Prime Minister Lester B. Pearson, Quebec Premier Daniel Johnson and Montreal Mayor Jean Drapeau. For Drapeau, particularly, this was a day of triumph. *(LAC/ Canadian Corp. for the 1967 World Exhibition fonds/e000990918)*

Expo's director of installations, Colonel Edward Churchill (left), battled long odds to get the exposition ready by the appointed date. With him is Director of Operations Philippe de Gaspé Beaubien (right of Churchill). *(The Montreal Star, Mar. 20, 1964)*

Philippe de Gaspé Beaubien, known as the mayor of Expo. Pictured here at a gala event with his American-born wife, Nan-b, they became Expo's most glamorous couple. *(Photo by Paul Taillefer,* The Montreal Star, *June 10, 1967)*

Expo's Deputy Commissioner General Robert Shaw (right) takes a ride on one of the many modes of transportation offered at the exhibition. His down-to-earth approach made him the perfect complement for the more flamboyant Pierre Dupuy. *(LAC/ Canadian Corp. for the 1967 World Exhibition fonds/ e000996038)*

The minirail passed through the geodesic dome or "Skybreak Bubble" that Buckminster Fuller designed as the U.S. Pavilion. The competitive Soviets dismissed the dome as a "soap bubble." *(LAC/ Canadian Corp. for the 1967 World Exhibition fonds/e000990869)*

Filled to its rafters with space hardware, the Russian Pavilion was an extremely popular destination. Among the less chauvinistic features was a sturgeon tank that produced caviar. *(LAC/Canadian Corp. for the 1967 World Exhibition fonds/ e000990955)*

U.S. President Lyndon Baines Johnson moved quickly through the U.S. Pavilion. Apparently the only item that really caught his attention was a cattle branding iron. *(LAC/ Canadian Corp. for the 1967 World Exhibition fonds/e000996587)*

These Vietnam War protesters were disappointed to learn that political protest, by a special bylaw, was not allowed on the Expo site. *(LAC/Canadian Corp. for the 1967 World Exhibition fonds/e001096649)*

Queen Elizabeth's minirail excursion with Prime Minister Pearson was a last-minute decision that caused a sensation for the delighted and surprised spectators. *(LAC/Canadian Corp. for the 1967 World Exhibition fonds/e000996579)*

Emperor Haile Selassie of Ethiopia, known as the Lion of Judah, enjoyed his time at the exhibition so much that he extended his stay. *(LAC/Canadian Corp. for the 1967 World Exhibition fonds/ e000996589)*

Moshe Safdie's McGill University masters thesis became the basis for one of Expo's most iconic structures—Habitat 67. *(Photo by Marcos Townsend, The (Montreal) Gazette)*

Designed as a prototype for a new style of urban living, Habitat 67 suggested a Mediterranean village in the middle of the Montreal harbour. Safdie hoped its modular or prefabricated nature would help revolutionize the housing industry. *(LAC/ Canadian Corp. for the 1967 World Exhibition fonds/e000990890)*

Île Notre Dame was the site of many significant pavilions. At the middle of the photo near the top is the truncated Union Jack of the British Pavilion and, to its left, the tent-like formation of Frei Otto's West German Pavilion. Also visible: the Canada, Ontario, Atlantic Provinces and Indians of Canada Pavilions. *(LAC/ Canadian Corp. for the 1967 World Exhibition fonds/e000990828)*

The former movie star Grace Kelly had become Princess Grace of Monaco, and here with her children and husband, Prince Rainier, in tow, she tours the Expo site. Pierre Dupuy can be seen in the background. *(LAC/Canadian Corp. for the 1967 World Exhibition fonds/e000996510)*

replied Fuller, he was fine, it was just that the pain in his knees had convinced him to drop some weight. So he ate only steak and orange juice, no carbohydrates, "and the weight had just fallen off pound by pound, and he was within ten pounds of his goal and feeling great, the knees just fine, what did I think of the Skybreak Bubble, did I know his new book of poetry, *Intuition*, was out now, he had a copy for me, meet Iqbal here, Iqbal is from Iraq, he has an absolutely brilliant idea about quasars, old man, wait till you hear it, have you had lunch?"[10]

"He had a great loving quality," Watson says now, many years later. "He was the first man who ever said to me 'I love you'—and it had no sexual connotation. He was the first man who kissed me. He always called people he liked 'old man.' So we were saying goodbye at the airport and he said, 'Well, goodbye, old man' and he kissed me."[11]

MOSHE SAFDIE WAS BORN in Haifa in 1938. His father imported textiles, but when the economic situation in Israel turned sour, affecting that trade, the family emigrated to Montreal in 1954. From an early age, Safdie wanted to be an architect. That ambition disappointed his father, who hoped his son would come into business with him. But Safdie decided to follow his own dream and enrolled at the McGill University School of Architecture, where he distinguished himself as a brilliant student with a singular vision. By then, he had met his future wife, Nina, and for a time they lived on her earnings as a secretary for the Bell Telephone Company while he continued his studies. Academic excellence earned Safdie a place on a tour of North America sponsored by a scholarship from the Central Mortgage and Housing Corporation. This tour offered him a look at both suburbia and public housing, high-rise towers and majestic single homes, and it led to meetings with prominent architects and planners. The trip profoundly affected the direction of his studies. Safdie now saw two problems that needed to be addressed: the essential inhumanity of high-rise public housing and the essential profligacy of the suburban dream home on its large lot. Instead of designing a parliament building for Jerusalem as part of his thesis, as he had planned, he redirected his scholarly energies to designing a housing system that offered both privacy and the space and sense of community found wanting in contemporary urban models. He called his thesis "A Three-Dimensional Modular Building System." The seeds of Safdie's Habitat had been planted.

Safdie's thesis won the gold medal at McGill, and with the medal came a two-month travelling scholarship. He and Nina bought an old car that broke down frequently as they travelled the California coast. The real eye-opener occurred as they ventured inland. The Grand Canyon with the Indian pueblos built into its cliff face and the adobe clusters that adorned its plains and mountain peaks fascinated Safdie: "the expression of people living harmoniously in nature and true to nature, building an architecture of unquestionable morphological truth in the context of the native material and the climate and the landscape."[12]

Next came a job working for the American architect Louis Kahn in Philadelphia. Safdie knew Kahn to be one of the great contemporary teachers of architecture. But the younger man found it increasingly difficult to keep his own opinions in check. The year with Kahn proved fruitful, but tensions between the two escalated to the point that Safdie felt he must move on. Fortuitously, his old boss and mentor, Sandy van Ginkel, came knocking in the summer of 1963 to invite him to join Claude Robillard and himself in devising the Expo 67 master plan. Safdie says he went to Expo because he wanted to work on a large scale and because he foresaw that his dreamed-of housing exhibit might become a reality there. And so he arrived back in Montreal, armed with a vision and enormous determination. The location of Safdie's exhibit became the first issue to be addressed. Safdie signed on after the decision had been made to focus the Expo site on the rebuilt Île Ste. Hélène and the newly created Île Notre Dame. Earlier, though, Safdie worked at van Ginkel's office on a city master plan whose emphasis focused on the redevelopment of the harbour areas. Safdie wanted his housing exhibit—as he kept thinking of Habitat at this point in time—to occupy a section of the Mackay Pier, but the Port Authority head, Guy Beaudet, initially offered resistance. Not coincidentally, Beaudet favoured the mayor's islands concept because it kept his harbour free and clear. But the Mackay lands belonged to the federal government and Beaudet was overruled. Once the federal government endorsed the Expo master plan in December 1963, the project could proceed. However—and this became typical of the back-and-forth process that plagued the creation of Habitat—Safdie's dream almost died stillborn. Habitat had not been included in the master plan budget presented to the federal cabinet, and Deputy Commissioner General Robert Shaw preferred dropping it rather than jeopardizing the whole scheme. Colonel Churchill convinced Shaw to reconsider. As far as Safdie was concerned, Edward Churchill became the indispensable link in the chain of command that got Habitat—not to say, Expo—built. [13]

When the president of the committee of cement companies underwriting the initial feasibility study of the Habitat project tried to claim ownership of the concept—Montreal architect Jean-Louis Lalonde, the cement companies' representative, had first come up with the name "Habitat"—Churchill stood his ground. He reminded the committee president that they had donated the money to the government to build Habitat and thus Habitat rightly belonged to the Expo corporation. Later, after the October 1964 decision to drastically scale back the Habitat plan from 1,000 to 158 units consisting of 354 prefabricated boxes and jettison the idea of a 22-storey commercial section while retaining only the 10-storey residential section, an outside advisory group's questioning of the structure's stability under earthquake conditions threw another spanner into the works. While Safdie relied on the wisdom of his engineer, Dr. August Komendant, many at Expo, including its chief engineer, Gilles Sarault, opposed going ahead. But Churchill did a quick calculus of Komendant's expertise and, with Shaw in agreement, backed Komendant and Safdie. [14] "They kind of adopted me," Safdie says of Churchill and Shaw. "They were straight shooters. You would expect them to be very practical men with little taste for risk-taking and yet, time and again, they took incredible risks, certainly on Habitat."[15]

Safdie decided to place his building at the northern end of the pier since that was where the best view was. He completely redesigned it so as to create a semblance of the public space conceived for the original twenty-two-storey section. And using the same modular box units, instead of cellular columns in inclined planes, he developed a cluster geometry. This was new. Clusters of eight boxes would be piled one on top of another.[16] The decision to cut back the Habitat concept was a bitter pill, though at least part of the plan would now survive. Yet, as Habitat actually began to take shape and Safdie resigned his Expo planning duties to fully concentrate, without conflict of interest, on his pet project, tragedy struck. His infant son, Dan, died of crib death. His son's death devastated him.

"The juxtaposition of such a tragic downturn in my personal life while at the professional level there was such an upturn—it was very hard to reconcile," he says.[17] Also during this period, Peter Barott, a partner in the architectural firm of David, Barott, Boulva, Safdie's associate firm on Habitat, died from a heart attack at the age of forty-two. But a brighter day dawned. During the seven-month period from November 1964 to May 1965, as the Safdie office on the thirty-eighth floor of Place Ville Marie produced the Habitat working drawings, Moshe and Nina Safdie welcomed the arrival of a new son, Oren.[18]

If much of the Habitat process seemed a succession of stops and starts, part of the blame for this could be ascribed to the caprice of Jean Drapeau. Drapeau longed for the Eiffel Tower—or, at least, his version of same—as the symbol of Expo, and the longer that dream persisted, the more delays stymied the progress of Habitat, itself in the running to be an official Expo symbol. Briefly complicating matters further was a ploy by a French cement manufacturer to pre-empt Habitat and claim federal dollars for its own Mackay Pier development plan.[19] Getting Habitat off the drawing board, then, was no simple thing, though even the green light to begin construction in the summer of 1965 did not mean the end of frustration.

Safdie had a factory built beside the Habitat site, containing steel moulds in which the units could be made. A steel cage was installed in each mould and concrete then poured in around the cage. The concrete phase completed, the hardware was installed, at which point the unit moved to an assembly line. A wooden subfloor was put in, with electrical and mechanical services beneath it. Then the windows and insulation, followed by pipes being laid for the bathrooms and kitchens. Finally, a crane lifted the unit to its position in the building. But the severely cut back version of the original Habitat design not only meant an inability to achieve economies of scale—in the end, Habitat cost $22,195,920 or about $140,000 per living unit—it likewise compromised Safdie's Brave New World plans to revolutionize architecture and the housing construction industry through assembly-line factory methods.

Mistakes happened. For example, only after construction started did Safdie realize that roofs ought to have been placed atop the units from the beginning rather than added later. Rain and snow bedevilled the builders, so that eventually a polyethylene sheet had to be draped across each box as it was worked on; this draping and undraping of the polyethylene sheet added further delays.[20]

Mistakes happened, yes—but such excitement! One week there was just a box and the next week you had two storeys, then three, and before anyone knew it, a street had been put in. Safdie felt the creator's special thrill, but also a satisfaction that this was something different and special. Habitat may not have been the first try at manufacturing a house through factory methods, but with Habitat the scale was more ambitious, the fifty-five-square-metre units larger, the finishes and detailing more sophisticated.[21] Units varied in size, depending on how many of the boxes were joined together.

In many ways, then, the creation of Habitat was an unforget-table experience, and those involved had a great many memories. One morning, soon after dawn, the project manager of contractor Anglin-Norcross, Bob Hughes, arrived to hear a strange sound coming from one of the boxes. Moving closer, he discovered the night shift dancing a sunrise dance on the subfloor before they left for home: many of the Habitat riggers were from the Caughnawega (now Kahnawake) reserve near Montreal.[22]

Doubt and worry dogged Safdie nonetheless, often traceable to the uncertainty surrounding the wishes of the political masters to whom the Expo Crown Corporation answered. The prime minister had made strenuous efforts to appease French Canada, and he well understood the resentment from other regions if special favours seemed offered to Quebec. Hence, the federal government insisted that none of its financial support for Habitat be classified as assistance for housing. Moreover, criticism of Expo's escalating costs caused fretting among the Liberals. When Robert Winters took over as minister of trade and commerce—the portfolio bearing responsibility for Expo—Safdie experienced a special pang. Safdie was aware that Winters was keen to be the next leader of the Liberal Party and sought to appear as the best pal of the taxpayer. Facing substantial press criticism for its cost, Habitat seemed a likely sacrificial lamb.[23]

Further demands for cost-cutting had to be fended off, be it the elimination of a garden irrigation system or public-area lighting fixtures, but Safdie says, in the main, he got his way. That epitomized so completely Safdie's wish to create human-friendly environments. For Safdie, a garden irrigation system was anything but a frill.[24]

Furnishing Habitat presented its own set of problems. Safdie and the prominent Montreal designer Jacques Guillon approached, on their own initiative, several top international interior designers and met with a positive response. Safdie and Guillon were ecstatic. But then the Canadian Manufacturers Association got wind of their plans and played the nationalist card. What were foreigners doing in a Canadian exhibit? Robert Winters bowed to this sentiment and applied the screws to Expo management, who opted to go with Canadian designers.[25] Meanwhile, over in Moscow, Andrew Kniewasser found himself trying to placate an indignant International Bureau of Exhibitions, whose counter-response had been: was not Expo 67 an *international* exhibition? The furor abated and nationalist sentiment prevailed. But other vexations loomed.

The exhibitions department of Expo organized an advisory group of members of the furniture industry to look into the matter of designing the Habitat interiors. Their solution? To offer free furnishings for the twenty-six exhibit units—provided the popular Canadian women's magazine *Chatelaine* was put in charge of the units' design. From a cost-conscious point of view, if not necessarily an aesthetic one, the idea perhaps had a certain logic. But not to Safdie and Guillon who, again, on their own initiative, approached several top Canadian designers. And as before when they had approached the international designers, the two were greeted enthusiastically.

Safdie had been appalled by the *Chatelaine* presentation, finding it "vulgar, ugly, bargain-basement stuff, pettily concocted." For Safdie, the dust-up with *Chatelaine* became misrepresented. It was not simply a matter of conflict between contemporary versus traditional furniture. It was a matter of understanding the effort to create a particular kind of environment. Pseudo–American Colonial did not exactly square with that vision.[26]

An exasperated Edward Churchill decided the matter by dividing up the assignments between the two groups: the designers chosen by Safdie and Guillon, and those selected by *Chatelaine*. In his memoir, Safdie offers a footnote to the affair. Following the meeting in Churchill's office, he had no further contact with the *Chatelaine* people. But several weeks later, Safdie arrived at the Habitat site to find a large, two-and-a-half-metre sphere made out of papier mâché with curious holes in it. The colour scheme for this object was pink and lime. In Safdie's words, "It looked like the cut-up kidneys of a Martian." Asking what this was meant to be, he was informed that *Chatelaine* had just delivered it and it was meant to be a play sculpture for the kids. A manufacturer had donated it. Safdie hit the roof, eventually resorting, in the company of his wife, Nina, to surreptitiously removing the thing in the middle of the night, only to be accosted and held by the Habitat security forces. The matter resolved itself, but only after weeks of pleading on Safdie's part to have *Chatelaine* remove the offending object.[27]

There were many fires to put out, many lessons learned on the fly. Most observers, whether or not they found fault with aspects of the final result, admired the bravery and ambition behind Moshe Safdie's Habitat. The visiting Italian architect Bruno Zevi had high praise. "In order to really appreciate Habitat one has to live in it," he declared, "because only then does one become aware of both the functional soundness and aesthetic appeal." (Of all Expo's features, Zevi singled out just Habitat and Fuller's dome; the other pavilions, he said, were merely "good answers to mediocre questions.")[28] Myrna Gopnik and Irwin Gopnik, two American-born professors and early residents of Habitat, concluded, "What has survived in Habitat 67 is not even a theoretical celebration of technology but a celebration of human values: those involving the perceptual and psychological and social elements of shelter. Safdie had hit upon a theory of design which completely eliminated the problem of aesthetic arbitrariness and simultaneously made possible a much greater variety of forms, and therefore, of choices."[29] Safdie himself saw Habitat in the tradition of a Mediterranean village, or like the Indian pueblos that so transfixed him during his travels through the American southwest: "Habitat is in the tradition of spontaneous self-made environments, the beginnings of a contemporary vernacular."[30] To a great extent, Safdie's vision has remained more a beacon of what *could* be in terms of choices we make about housing in our urban environments than choices that we've actually elected to make. But his vision and its incarnation continue to intrigue and stir debate. At Expo 67, Moshe Safdie and Habitat became part of the cultural conversation. Forty-five years on, they still are part of that conversation.

TEN

Screenings

Film was no stranger to world expositions, but never before Expo 67 had film in such variety, scope and sheer quantity been on such overwhelming display. At the 1900 Paris Exposition, Raoul Grimoin-Sanson's simulated balloon flight, using a process that prefigured Disney's multi-screen Circle-Vision 360, caused quite a stir—though mainly with the authorities, who shut down the exhibit after only three days because of dangers posed by the projectors' arc lamps, the lack of ventilation and the flammable film stock.[2] Film as an integral part of the exhibition process made a breakthrough at the 1915 Panama-Pacific International Exposition in San Francisco, and the first demonstration of what became known as CinemaScope took place at the 1937 Paris Exposition.[3] The multi-screen film created a splash at the Brussels fair in 1958, but it was at the New York World's Fair of 1964–65 that the shift in emphasis from exhibiting objects to exhibiting images really began.[4] Crass and commercial though they may have regarded it in other respects, the film-savvy New York fair exerted a major influence on Expo planners.

"Expo is a many-screened splendour," wrote Wendy Michener in *Maclean's*. "Everywhere you look there are movies, movies, movies. The whole site is a mass of reflecting surfaces, flashing lights and refracted images." For instance, in the Cuban Pavilion, projectors hung from the ceiling presenting scenes of that country's recent revolution onto outdoor screens. Over at the Czech Pavilion, slides were projected onto moving plastic blocks, while hidden projectors at the Quebec Pavilion conveyed images of furs, forests, water and textiles via cubes and tubes. British designer Sean Kenny's arresting combination of sound and film managed to compact a thousand years of history into an exhibit that became an Expo talking point. "There's no avoiding the great visual onslaught," concluded Michener. "It might just as well have been an experimental film festival as a world's fair."[5] Observed *Film Quarterly's* Judith Shatnoff: "At Expo one saw the technological advances in optics, electronics, computer programming, and film production that allow explorations the first experimenters only dreamed of; and, significantly, one saw a huge, ready, and responsive audience."[6]

People tended to go a little gaga about the films at Expo, even though a number of them seemed to run together in the mind soon after viewing. Who could deny the hot, giddy impress of the new? One year after Expo, Stanley Kubrick's *2001: A Space Odyssey* seemed to capture some of this Expo spirit. Through the interest in space travel, yes, but also in the trippiness of its light-show effects, a phenomenon abetted by a burgeoning marijuana subculture: movie theatres had smoking sections in those days and a growing legion of "tokers" discovered in *2001* a great new excuse to get high.

Among all the films at Expo, one, by virtue of its ambition and cost, invited the greatest initial attention. Director Roman Kroitor's *In the*

Labyrinth, made for the National Film Board of Canada and shown in the NFB's own specially designed five-storey Labyrinth Pavilion on Cité du Havre, melded the Minotaur myth with the theme of humanity's continual search for meaning. Fittingly, Northrop Frye served as an advisor on *In the Labyrinth*. Frye, a world-renowned scholar of mythology, was a professor of Kroitor's from his days as a student at the University of Toronto.[7] The Labyrinth experience required an audience to pass through three chambers. In the first, one watched as images alternated back and forth between a twelve-metre vertical screen at eye level and a twelve-metre horizontal screen twenty metres below. The viewer followed human progress from birth and the innocence of childhood to maturity and a greater questioning of life's purpose. The second chamber consisted of a mirrored maze of dark and winding corridors and blinking lights that led to a third chamber, where five screens were arranged in a cruciform pattern. Here, we were told, was depicted humanity's universal struggle against the beast within. In one spectacular sequence, an Ethiopian hunter spears a crocodile on the centre screen while the surrounding four screens throb with images of painted death masks. "The conquest of the beast is a conquest of perspective and the return in triumph is indicated by the central image of a newborn infant surrounded by smiling faces, all races, young and old," noted Judith Shatnoff. "If, on reflection, conquest seems too easy, triumph too neat, the setting nostalgic, in experience the conclusion is deeply moving."[8]

Joseph Morgenstern, writing in *Newsweek*, looked beyond what he considered "some high-flying bunk about accepting our mortality and finding the Minotaur within ourselves" to the sheer beauty of the images and the ingenuity in the design of its showcase building: "Labyrinth is a fun house, even though there are no air jets for the ladies' skirts. It gives us mystery and grandeur, hallucination without toil, and when it mixes its media and surrounds us with flashing lights, mirrors and electronic jungle noises, it becomes a *son et lumière* spectacle on the site of a castle yet to be built."[9] Others seemed more skeptical. Two years of filmmaking, at a cost of four and a half million dollars, had resulted in a film that, to Mordecai Richler, "seems both portentous and inadequate."[10]

Hugh O'Connor, the forty-six-year-old Montreal native who, along with Kroitor and Colin Low, produced the film and directed several sequences in *In the Labyrinth*—notably those set in India—was later shot and killed in eastern Kentucky. In September of 1967, O'Connor and a four-man crew were filming scenes of poverty in that state for a documentary. According to crew members, they had finished filming a cluster of shacks when the owner of the property accosted them, warned them to clear off, fired two shots above their heads, and then shot O'Connor in the chest. O'Connor thought he had obtained permission to film on the property but had not realized that permission came from a renter and not the actual property owner.[11] O'Connor had headed the NFB's science unit for five years and was brought into *In the Labyrinth*, according to filmmaker Graeme Ferguson, because neither Kroitor nor Low were forceful enough. "Well, they're pushy in some ways, but if you say, 'Go out on that street and get people to cooperate with you,' they weren't comfortable with that. Hugh had that brashness and they did not."[12]

Content to leave the heavier existential musings to *In the Labyrinth*, the film *Canada 67* at the Telephone Pavilion shamelessly—and enjoyably—played the patriotism card. Produced by Walt Disney Studios, whose founder and namesake died several months prior to Expo's opening, the twenty-two-minute Circle-Vision 360 film was presented in an auditorium designed to hold 1,500 people at a time, featuring nine projectors and a 360-degree screen. "In terms of architecture, it was a very simple building," says Gar MacInnis, who worked for Toronto's Adamson and Associates, designers of the pavilion. "It was a matter of moving people through."[13] The building required plenty of aisle space in an adjacent chamber, where Bell product was displayed.

Metal railings divided the auditorium and served to channel people in and out. They provided another function, too—something to grab on to when the aerial camera banked steeply while flying over Niagara Falls and audience members succumbed to the camera's vertiginous pull. Quebec's Winter Carnival, a Toronto Maple Leafs game, lakes and prairies and national parks—the filmmakers covered all the bases. As the RCMP Musical Ride approached them from all directions, a whoop of delight usually erupted from the spectators. *Canada 67* left nary a cliché unturned and, at the conclusion, it pulled out the emotional stops by playing "O Canada." Nan-b de Gaspé Beaubien says she took all her visitors to see it. "Everybody in the audience," she says, "was in tears."[14] Prime Minister Pearson loved the movie as well, and wanted it shown in theatres across the country.[15] A few resisted the film's appeal. *Newsweek*'s Joseph Morgenstern compared the experience to diving in hot fudge. It had to have been made by Americans, said Canadian Kodak public relations official Jeremy Ferguson, because Canadians would be too skeptical to produce something as "rah-rah" as that.[16] Nevertheless, most viewers appeared to love the movie, hot fudge and all, and the Telephone Pavilion proved enormously popular.

Among the other films attracting attention were the Canadian National Railway's *Motion*, using wide-screen 70-mm stock that, now and then, would divide into three images; its director, Robert Gaffney, had made *Windjammer* for Cinerama. Nick and Anne Chaparos's *The Earth Is Man's Home* was an eleven-minute film in which the nine-metre-high and four-metre-wide screen was divided into three sections that now and then combined into a single image; Morley Markson's *Kaleidoscope* at the Canadian Industries Pavilion examined, using mirrors, the theme of man and colour; and John and Faith Hubley's witty five-minute *Urbanissimo* at the Man in the Community Pavilion illustrated the lure of the big city for a young man from the countryside. At the Meditheatre exhibit in the Man and His Health Pavilion, a film depicting open heart surgery became notorious for prompting viewers to faint.[17] The fainters became a familiar sight around Expo clinics. So, too, did those who pretended to need wheelchairs in order to skip the pavilion lineups. Clinic workers began to develop a healthy dose of skepticism.

One of the bona fide smash hits of Expo, and a propaganda bonanza for the province of Ontario, was Christopher Chapman's *A Place to Stand*. James Ramsay, director of the Ontario Pavilion, had been greatly impressed by the Telephone Pavilion's 360-degree Circle-Vision process, but Walt Disney owned it and Ramsay says he "didn't want Disney because it would be 'Walt Disney Presents Ontario.'"[18] He turned instead to a Toronto company called TDF, one of whose partners, David Mackay, became instrumental in setting up *A Place to Stand*. All its images went onto one 70-mm strip of film, meaning that ninety minutes of images were squeezed into a movie whose ultimate running time was a little over seventeen minutes. Projected on a twenty-by-nine-metre screen, it covered a variety of aspects of Ontario, its farm and city life, its culture and sports, industry and natural splendour, and it did this in a beguilingly breezy and multi-imaged way. Jim Ramsay knew what he *didn't* want: "the joys of steel making and all this stuff." And he paid close attention. "I didn't want anyone slipping in the *Joy of Sex* in Yorkville," he says. "That had happened to me before." *A Place to Stand* employed no narration, but there was music and there was a song ("Ontari-ari-ario") that became, along with Bobby Gimby's "Ca-na-da," a touchstone of the period. Dolores Claman wrote the music for the song and her husband Richard Morris did the words.

"I was bursting with pride at the Ontario Pavilion," says artist Charles Pachter. "The song, silly as it was, was memorable." More memorable, anyway, than the official Expo song, whose English title was "Hey Friend, Say Friend." (The song's French title was "*Un jour, un jour.*") "It was better in French," says Pachter of that Stéphane Venne composition. "It's very elliptical anyway—but in English it was ridiculous."[19]

A Place to Stand took more than two years to complete and cost over one million dollars. It would win Christopher Chapman an Academy

Award for best short film, and its multi-image influence could be seen in at least two mainstream films the following year—Norman Jewison's *The Thomas Crown Affair* (that movie's star, Steve McQueen, attended an early screening of Chapman's film and loved it)[20] and Richard Fleischer's *The Boston Strangler.*

Chapman later explained to Leslie Scrivener of the *Toronto Star* how at one point in the process he reached a terrifying impasse when he realized he hadn't gotten the emotion of the piece and he was working without a script. Instant trauma. "I realized my fear was blocking everything. I had to believe in the film so much that it would come to life again, and it did. Suddenly, it clicked. It was as if every single piece of film was cheering at me, as if the film was telling me what to do, and I was able to go on!"[21] His fellow filmmaker Graeme Ferguson notes that the film had to be put together in the optical house because he had no way of screening it—that is, he could screen the individual images but he could not screen them in juxtaposition. "That was a very big achievement," says Ferguson. "I don't think any other filmmaker at Expo overcame such a big problem and overcame it so successfully."[22]

For those of a certain generation, *A Place to Stand* became iconic. It had an afterlife, too, as it was exhibited soon after Expo as a short feature in regular movie houses. This aroused the ire of opposition members at Queen's Park, who claimed Ontario premier John Robarts—said to tear up when he heard the film's song[23]—was riding its coattails in that fall's election campaign.[24]

A very different sort of film entertainment could be found at the Czech Pavilion and its Kinoautomat. In a small auditorium, the cinematographer Radúz Činčera unveiled his computer-programmed push-button comedy, *One Man and His House.* At the centre of the forty-five-minute film's plot were a mild-mannered man, his voluptuous blonde neighbour and his jealous wife. At a series of junctures during the running of the film, the audience had to choose between two courses of action. For instance, should the man allow his buxom neighbour, clad only in a small towel, into his apartment? If yes, one pushed the green button; if no, the red. Invariably, audiences tended to choose the riskier option and the story continued. And each time, the hero of the piece, Mr. Novak, appeared on stage and spoke to the audience about its decisions. Except that, according to the daughter of Činčera, the actor playing Mr. Novak did not understand English and essentially uttered "a collection of sounds." "A lot of journalists came to him and wanted to do interviews," she told one writer, "but he wasn't able to reply. He didn't understand. Then he asked my daddy to teach him one more sentence, which was, 'I cannot talk with you, but I can drink with you.'"[25] The celebrated CBS news anchor Walter Cronkite tried to speak with the actor playing Mr. Novak. Journalist-broadcaster Fred Langan, then an Expo press aide, escorted Cronkite about the exhibition and says Cronkite grew quite irate when the actor wouldn't give him the time of day. "Cronkite thought the guy was snubbing him," says Langan. "He couldn't believe the guy didn't speak English."[26]

Činčera received a lot of attention, and interest was high for his interactive film process, but hopes of building on its Expo success went up in smoke the next year when Communist authorities clamped down on the Prague Spring and Kinoautomat became collateral damage of the Cold War.

In addition to Kinoautomat, the Czech Pavilion amazed with its polyvision slide and film show outlining the marvels of industry and its Diapolyecran which, in like spirit, celebrated the wonders of technology through a blizzard of images controlled by 224 projectors and 15,000 slides that flipped every fifth of a second.

One of the stellar works in Expo's multi-screen universe was Graeme Ferguson's *Polar Life*, made for the Man the Explorer Pavilion. Ferguson shot in Canada, Greenland, Alaska, Finland, Sweden, Norway and the Antarctic; not permitted to film in the Soviet Union, he hired a Russian cinematographer to obtain the Russian Arctic footage. Filming took eighteen months. The completed film ran eighteen minutes and was shown in an auditorium divided into four sections, each section seating one hundred and fifty people. The sections were on a turntable that revolved as eleven projectors projected the film onto eleven stationary screens. Ferguson shot his movie, containing stark and beautiful images of the polar regions, with the specifics of the theatre in mind. According to the original design, the theatre would rotate clockwise, meaning the images would appear on the audience's right. Halfway through filming, however, the plan changed. Now the plan called for the theatre to rotate in a counter-clockwise motion. "From an artistic point of view it didn't really matter," says Ferguson, "because the rotation was so slow."[27]

Ferguson was thirty-eight years old when he took on *Polar Life*. He had been working in New York as a freelance filmmaker. Starting out at a time when film schools were still in their infancy, the young Canadian apprenticed with noted filmmakers Maya Deren and Arne Sucksdorff, each of whom also acted as cinematographer on their own films. Deren's second husband, Alexander Hammid, with Francis Thompson, created the Oscar-winning multi-screen *To Be Alive*, the hit of the New York World's Fair of 1964–65. The Thompson-Hammid success influenced Ferguson's and other Expo films. "Somebody said, 'After New York, you've got to use multi-screen,'" says Ferguson—which, actually, had not been his plan at all: "I didn't want to use multi-screen," he says, "I wanted to make a 3D film!"

Thompson and Hammid were also represented at Expo. Their six-screen look at Canadian youth, *We Are Young!*, showed at the Canadian Pacific-Cominco Pavilion, while their earlier effort from the New York fair could be seen at the United Nations Pavilion. Hammid had been with *In the Labyrinth*'s Hugh O'Connor on that ill-fated project in eastern Kentucky; the film they were making was for Thompson's company. Graeme Ferguson took over O'Connor's duties on the project.

Thinking ahead to what they might do after Expo 67, Ferguson and his brother-in-law Roman Kroitor, director of *In the Labyrinth*, set their sights on bigger things. Over drinks at Kroitor's Montreal home, the two of them discussed an idea that led ultimately to the development of the IMAX system. Ferguson gives much credit to the indefatigable Roger Blais, a filmmaker with the NFB and an architect by profession, in charge of the selection and supervision of all the films at Expo. It was Blais who pushed the Disney people to hire Canadian personnel for their Expo movies and chose to rent rather than purchase projection equipment, a decision that, according to Blais, saved 35 percent of the budget.[28] And it was Blais who laid down a general rule that had a great impact on Ferguson and Kroitor. "I didn't report to him, but he laid down the law in a way that was very important to IMAX," says Ferguson. "At the New York fair, some pavilions had been built using technology that had completely failed. New York didn't have anybody to say, 'You will have to prove that it will work.' Roger says, 'You can only use technology that exists—you can't invent it at Expo.'" So when Ferguson and Kroitor were having those drinks and tossing ideas back and forth, the question arose: "What would we have done if Roger Blais had not laid down the rule that we could only use existing technology?" The answer came quickly: a larger screen, with one projector. "Within forty-five minutes," says Ferguson, "we roughed out the first format that would have been required."

The first film shot in the IMAX process—where the film in the camera is 65 mm and in the projector is 75 mm—would be *Tiger Child*, made by Kroitor and Donald Brittain and shown at Expo 70 in Osaka, Japan. Ferguson then followed with *North of Superior* for Ontario Place in 1971. "The moment you expanded cinema," he says of this new process and how he learned from it, "you have a new art form." IMAX proved one of Expo 67's notable legacies.

THE FILMS OF EXPO riveted worldwide attention, but it is worth remembering a footnote of some importance on another front. Amid all the multi-screen, interactive flash and dazzle, a more conventional movie had its world premiere at Expo, a movie that, as it turned out, was not conventional at all, but instead was the cultural equivalent of a hand grenade. It made its way to world attention by way of the annual Montreal International Film Festival, which, for the summer of 1967, was extended to two weeks instead of one and held under the aegis of Expo. Patrick Watson was a founding board member of the festival, and he and his first wife and their three children stayed at Secretary of State Judy LaMarsh's Habitat apartment during the festival's run in early August.[29] One of Watson's favourite hangouts was the Windsor Hotel, which served as festival headquarters. That Victorian palace first opened its doors in 1878, and among the great and glorious calling it a home away from home was famed tragedienne Sarah Bernhardt, who stayed there in 1880.[30] "What persists in the memory," says Watson, "are the wonderful conversations in the Windsor Hotel and the talks that were given in there: it became a kind of magic cave." This magic cave also featured a great bar, like the Mayflower in New York: "big room, windows opening onto the street, there was a real buzz to it," says Watson.

One of the films in competition at the festival that year was the Québécois filmmaker Michel Brault's *Entre la mer et l'eau douce (Drifting Upstream)*, a story about a rural youth in the big city, a metaphor in its way for the growing urbanization of French Canada. The movie's stars were the *chansonnier* Paul Gauthier and Montreal-born Geneviève Bujold, an actress of gamine sensuality and arresting intelligence, already an international name through her work for directors like Alain Resnais, Philippe de Broca and Louis Malle. Bujold had returned to Montreal for the Brault film's festival showing.

Brault established his cinematic roots at the French section of the NFB in the documentary tradition known as *cinéma verité*. *Entre la mer et l'eau douce* marked his first attempt at fiction, though it remained grounded in Brault's documentary beginnings. Much of its dialogue was improvised and pioneered the introduction of Quebec slang or *joual* into movie conversation.[31] The indigenous film industry in Quebec blossomed in the mid-sixties and Michel Brault was one of those in its vanguard.

Bujold had been in Montreal the previous year to participate in a panel selected by the Montreal festival, its job to choose the best fifty-second film on the theme Man and His World. There were 265 entries, and the winner, a Czech, received ten thousand dollars.[32] Others on the jury besides Watson and Bujold included Habitat architect Moshe Safdie and filmmaker Claude Jutra. Safdie says that they all became fast friends.[33] Watson briefly became a neighbour of Safdie's that summer of 1967 while Watson and his family lived at Habitat. "His apartment was just below us," says Watson, speaking of summer evenings out on the balcony. "At drink time he would be down below and I would be up above and we'd chat."

The Montreal festival in the Expo summer of 1967 had its share of controversies. The Quebec Censor Board banned Vancouver filmmaker Larry Kent's *High*, described in one synopsis as being about "a young couple of the 'hippie' set who team up in permissive love-making and crime,"[34] with the result that it could not be shown in the Canadian Film Festival portion of the program. When the awards for best feature film at the Canadian Film Festival portion were bestowed on Allan King for his documentary *Warrendale* (originally commissioned by Patrick Watson for broadcast on the CBC, which later rejected its depiction of emotionally disturbed children at a mental health facility as too hot to handle)[35] and Jean-Pierre Lefebvre for his *Il ne faut pas mourir pour ça*, the winning filmmakers, out of solidarity, and in protest against the ban on Kent's film, agreed to share the five-thousand-dollar prize money with the directors of the other films in the feature competition. Jury president Jean Renoir, legendary director of *La règle du jeu* and *La grande évasion*, registered his own protest, calling the Quebec Censor Board "out-dated and barbarous."[36]

Renoir was not the only big name around. The Austrian-born director Fritz Lang (*Metropolis, M*) showed up, as did the American director John Ford (*Stagecoach, The Searchers*). A young man named Moses Znaimer escorted Ford about Expo.[37] Patrick Watson had brought Znaimer into Watson's CBC Television news program *This Hour Has Seven Days*, where Znaimer had soon established a name for himself, and proposed him as a greeter and guide because of his command of French and Russian.[38] Moses Znaimer went on to become a zeitgeist darling, first as co-founder of Toronto's Citytv—the first Canadian station to truly exemplify the multicultural approach in its selection of on-air personnel, its offshoots including MuchMusic and Fashion Television—and then, more latterly, as the force behind Zoomer Media, whose principal demographic is aging baby boomers.

Expo and the Montreal festival also provided the occasion for the world premiere of a movie that changed forever the vernacular of mainstream filmmaking. The movie was *Bonnie and Clyde* and its impact was immense. The director of *Bonnie and Clyde*, Arthur Penn, and its stars, Warren Beatty and Faye Dunaway, came to town and hung out at the Windsor Hotel.[39] Character actor and *Bonnie and Clyde* co-star Michael J. Pollard—whose round face and smudged features suggested a Campbell's Soup kid on acid—popped into Montreal and is said to have left behind a valuable book at the Rainbow Bar and Grill on Stanley Street as a deposit against his bill there.[40]

Bonnie and Clyde broke new ground in a number of ways. Its screenwriters, Robert Benton and David Newman, were *Esquire* magazine journalists fascinated by the French New Wave filmmakers of the sixties, directors such as Jean-Luc Godard (*Breathless*) and François Truffaut (*Jules and Jim, Shoot the Piano Player*). These creators inspired a new idiom in movies with greater sexual candour and a freer and looser style and story structure. Benton and Newman attempted to capture that spirit in their screenplay about the Depression-era bank robbers Clyde Barrow and Bonnie Parker. In fact, at one time or another, Benton and Newman toyed with the idea of Godard or Truffaut as director for their project—that is, until Beatty (who also served as producer) and Penn took it over and made it theirs.[41] Did it glamourize its title characters, as some suggested? In the sense that two attractive actors played them, the answer has to be yes—but only to a degree. *Bonnie and Clyde* made it clear—and quickly—these were not bright people and their fecklessness commanded a terrible price.

The movie became a landmark and critical lightning rod for the manner in which it treated its subject matter. Bullets tore into flesh. People suffered awful, messy death agonies. The depiction of movie violence could never be the same again. Moreover, beginning as it did in a vein of what could even be termed slapstick—the ineptitude of the robbers counterpointed by the banjo music of Flatt and Scruggs, a duo best known for providing the theme for the lowbrow TV sitcom *The Beverly Hillbillies—Bonnie and Clyde* completely jangled expectations, moving in a millisecond from comedy to carnage. It kept the viewer off-balance and in a state of dread anticipation. And the sting of its violence, during a period in America when violence moved ominously to the forefront of people's consciousnesses, proved altogether unnerving. As black activist H. Rap Brown proclaimed, at a time of war in Vietnam and race riots in the streets of America, "Violence is part of America's culture and is American as cherry pie." [42]

A Montreal reviewer who attended the world premiere dismissed it as "not the kind of film that Montreal Film Festival audiences would go to the commercial cinema to see and it is certainly not the kind of film they expect to see in a festival organized to introduce the great films—or even the unusual films—of world cinema."[43] Indeed, the dean of American film reviewers, Bosley Crowther of *The New York Times*, offered a scathing denunciation. But Pauline Kael, in a lengthy piece for *The New Yorker*, praised the film's aesthetic outlawry, and if *Bonnie and Clyde* altered the movies—it became a box office hit and Warren Beatty became Prince of Hollywood—it likewise altered the world of movie criticism. Kael's star ascended, Crowther's declined. People found themselves taking a second look. Tastes shifted. The movie was part of a revolution occurring on a number of fronts—political, social, artistic—and in the closing years of the sixties, this revolution gathered in momentum and ferocity. Few remained untouched by its demands for change. Even in the bubble that was Expo 67, they had begun to feel its tremors.

ELEVEN

Altered States

In the mid-sixties, change—profound social change—was in the air, and for many Montrealers, Expo seemed one of the harbingers of that change. Architect Marianne McKenna's family were English-speaking Catholics—a group her mother referred to as the "real minority" in Montreal—and in 1967 she was eighteen years old and a United Nations Pavilion guide at Expo. By her own admission, she had until then led a reasonably cloistered sort of existence—but that was about to change. "Here you were, locked up in a private girls school, with skiing on the weekends," she says. "That'll keep you chaste!"[1] McKenna's mother had instructed her never to venture east of Morgan's department store (now The Bay); for certain properly brought-up anglo girls, Morgan's marked the dividing line between French and English Montreal. "No French-Canadian boyfriends, for sure," she remembers, "the mixing was not there." Still, she refused to feel entrapped. Her Expo duties helped in this quest for freedom. As a UN guide who escorted VIPs around the Expo site, McKenna could take in performances at the Czech Pavilion before moving on to sample exotic dishes at one of the

African pavilions or sip cocktails in the hospitality suite at Habitat. Expo offered the perfect transition between a sheltered high school life in Montreal and the university life in the United States awaiting her in the fall. "It changed attitudes," Marianne McKenna says of Expo. "It opened up Montreal to the world. For the adventurous, it was incredibly stimulating."

The difference between the old Montreal and the Montreal of Expo 67 was particularly noticeable to one native son who had returned home. Mordecai Richler confessed himself overwhelmed by the change in the city that had occurred in the space of a mere three years since his previous visit. The skyscrapers and the high-rise apartments and the slum clearance projects and the new Métro—not to mention the Place des Arts and the new hotels and the express highways—astonished him. "Home, suddenly, is terrifyingly affluent. Montreal is the richest-looking city I've seen in years."[2]

Place Ville Marie was a collaboration between architect I. M. Pei and the flamboyant American developer William Zeckendorf. Placed atop a new underground city of shops and restaurants (revolutionary for the time and ideal as an escape from the bitter Montreal winters), it had the effect of expanding, not to say transforming, the venerable Central Station and Queen Elizabeth Hotel that it served to connect. Place des Arts, the Stock Exchange Tower and architect Peter Dickinson's Canadian Imperial Bank of Commerce tower preceded the Expo 67 building boom. Place Bonaventure and Place du Canada, though, had been explicitly motivated by Expo. One Montreal historian suggested that for four years the city was really just one big construction site.[3] Zeckendorf praised Mayor Jean Drapeau as the developer's friend.[4] "If you wanted to build something in Montreal you had to get your architectural plans approved by *Maître* Drapeau," says Jack Rabinovitch, then an executive with the development company Trizec. "He was very particular on how things looked. Once he had approved it, you had no problem with the city."[5]

Says Fred Langan: "The one word you remember from a Jean Drapeau council meeting was 'adopté,' 'adopté,'—a room of trained seals raising their hands."[6] Yves Jasmin concedes that Drapeau was highly autocratic and surrounded by yes-men, but things got done and, contrary to the Duplessis administration, says Jasmin, there was no corruption in the Drapeau administration.[7]

Long-time Montreal Gazette journalist Bill Bantey credits Drapeau with great imagination, not to say great determination. "Hours meant nothing to him," says Bantey. "He was in the office at 6 a.m. and still there at 11 p.m. at night. It was just incredible the amount of work he put in."[8] A Drapeau breakfast usually consisted of a glass of hot water. Lunch might be a sandwich or—if he got really daring, says Bantey—he might send his chauffeur over to The Main to purchase a steamed hot dog. Dinner was the big meal of the day, but even here Drapeau watched carefully what he ate. Not much of a drinker, he enjoyed a glass of wine now and then.

That spring of 1967, the Royal Architectural Institute of Canada awarded Jean Drapeau a gold medal for distinguished service—the first time the award had been presented to an individual.[9] But Drapeau also had critics who blamed him for inadequate city planning and for gutting neighbourhoods to make way for eyesore expressways.[10] Many could not forgive him for demolishing some of the wonderful mansions on Sherbrooke Street to make way for skyscrapers in the name of "progress." "For example," says Bill Bantey, "the Van Horne house was demolished because no one could afford the bloody taxes on it. On the other hand, Montreal has museums they've never had before."[11]

No better emblem of the new Montreal existed than its new Métro. Started in October 1960 and completed by late fall of 1966, the Montreal subway's completion date was one more civic milestone accelerated by the prospect of Expo 67. Extending thirty-three kilometres and built at a cost of $213.7 million, the Métro featured twenty-six stations, each designed by a different architect. Its blue train cars moved along a track on rubber Michelin tires (as in Paris). A subway with rubber tires! "It just blew your mind in terms of modernity," says William Thorsell of the Montreal renaissance. "The Quiet Revolution, *Maîtres chez nous*, modernity coming to Montreal. Tremendous competitive advantage— Toronto was just waking up. Its technology, its economy, Expo being the big stage door opener—you really thought Montreal was going to be the city of the future in this country."[12]

The Métro's rubber tires emitted great heat, sometimes a problem as you descended by escalator into the station. "The awful part was to be dressed for winter and descend into it," says Charles Oberdorf—but this was a quibble. The style of these stations! The Toronto subway, he says, "was just a hospital waiting room by comparison."[13] According to Marianne McKenna, the Métro changed the configuration of the city: "You could travel through the city—and it brought the city together on the Expo site."[14]

In ways metaphorical as well as literal, the Métro was bringing together a city long marked by what the novelist Hugh MacLennan immortalized in the title of his 1940s classic novel *The Two Solitudes*. "The whole universe in our growing up was between *les français* and *les anglais*," says Louise Arbour. "The whole world was divided between Catholics and Protestants."[15] And, adds Mark Starowicz, who would later become an influential CBC Television producer, "It was a sort of East Berlin–West Berlin—without a wall. It was shocking! There was no cultural crossover."[16]

Tony Robinow moved from Toronto to Montreal in 1963 and remembers a luncheon held at the Senneville residence of author Philip Stratford and his wife. He observed that people at the table spoke both languages comfortably and he thought that was what Montreal was going to be. He learned differently—in his eyes, it was still the "Two Solitudes." For student activist Donna Mergler, growing up in Montreal in the sixties, the true dividing line between French and English was Rue Saint Laurent, or The Main—a "sort of no man's land." Mergler, though, was determined to cross that boundary: "And I crossed over Saint Laurent and discovered this exciting society where all these exciting things, politically, socially, culturally, were happening."[17] In general, however, the twain refused to meet—though a new assertiveness existed among the Québécois—a term that in itself was relatively new.[18] The *Fleurdelisé* now flew beside the Canadian flag in front of provincial buildings and public schools;[19] Montreal cabbies now had to speak both English and French by order of a new by-law;[20] and anglo arrogance was confronted more directly. In the early 1960s, when Canadian National Railway president Donald Gordon declared that the reason French-Canadians were not found in executive suites was because they lacked the requisite skills—not altogether untrue because of the antiquated educational system, but a decidedly tactless comment nonetheless—thousands of French-Canadians took to the streets in protest.[21] The days of the Eaton's saleslady said to have instructed her French-Canadian customers to "Speak white!" were clearly numbered.[22]

IN OPENING UP MONTREAL to the world, Expo may have further encouraged the autocrat in Drapeau. He wanted to ensure his city made a good impression and, to that end, he went all out in efforts to remove offending objects in whatever form they took, rounding up the city's homeless[23] and erecting fences to hide the poorer and seedier sections of town from the gaze of tourists. The fences provided a canvas for counter-protesters: "FLQ" could be found on some, and one cheeky wit invited tourists to "*Visitez les slums*," which no doubt infuriated the mayor. Extending a crusade that brought him and the Civic Action League party to office in the late fifties, Drapeau remained vigilant in trying to close down those vestiges of Montreal's lurid "sin city" reputation, the small strip clubs and bars. "I won't say you can't sin in Montreal any more," he told a reporter, "but you can't do it in an organized way."[24] Some called him on this. "The double standard in police permissiveness regarding entertainment in Montreal apparently still stands," wrote *Montreal*

Star columnist Bruce Taylor, who noted that while topless dancers were forbidden in Montreal nightclubs, the Garden of Stars at Expo was still promoting its *Prestige de Paris* show with the tagline of showgirls "in attractive undress at times."[25] Another voice critical of this Drapeaunian double standard comes from the narrator of Michel Tremblay's *The Red Notebook*, a fictionalized account of the denizens of a transvestite brothel during Expo year in Montreal: "The Morality Squad so dear to the heart of Mayor Jean Drapeau has come calling, with its stream of undeniable injustices, its blatant bad faith and its despicable hypocrisy, content to cloud the issue, to shake the cage without offering anything new … Montreal looks like somebody's old auntie who usually lives in her kitchen and insists on entertaining company in the living room, which she doesn't really know and where she never feels at home. A provincial city that likes to think of itself as a capital: welcome to the Vienna State Opera—that's culture—but forget about the Main, it has to be kept under wraps, its very existence denied."[26]

Nor did the morality squad confine itself to topless go-go bars. Nine dancers were arrested at the Youth Pavilion for what was described as the performance of indecent gestures. The police action so incensed venerable Quebec actor-playwright Gratien Gélinas that he donated the five-hundred-dollar prize that he received from the Montreal Saint-Jean-Baptiste Society to the dancers' defence fund. "There is something to get deeply saddened and indignant about when a small foul wind, coming straight out of the Middle Ages, blows over our metropolis," declared Gélinas. "And this takes place 'chez nous,' in this year of grace and collective pride of Expo 67, when Montreal is understood to proclaim itself … the capital of the world."[27]

The affronted petit bourgeois in Jean Drapeau could stem the tide only so far. Emerging social and political currents and cross-currents swirled and eddied about his city such that even a determined mayor could hardly stop them, no matter how much he might have wished them away.

EXPO DIDN'T IMPRESS Judy Rebick. The feminist commentator and activist was then a student at McGill University and living with her boyfriend in a house they shared with another couple on Hutchison Street in the "McGill ghetto." They may not have called it such—in truth, the word did not enter the vernacular until two years later—but Rebick and her friends lived what we might now call a counterculture life. "We were very cynical about Expo because we saw it as the cops cracking down," she says. "They're spending all this money on this circus and not spending it on poor people."[28]

Nor, in this flowering of the hippie phenomenon known as the Summer of Love did hippies much impress her. "Montreal had a bohemian culture," Rebick says. "We were taking acid in 1965 but the cops didn't know about it, so it wasn't illegal then. The hippies brought down the heat. The bohemian culture was rooted in an artsy thing, whereas the hippie culture was a mass popular culture." According to her, the Montreal police were "very repressive around drugs." In that attitude, they were hardly alone. In this summer of 1967, a British court sentenced Mick Jagger and Keith Richards of the Rolling Stones to jail terms for possession of pep pills, in Mick's case, and in Keith's case for allowing his house to be used for the smoking of marijuana,[29] while ballet stars Margot Fonteyn (who would be performing at Expo) and Rudolf Nureyev made headlines by becoming found-ins at a pot party raided by the San Francisco police; no charges were laid.[30] The Beatles and novelist Graham Greene were among those signing a petition that called for an easing of the laws regulating marijuana possession.[31] Meanwhile, the new "in" drug was LSD, lysergic acid diethylamide, generally referred to as "acid," popularized by Harvard professor Timothy Leary, who invited everyone to "tune in, turn on, and drop out," an invitation that provoked and terrified the powers that be.

In Toronto during this summer, a hippie self-help organization known as the Diggers led a protest to shut down Yorkville Avenue to traffic; Yorkville by then had become a mecca for the city's hippie and coffee house population. In Vancouver that August, thousands of hippies converged for a "super be-in" in Stanley Park. The same month, as part of Youth Day, Expo organizers programmed a love-in for Place Ville Marie, featuring the groups Jefferson Airplane (whose song "White Rabbit" became an LSD users' anthem) and the Grateful Dead. People at the Montreal concert wore flowers in their hair and painted daisies on their faces, though perhaps the hippie phenomenon did not exert the same hold here that it did in the other two cities. "In Montreal, because of the francophone factor, youth was much more directed to nationalism than hippies," says Judy Rebick. "It was much more political in Montreal."[32]

Novelist Susan Swan, a self-described "traditional Southern Ontario girl" who, as a student at McGill, had fallen in love with Montreal, was a friend of Judy Rebick's. "I used to talk to her about drug trips and write down every word for my notes," she says. "We both had missions. I was going to be a great writer and she was going to be a great activist. We couldn't afford to destroy ourselves on drugs and sex, although we were certainly in their thrall."[33] Much of that talk and note-taking occurred in a greasy-spoon restaurant named, appropriately, The Grease, a hangout on Milton near The Main. Nancy Sinatra's "These Boots Were Made for Walking" played on the jukebox and, remembers Swan, "I could have a beer with my pizza, and I thought that was the most sophisticated thing."

The summer of Expo 67, Swan rented out her Montreal flat at a handsome rate in order to work as a reporter in Toronto at the *Telegram*. Rebick and her boyfriend, meanwhile, played host at their Hutchison Street house to both Jefferson Airplane (minus lead singer Grace Slick, who bunked elsewhere) and the Grateful Dead, in town for their Place Ville Marie performance. Rebick's boyfriend had met U.S. satirist-provocateur Paul Krassner, who tipped their house as a place where the groups could spend the night. Krassner, himself, came to speak about the hippie phenomenon at the Youth Pavilion and is possibly best remembered for burning his draft card during an interview with CBC Television at the U.S. Pavilion, to the fury of pavilion personnel gritting their teeth on the off-camera sidelines.[34] "They were like a Monty Python skit of a rock band, they were so full of themselves," says Rebick of Jefferson Airplane. "But the Grateful Dead, they were interesting to me. Jerry Garcia walked around with his guitar all the time. He was constantly practising. They were good guests, though. They cleaned up afterwards."

The Jefferson Airplane members asked her to accompany them on a tour of the Expo site. She accepted and took the VIP tour of the grounds with them. They read their reviews as they were being driven around. They were fun guys, but in small doses. "Too much testosterone for me," says Rebick, "so I got off the bus." Jefferson Airplane was on its way to meet Dr. Timothy Leary at his farm in upstate New York; they invited her to join them, but she declined. Asked if she has any regrets about that decision, Rebick shakes her head. "They were on acid constantly," she says. "I was twenty-one years old—*but I was sensible!*"

ANOTHER TWENTY-ONE-YEAR-OLD, in Montreal for the first time, was Alan Hustak. Working for an Ottawa radio station, he arrived to cover the opening of Expo. As he drove his red sports car along Sherbrooke Street that perfect April morning, "it was as if the streets were paved with gold. I've often said if God allows me to come back to earth for one day after I die, make it that morning."[35] As he moved about Île Notre Dame, as a light mist rose off the river, sounds of music wafted from a place not immediately discernible. Hustak rounded a corner to discover a group of hippies about his own age. He figures they were students from the McGill music school. They were playing Vivaldi and it was spring and they were toking and the whole mood seemed somehow magical.

A chance encounter with the director of English TV news for Radio-Canada led to Hustak being hired as an Expo reporter. "I'm a kid from Saskatchewan and I'm let loose at Expo 67!" he says. "I came for a weekend and I stayed forty years." He arrived with somewhat redneck notions of French-Canadians being effete and quickly learned to discover around him an incredible dynamism. "This man Dupuy! This man Beaubien! There was this undercurrent at the fair. Underneath the joie de vivre, there was this ferocious kind of pride, Frenchified. While everybody visiting saw this as a Canadian effort, the people who were working, particularly the French-Canadians, this was their defining beginning of a Quebec accomplishment."

Hustak eventually became a reporter at the *Montreal Gazette* and later worked as a researcher for Drapeau when the latter considered writing his memoirs. (Of the mayor, Hustak says simply, "He *was* the city!" [36]) Hustak became a friend of Nick Auf der Maur, a legend of the city's press corps who worked hard, played harder and died far too young. Today, an alley off Crescent Street commemorates his name and is not distant from the Winston Churchill Pub, a favoured hangout of his. There are nothing but outrageous stories about auf der Maur, and not least the one about his wager that he would sleep with a hostess from every national pavilion at Expo. "It made for a good story whether it happened or not," says Mark Starowicz, another *Gazette* colleague at the time. "Certainly he tried."[37] Another story told how the dancer Rudolf Nureyev spent an evening at the Rainbow Bar and Grill on Stanley Street hitting on the straight, but mischievous, auf der Maur. "Nick," says Hustak, "could seduce anybody with his wit and personality."[38]

Contrary to the jaundiced opinion of Montreal nightlife offered by the narrator of Michel Tremblay's *The Red Notebook*, the young Canadians who found themselves working at Expo—many from out of town, some in their first jobs away from home—discovered in Montreal after dark a proverbial garden of earthly delights. For William Thorsell, from Edmonton, Montreal meant his first visit to a disco, "where you could actually drink beer." Thorsell found an apartment on Durocher, just north of Sherbrooke: "One big room on the roof, walls of glass, looking over the city." He rented it with two friends. Their apartment, he says, became "party central."[39] But then Montreal, itself, during the summer of Expo 67 was pretty much one big party central.

Architect Rod Robbie's firm had rented an apartment in Montreal, decorated by one of the partners, according to Robbie, in the style of a bordello. A married man, and not into the wild life, Robbie recalls one party at that apartment where he ended up, fully clothed, in the shower with another man and woman, who were wearing what one usually wears in a shower, which is to say nothing at all.[40]

In between escorting VIPs around Expo, Prudence Emery found time to have an affair with a visiting Russian named Leo, who arrived on her doorstep bearing a huge bouquet of roses. Emery, who would in time become one of this country's premier film publicists, lived on lower Stanley Street and tooted about the city in a red MG, occasionally enjoying a jumbo martini at the Beaver Club (an institution originally established by members of the North West Company and legendary for its hard partying), then located at the Queen Elizabeth Hotel. "I woke up every morning feeling excited," she says. "And I've never felt like that on any other job."[41]

Everyone had his or her favourite nightspot. For Charles Oberdorf, there were the two discos on Mountain Street, one near Sherbrooke and the other near Saint Catherine, and there was also another, in Old Montreal, which was a real mash-up of English–French, black–white, straight–gay. [42] Adrienne Clarkson covered Expo for her CBC Television talk show. "The painter Mousseau opened a disco on Crescent Street with a stainless steel floor," she says. "Everybody danced in their bare feet. To me, Expo meant walking home at three in the morning and you have to get up at seven. But who cares because you're twenty-seven years old!"[43] John Uren, who worked at the World Festival, used to frequent Le Patriote, where he listened to Monique Leyrac, as well as a black nightclub south of Saint Catherine, where he caught Otis Redding and B. B. King. Black performers, says Uren, "loved Montreal because it had little prejudice. Why do you think [baseball star] Jackie Robinson played there? When you grow up in Toronto and go to Montreal, you understand there's a big city and a *big city*."[44]

Reporter Mark Starowicz remembers how suddenly Montreal seemed to become a major cosmopolitan centre. "The city just overnight became an international city, and remained so from that summer onwards," says Starowicz. "The civil rights movement in the U.S., Vietnam—suddenly we became relevant to all that. It became a city you came to to advance your cause. Suddenly there seemed to be Algerian poets everywhere."[45]

While Drapeau may not have enjoyed all the changes that came with Montreal becoming this international destination ("He hated beards," journalist Bill Bantey once observed, "it was *hippie*!"),[46] the mayor had to beam with pride at the city's, as well as his own, newfound stature.

TWELVE

Spectacles

The key thing about Expo—I don't think we would have had the art. At the end of Expo, art was extremely important to Canadians. Painting, sculpture, architecture, music—not just film. We had, that one year, a combination of the work of artists that has never happened before or since. Artists speaking to people and people absorbing their art.

—FILMMAKER GRAEME FERGUSON

Expo 67 was a cornucopia of a lot of things, and certainly this statement applied to the variety and scope of its display of the visual arts. "The relevance of the visual arts to man and his world was never more broadly defined nor more clearly illustrated than at Expo," wrote art historian David P. Silcox. "The confidence that came from knowing that others thought that what you did was valuable was a benefit for the present. But perhaps more important for the future, Expo presented to the Canadian public, in a way that would have been impossible otherwise, the achievements of Canadian artists, architects, and designers."[1]

That education in the visual arts began at the extraordinary fine arts exhibition assembled at the Man the Creator fine arts gallery at Cité du Havre. Grouped under various theme ideas (Man and Play, Man and his Conflicts, Man and His Ideals, etc.) were masterworks from around the world as well as a selection of more contemporary works. Though he found some of these groupings could lead to "thought-provoking juxtapositions," an art critic for *The Washington Post* concluded, "It's probably best to ignore the 'theme' idea, or to view it as an excuse to bring together an exciting collection of masterpieces."[2] Indeed, the show virtually commanded jaws to drop, with its inclusion of, among others, Rubens and Van Dyck from the Hermitage Museum in Leningrad (now St. Petersburg); Cézanne and Gauguin landscapes; African masks and Indian carvings; Persian ironwork and Japanese bronzes; Constable and Gainsborough; Hogarth and Rembrandt; Velázquez and Turner; Monet, Miró, and Pissarro; Borduas and de Kooning. There were two hundred works in all.

A large international photography exhibit organized by Philip J. Pocock was located nearby. *The Camera as Witness* featured five hundred photographs selected from forty thousand works, which included such celebrated photo-artists as Brassaï (the pseudonym for the Hungarian-born photographer), Jacques-Henri Lartigue, Edward Steichen, Robert Capa and Bill Brandt.

Before Expo opened, however, controversy clouded *The Camera as Witness*. A wrenching photograph by Donald McCullin depicting a tearful Turkish Cypriot woman who had just learned her husband had been killed in a Greek raid on their village in 1962 brought forth the ire of the director of the Greek Pavilion. "For every Turkish woman who has lost her loved one, there are hundreds of Greek women in the same situation," this official complained, accusing Expo management of a lack of tact and consideration.[3] Dark hints ensued. An offended Greece might refuse to participate in the opening of Expo—and the continued presence of the offending photograph might even imperil a September visit by King Constantine, the Greek monarch. Pierre Dupuy reacted swiftly. The photograph was removed and the exhibition catalogue pulped and replaced by another—this time minus not only the discomfiting picture but *all* photo captions.[4]

Expo was also a playground for sculpture. In the rose garden on Île Ste. Hélène, as well as on the grounds adjacent to the U.S. Pavilion, an astonishing array of international sculpture had been assembled, works by Picasso, Braque, Matisse and Rodin among them. The Scandinavian countries had their own sculpture garden, while the Swiss Pavilion featured the imposing shapes of Alberto Giacometti. A Henry Moore bronze stood outside the British Pavilion. Canadian artist Gerald Gladstone had a number of pieces at Expo, including Uki, the fire-breathing dragon at the Canadian Pavilion, and a mammoth something-or-other at La Ronde. And in Inco Plaza on Île Ste. Hélène stood the twenty-metre-high stabile by the American sculptor Alexander Calder. Supervision of this artistic bounty presented its particular challenges. "The other day two youngsters climbed Berta Lardera's 'Dramatic Occasion XI'—and it nearly was a dramatic occasion when the guard approached," noted a reporter.[5] Among the concerned custodians was artist Charles Pachter, then just returned from art school in the United States and hired to assist Guy Robert from Montreal's Musée d'Art Contemporain, who was in charge of the sculpture exhibits. Pachter remembers taking beer and sandwiches to Calder. "He was in his seventies," says Pachter, "very down-to-earth and single-minded and focused on the piece."[6] The Calder piece, bearing the simple yet grandiose title *Man*, reminded some spectators why Calder remained more noted for his mobiles than his stabiles. It was "a great knobby chunk of steel," complained Robert Fulford, "an ungracious mass of ungainly angles, a totally earthbound work of art … a vain and empty gesture."[7]

Among Canadian art critics, the greater disappointment lay with the Canadian sculpture represented. For David Silcox, only a half-dozen of the twenty pieces commissioned seemed significant works, and he included Michael Snow, Sorel Etrog, Armand Vaillancourt, Ted Bieler, Robert Murray and Elza Mayhew in this select group. At the same time, he noted those missing from the exhibition—the likes of Harold Town, Iain Baxter, Les Levine and Gino Lorcini among them. "All in all," declared Silcox, "it was a splendid occasion for which our sculptors were less prepared than they should have been, but they have had little opportunity to work on a grand scale."[8] He was echoed by art critic Harry Malcolmson. "Most of our sculptors begin as painters and they don't get over it easily," wrote Malcolmson. "At Expo, without the accustomed rectangular setting, this kind of linear, silhouette-sculpture looks pitiful indeed." It did seem rather that Expo's wide open spaces almost defied anyone unprepared to make a bold statement. In fact, for Malcolmson, the one great sculpture at Expo happened to be a building—the Venezuela Pavilion: "The building has coherence, unity, breathtaking discipline and clarity, and a marvellous contact with the earth."[9]

Like David Silcox, Malcolmson had kind words for Robert Murray and Sorel Etrog ("who *think* as sculptors") and a special mention for Michael Snow. "Michael Snow's *Walking Woman* harem at the Ontario Pavilion is strong too, but for reasons personal to Snow's idiosyncratic art," noted Malcolmson. "Snow's work is really an idea made visible. When Snow extracts his Walking-Woman shape from a painting, he never pretends it's a 'sculpture' he has made. It is clearly a painting-shape let loose into the world. The disconcerted spectator finds himself mentally clothing the Woman with a picture-frame to restore her to her natural habitat."[10]

Snow's eleven stainless steel *Walking Woman* sculptures, placed strategically about the Ontario Pavilion, became a talking point in their ambiguous ubiquity. By the time of Expo, they were already familiar images through other, non-sculptural, media. Snow had used the contour in his work as early as 1961. Asked about his inspiration, Snow offers an amused smile. "Probably sex," he says. "It was just trying to set up a situation that would involve figuration but wouldn't be using some of the traditional means of depicting a figure." He got the idea of making cut-out figures that would be independent of any specific location; their background was the wall against which he happened to place them. One day, using a 1.5-metre-tall piece of cardboard, he drew the outline of a figure and then cut it out with a knife. This time it really sank in that it was a reproducible thing: "The idea of using it as a constant *and* as a tool ..."[11]

At that time, Snow and his then wife, artist Joyce Wieland, lived in New York, first in a loft on Greenwich Street and then later in a loft on Chambers Street. Because loft dwelling then was illegal, certain kinds of work had to be performed in an underground way. "Joyce and I moved into our loft on Chambers Street," he says, "and we wanted a bathtub and some changes made in the kitchen." In their case, the part-time plumbers showing up at their door were Richard Serra and Philip Glass, later recognized, respectively, as a famous sculptor and a famous composer. New York offered a "fantastic period of creativity in art" and Snow found himself caught up in it. He was also attempting to redefine his goals.

"I thought," he says, "I was doing too much in too many areas." In the mid-fifties, most of his income came from his prowess as a musician. "One of my decisions was to stop being a musician and be a visual artist," he says, "but even there I had worries that perhaps I should be concentrating on one particular thing." The sixties work meant mainly *Walking Woman* and films, "but there was an overlapping transition into the kind of work I started to do after *Walking Woman*, which was mainly sculpture." He got the Ontario Pavilion assignment after winning a competition. To him, it seemed the perfect way to bid farewell to this iconic image. "It really was like a kind of final, very public appearance of *Walking Woman*," he says. "I felt it was coming to an end anyway and this seemed a fantastic way to end it."

The same year, he won a prize at Brussels with his experimental film

Wavelength. "The medium in painting is oil paint," he says. "In this case, it's coloured light." *Wavelength* is a study of the medium of film and its possibilities, illustrated by a camera that moves in ever-closer to a picture of waves as the soundtrack bubbles with various auditory effects. A film, in other words, guaranteed to have certain viewers clamouring for the exits, a reaction fazing Michael Snow not at all. Given his background as an experimental filmmaker, it is perhaps no surprise that he offers a more qualified take on the films of Expo. "It's really a form of commercial art," he says, "there's an appeal made for your participation. It was rather shameless in its invitations ... This '67 group of films was really a predecessor for what's happening in the art gallery where gallery projection installations have become a very strong form. A gallery viewer is ambulatory and so you have to make something which might be of interest for a short time or for a long time. It's very hard to make something that has a beginning, middle, and end—simply because people won't stick around."

Snow found himself greatly impressed by the U.S. Pavilion, particularly its exhibition of pop and abstract expressionist paintings by artists such as Jasper Johns, Robert Rauschenberg, Robert Indiana, Andy Warhol, Helen Frankenthaler and Barnett Newman. These paintings were exhibited on large vertical swaths of canvas that had been suspended from the roof of the dome. "The paintings resembled enormous banners more than works of art," observed art historian Virginia Anderson. Anderson points out that a number of factors contributed to this effect. The actual size of the paintings, for one thing, but also the pop aesthetic of the artists chosen and the fact that they were presented in a context that included spacecraft and giant blow-ups of movie stars. Not incidentally, the U.S. Pavilion was meant to accommodate five thousand visitors an hour. As Anderson says, "This was not the venue for close and careful viewing, to put it mildly."[12] Today, these artists are considered masters of the form. In 1967, they invited a more dismissive reaction. "Bold," "shallow," and "decorative" summarized a *New York Times* critic.[13]

Not without controversy of its own was the Painting in Canada exhibit at the Canadian Pavilion. The critic for *The Washington Post* complained that it was "badly selected" and "'artily' hung."[14] But then Barry Lord, who curated and hung the exhibition, liked to court controversy. The show, historical as well as contemporary, featured forty-two paintings from artists such as Emily Carr, Jean-Paul Riopelle, Paul-Émile Borduas, Jack Bush, Harold Town, Jack Chambers and Claude Breeze. Breeze's *Sunday Afternoon*, with its portrayal of the lynching of a black man in the American South, was one of the more politically charged works. Conspicuously absent from the show was the high-profile Alex Colville, an absence that displeased a few pavilion higher-ups. "They were shocked," Lord notes gleefully, adding he decided on the lesser known painter Miller Brittain instead.

Lord compares what happened at Expo with what happened at the Tate Modern gallery in London. Avant-garde started to become mainstream. The sculptor Sorel Etrog, a known commodity before Expo, became, according to Lord, a powerhouse afterwards. "It had the effect of putting Canadian art out as a mainstream concern as opposed to a marginal concern," he says.[15]

For much of 1967, Lord served as the editor of *artscanada* magazine. Its publisher, and Lord's boss, was Paul Arthur, the design eminence whose signs and pictographs blanketed Expo. Their relationship grew strained: Lord's protest against President Johnson and his subsequent arrest ensured a degree of fallout. Arthur had difficulty with this notoriety, says Lord, adding that he was let go from the magazine in September 1967 with notice to be gone by year's end. Lord suggests he posed another problem for Arthur by slagging a photo exhibit by Roloff Beny in the VIP section of the Canadian Pavilion. "Roloff had made a deal with [Canadian Pavilion commissioner general] Leslie Brown and the pavilion," he says, "and 'given' them the exhibition." Beny had friends in high places—not least the supremely elegant Signy Eaton of the department store Eaton's, who were major supporters, as it happened, of the Society of Art Publications that Paul Arthur headed and that published *artscanada*. In Barry Lord's interpretation of events, push came to shove—which meant goodbye Barry Lord.

THERE ARE THOSE WHO CLAIM—and they have a point—that the centre-piece of Expo 67 was its abundance of opera, theatre, ballet, symphony and revue, all gathered under its World Festival big tent. Memorable acts and performers appeared elsewhere—the programs at the Canadian Pavilion organized by comedians Wayne and Shuster and actor-playwright Gratien Gélinas, for instance, or Leonard Cohen reading from his poetry at the Youth Pavilion. But Expo's World Festival represented an assemblage of talent from around the globe like no other before or (surely) since. Consider just this sampling of the artists on offer: The Red Army Chorus. The Kabuki Theatre of Japan. The Royal Opera from Stockholm (its first tour of the western hemisphere). The Bolshoi Opera. The La Scala Opera Company from Milan. The Vienna State Opera performing *Elektra* with Birgit Nilsson. The Montreal Symphony's production of Verdi's *Otello* with Jon Vickers, Teresa Stratas, and Louis Quilico under the direction of Zubin Mehta. The National Theatres of Britain and Greece, the former led by Laurence Olivier. Gilles Lefebvre's Jeunesses Musicales. The Mormon Tabernacle Choir. Duke Ellington. Isaac Stern. The Supremes. The Canadian Opera Company performing *Riel*, a new work by Canadian composer Harry Somers. The Royal Winnipeg Ballet, the National Ballet of Canada, and Les Grands Ballets Canadiens de Montréal. Britain's Royal Ballet Company with Dame Margot Fonteyn. Canada's Stratford Festival performing *Antony and Cleopatra* with Christopher Plummer and Zoë Caldwell. Maureen Forrester performing Mahler's "The Song of the Earth." Jean-Louis Roux's Théâtre du Nouveau Monde. The Australian Ballet, whose star and co-director Robert Helpmann commented: "Eighteen months ago when I was in Montreal, I found the Expo 67 site a sea of mud and a scene of confusion. When I returned some months later I found it to be a sea of snow and the scene of even greater confusion. Now I am back again I find that a miracle has taken place and I feel honoured at being able to play a very small part in what obviously will go down in history as the greatest of world's fairs."[16]

And still there were more: Broadway star Carol Channing; Marlene Dietrich; Jack Benny; Maurice Chevalier; as well as native talents like Quebec's Monique Leyrac and Gilles Vigneault and the Maritimes music maestro fiddler Don Messer (a homey touch), all of them dispersed among halls and auditoriums of varying capacities in Place des Arts, the Expo Theatre, the Autostade, and the Garden of Stars at La Ronde. Expo's World Festival tried to offer something for everyone.

Veteran public relations and communications czarina Mary Jolliffe, who cut her teeth launching Canada's Stratford Festival in 1953, arrived in Montreal at the eleventh hour from a position as director of communications for the national company of New York's Metropolitan Opera to head up the World Festival communications department. "I think I only got about three months notice and one went like Billy-be-Damned," she says. "They had no awareness of the scope of what they were tackling. They didn't know how to run a box office properly. They didn't have a media list!"[17] Yet possibly because of this sense of challenge and quasi-chaos, there did exist a definite *esprit de corps*. "There was great joy and wonder," says Jolliffe. "Nobody had ever been exposed to anything like this. I could touch base with that feeling because that was the feeling we had with Tony [Sir Tyrone] Guthrie and Stratford."[18] Her biggest fear was that they couldn't pull it off. "I don't think I was afraid I didn't know enough—but I had doubts about the viability of it … I had a wig, made of natural hair, and I used to get so frustrated I'd tear it off!"

Commissioner General Pierre Dupuy arrived late for the World Festival's initial press conference, but the renowned actor-producers Laurence Olivier and Jean-Louis Barrault, bilingual both, stepped in and moderated the event. "They took it over," says a grateful Mary Jolliffe. In his Expo memoir, Dupuy, who eventually did turn up, spoke delightedly of how Olivier read in French one passage of a poem Dupuy wrote specially for the occasion and how Barrault followed suit by reading another passage of the poem in English. "*Quel exemple d'harmonie,*" noted Dupuy, "*pour notre pays bilingue!*"[19] Mary Jolliffe remembers only that Dupuy's poem seemed "interminable."[20]

John Uren, a member of Jolliffe's team, once ran a coffee house in Calgary called The Depression (singer-songwriter Joni Mitchell received one of her first breaks there). The Stratford Festival's Vic Polley, for whom Uren worked in publicity, recommended him to Jolliffe. Uren had taken on the role of general manager of Toronto's Crest Theatre in the spring of 1966, only to have the Crest expire in the summer of that year. He recalls going to the family cottage at Lake Simcoe and telling everyone about his new job at Expo and being met with blank looks. "I'm going to Expo," he says, "and nobody had heard of it!" Uren worked in advertising and promotion on paid ticket entertainment. Those in attendance at weekly planning meetings included Philippe de Gaspé Beaubien, David Haber, Jean Coté, and Gordon Hilker. Haber and Hilker booked the shows and Coté was responsible for the day-to-day operation, says Uren. One time, the dapper Haber appeared in a dinner jacket, garb he was still wearing from the previous evening. It was Haber who got off a lovely line at the expense of Soupy Sales, the American television comedian who fronted a revue entitled *Hellzapoppin '67* playing at the Garden of Stars and lagging at the box office. "*Hellzapoppin* is going down the tubes," remembers Uren, "and Haber says, 'We've gotta *stop* the word of mouth!'" Soupy Sales turned up as a guest at a party Uren hosted at his apartment in the Old Port area. "He was quite rude, not charming at all," says Uren. "And Susan—the daughter of my landlord—ordered him out of the party. I don't know why. All I remember is that Soupy Sales was thrown out and [actress] Jill St. John stayed." At midnight, Uren sent out for hot dogs and *patates frites* from The Main.[21]

There were other misses besides *Hellzapoppin*. Dancers from Ethiopia, booked into a small venue at Place des Arts, played their first night of a one-week engagement and then vanished. "Something happened and they all flew out the next day," says Uren. "They were there—and suddenly they weren't there." Expo organizers booked the Ringling Bros. and Barnum & Bailey Circus into the open air Autostade in April, but chill winds and freezing rain meant the deletion of certain acts: you don't necessarily want to walk a high wire when it is April in Montreal. And—another questionable call—Uren swears someone in administration discussed the idea of issuing condoms to the paid entertainment. "The prejudice against actors and performers was such that they thought they were going to deflower the city," says Uren. "It didn't happen—but it *was* proposed."[22]

By the time he arrived at Expo to headline a revue called *Flying Colours*, Maurice Chevalier was nearly eighty years old and trading on an *ooh-la-la* Gallic charm by then a little rusty. "He is ridiculous singing at his age with that stupid boater," pronounced Coco Chanel, the venerable but testy Paris fashion queen. "He is plain awful—at his age, he ought to retire." Yet Chevalier remained a name (best known, by then, for his role in the film *Gigi* and his rendition of the song "Thank Heaven for Little Girls") and Uren remembers how greatly impressed he was when he first watched Chevalier perform. "He comes on and immediately dances up—what?—eighty or a hundred steps and then starts to sing. And I thought to myself, 'This guy is fit!' I found out later he was lip-synching, so I wasn't quite so impressed." As a public relations ploy, World Festival organizers, armed with two thousand plastic boater hats, took their star up to Place Ville Marie to heighten awareness for the show. The stunt backfired, however, as onlookers urged Chevalier to perform and, when he refused, started to boo him. The same organizers took Duke Ellington up to Place Ville Marie and he played for over an hour. Ultra-cool Duke, resplendent in sky-blue suit, navy shirt and maroon suede loafers, thrilled the lunchtime crowd with Ellington standards like "Mood Indigo" and "Sophisticated Lady."[23]

Another trouper—and, compared to Chevalier, a mere child at sixty-six years old—was legendary German-born actress-singer Marlene Dietrich, who arrived at the airport to announce that her hundred-thousand-dollar wardrobe had been stolen from her New York hotel.[24] At that point, Dietrich had not performed in North America for quite a while. David Haber booked her for a week and she sold out in a flash. "Opening night was the biggest night of Expo—the whole gay, trans-vestite demimonde showed up," says John Uren. "The day Marlene Dietrich opened happened to coincide with Germany's national day at Expo. They were not amused because she got more publicity."[25]

Asked by a reporter how she managed to look so young, Dietrich retorted, "Because I'm not that old!"[26] Mary Jolliffe adored Dietrich; they first met at Toronto's O'Keefe Centre, where Jolliffe had worked. Jolliffe still has the scarf Dietrich gave to her. She was tough and sharp, remembers Jolliffe. She even mended her own tights. In fact, she was mending her tights when Jolliffe first met her. "And she said to me," says Jolliffe, "'I do this because I do this *better* than anyone else.'"[27] Krystyne Romer marvelled at the way Dietrich demanded a lighting rehearsal that lasted eight hours—the rehearsal not about the music but about showcasing her famous legs beneath that flesh-coloured dress.[28]

Documentary filmmaker John McGreevy, then an assistant director in the CBC Television variety department, had joined the CBC five years earlier when he moved to Canada from Britain with the ambition of becoming a filmmaker. When the CBC decided to broadcast popular programs like *Front Page Challenge* and *Wayne and Shuster* from Expo, McGreevy got the assignment of preparing the opening montages for each of these shows. "It gave me terrific access to the site," he says. "It was the ideal opportunity for a young budding filmmaker to cut his teeth. Also it confirmed me in my belief that Canada was the best possible place to be." The Expo films dazzled him. He had never seen films projected on ceilings and floors before, so that when a pebble is tossed on the upper screen, it is next shown dropping into the pond projected on the screen on the floor below. The array of World Festival offerings dazzled him as well. Ingmar Bergman's Swedish Opera Company put on Stravinsky's *The Rake's Progress* on a raked stage that seemed to shoot right into the audience—"very black and white and, as you would expect of Bergman, *searing.*" Another highlight was the Bristol Old Vic's production of *Hamlet* with Richard Pascoe. It was the first production of the play McGreevy had ever seen—and he emerged from the experience completely sold on the contemporary relevance of the play and on Shakespeare.[29]

OVER AND ABOVE ALL ELSE, Expo itself was the main show and, as such, a magnet for celebrated visitors. Ed Sullivan twice broadcast his Sunday evening variety program from the Expo site in May. Sullivan, an American television institution whose constricted body language seemed bizarrely at odds with a tendency to elongate his vowels, could thus introduce not once but twice from the audience his newfound friend Mayor "Gene" Drapeau.[30]

Actor Cary Grant dropped in for a look, as did the Aga Khan and car magnate Henry Ford. Singer and actor Harry Belafonte—who performed at Expo with Miriam Makeba—also brought his family along. Former Disney child star Hayley Mills came with her boyfriend, British director Roy Boulting, more than thirty years her senior. Actors Jack Lemmon, Henry Fonda, Kirk Douglas, Gregory Peck and Vincent Price were present and accounted for and, likewise, Sidney Poitier, who, in 1967, established himself as the first major black movie star with the box office hits *To Sir, with Love; In the Heat of the Night;* and *Guess Who's Coming to Dinner,* an ascension coinciding with a time when the United States was engulfed in racial turmoil.

Many celebrities received escorted tours from Expo personnel. One of these guides was Robert McDonald, a Toronto man in his early twenties, described as "fast-talking, hyper, very intelligent, lots of weird, funny cultural references—a great PR guy."[31] Among those he escorted around was Laurence Olivier, the pre-eminent actor of his generation, who, that year, suffered through a serious health crisis, while the death that year of his troubled fifty-three-year-old former wife, actress Vivien Leigh, probably added an extra layer of emotional complication. The great Olivier is supposed to have offered Bob McDonald this imperishable advice. "Remember, Bob," he told the younger man, "don't get married just to legitimize your fucking."[32] What prompted the admonition is not clear. It suggests, though, that Bob McDonald was the sort of person who put people at ease and invited confidences, not to say trenchant life wisdom, from strangers.

Another young Expo escort was Prudence Emery, and to her fell the task of looking after the flamboyant entertainer Liberace, a man whose Las Vegas act pivoted heavily on sequined capes and smarmy innuendo, and whom Emery describes as "a complete delight. He had this New York agent with him and they went into the Czech Pavilion, which had a very good restaurant. Anyway, after the meal the New York agent picked up the cutlery and put it in his pocket."[33] (This wasn't the only instance of such souvenir-keeping. Beer steins, stones from the Atlantic Provinces Pavilion—all sorts of Expo paraphernalia had a habit of disappearing.[34]) Emery also acted as guide for another, more recent, phenomenon, the model-actress Twiggy. Rake-thin, with a charming smile accented by heavy eye makeup and a cockney accent by way of Eliza Doolittle, Twiggy was the new "it" girl, avatar of the "waif" look. Everyone talked about the Twig. "You see, she's not a picture, she's an X-ray," declared media savant Marshall McLuhan, attempting to explain the fascination. "She's geometrical, abstract."[35] (A fanciful prefiguring, perhaps, of New Journalist Tom Wolfe's later description of women of a certain class and thinness as "social X-rays.") Emery says the paparazzi dogged them at every step and, in order to escape, she commandeered one of the Expo gondolas—only to encounter paparazzi, in another gondola, approaching them from the opposite direction.

Political figures couldn't stay away either. Likely contenders for the Republican presidential nomination, New York Governor Nelson Rockefeller and Michigan Governor George Romney arrived, as did New York Senator Robert Kennedy, his wife, Ethel, and their many children. Kennedy, perceived as the leading challenger of incumbent Lyndon Johnson for the Democratic presidential nomination, remained coy about his political intentions. "He was magic," says Monique Simard, working as a hostess at the Youth Pavilion where Kennedy paid a visit.[36] It is reported that when the senator and his wife, family and friends emerged from Labyrinth, Kennedy announced, "Enough of this educational stuff! Let's go to La Ronde and have some fun!"[37] Those observing the playfulness of Kennedy and his clan would recall that day with a start a little more than a year later, after Kennedy had been gunned down in a Los Angeles hotel by an assassin's bullet. Canadian political figures were much in evidence, too. John Diefenbaker's negative attitude toward Expo changed once the exhibition opened to generally rapturous acclaim. Diefenbaker was quick to point out that Expo actually began on his watch. Prince Albert, Saskatchewan's favourite political son, arrived in early July, before the queen's visit, to celebrate Saskatchewan's special day at Place des Nations.[38] Pierre Sévigny also attracted autograph hunters as he was driven about the grounds in a pedicab.[39] Minister of Trade and Commerce Robert Winters became playful and switched roles, pedalling his wife and their pedicab driver about the site.[40] Justice Minister Pierre Trudeau, a relative newcomer to the political scene, attracted his share of interest from passersby. "He already had star power," says John McGreevy. "I remember one day he visited the site, and it was like Obama today. He had a following already and he certainly impressed one as a man who was going to make his mark on the Canadian scene. I perceived him to be somebody who was watching everything around him and how to take advantage of any given moment. He knew where the cameras were and, like Princess Di, he knew how to play them."[41]

The Maharishi Mahesh Yogi arrived to give a lecture at the Youth Pavilion before jetting off to India to provide guidance on transcendental meditation to the Beatles and actress Mia Farrow.[42] *Playboy* editor and publisher Hugh Hefner came by, entourage in tow, and, according to one Expo official, "in eight hours he saw more than most people see in three days."[43] Hefner's visit coincided with the opening of a new Playboy Club in Montreal—a success to judge by the eighteen thousand memberships already sold by September 1967.[44] Reportedly, Hefner met, in passing, *Cosmopolitan* editor Helen Gurley Brown, whose motto was "Good girls go to heaven; bad girls go everywhere."[45] Hefner and Brown both promoted lifestyles aimed at taking advantage of the sexual revolution they helped pioneer. One *wants* to believe that meeting took place. Their crossing paths at Expo seems a necessary moment, the pop-cult equivalent of Stanley-meets-Livingstone.

ONE VISITOR HIGHLIGHT OCCURRED when Prince Rainier and Princess Grace of Monaco arrived for the celebration of Monaco Day in mid-July. Record crowds turned out to greet them. And no one could deny the appeal of Princess Grace, who, a decade earlier, was known as the movie star Grace Kelly. This transition from films to royalty was the stuff of real-life fairy tales and Princess Grace adapted to her new role with ease and skill, delighting spectators who craned their necks to catch a glimpse of her and Rainier and their three children, Caroline, ten; Albert, nine; and Stephanie, two. Princess Grace was expecting a fourth child in January.

Earlier in the day, Monaco had announced it was donating its pavilion to the City of Montreal, a gesture repeated by other nations, including the United States, Australia, Belgium, Ethiopia, Iran, Mauritius and Tunisia. The buoyant mood of the Rainier visit was capped by a dinner for two hundred guests at the Chateau Champlain Hotel, decorated with the gold and red coat of arms of the French Riviera principality. Mayor and Mme Drapeau sat on either side of the royal couple. The champagne flowed. And, in a weird flourish of culinary showmanship, as the dessert was about to be served, lights dimmed and in marched waiters to the "Colonel Bogey March," bearing strawberry mousse topped by sparklers.[46] One newspaper account reported that dancing began after the fish course, the prince and princess moving about the dance floor to "Up a Lazy River." But Expo's PR head Yves Jasmin suggests dancing started with the prince leading Mme Drapeau while the mayor begged off with an apologetic "*Je ne sais pas dancer*,"[47] a demurral the princess accepted good-naturedly. Several hours after the dinner, the Hon. Lionel Chevrier, commissioner general for state visits to Expo 67, received a call from the Rainier entourage requesting medical assistance,[48] and the next morning there came the unhappy news that Princess Grace had suffered a miscarriage and was resting at the Royal Victoria Hospital. On the crowded Expo social calendar, the Rainier visit, despite its sombre resolution, provided a blessed calm before the storm. The storm in this case meant the imminent arrival of French president Charles de Gaulle. Hurricane Charles would create quite a stir.

THIRTEEN

Significant Birthdays

While Expo 67 came to be regarded as the crown jewel of the country's centennial celebrations, or, in the words of Canadian centennial commissioner John Fisher, "the frosting on the cake,"[1] a host of other projects and events under the aegis of the Centennial Commission took place as well. By May 1964, the federal government had committed to spending one hundred million dollars on a centennial program, and a chunk of this money went toward the National Capital Construction Program in Ottawa, which would result in the building of the National Library and Archives, the Canadian Museum of History and the National Centre for the Performing Arts. Under the Centennial Grants Program—consuming twenty-five million dollars of the overall budget—one dollar for every man, woman and child would be allocated toward the construction of a centennial project of "lasting significance," on condition the federal contribution was matched dollar for dollar by the provinces and municipalities involved. The commission also ran the Federal/Provincial Centennial Grants Program, which was allotted twenty million dollars "for the acquisition, construction or restoration of buildings or other capital works of historical or architectural merit." By 1967, over two thousand projects under these schemes had been completed. Another federal-provincial program led to the building of the provincial archives in Victoria and the Manitoba Cultural Centre in Winnipeg. Nor was the commission simply about bricks and mortar. A youth travel exchange program proved a success, as did the program to encourage and reward physical skill and agility in school children. Festival Canada, an entity run semi-independently of the commission, promoted cultural awareness through the funding of tours by national and international performing artists and the creation of new works.[2]

Perhaps the highest-profile features of the Centennial Commission's mandate were the fifteen-car Centennial Train and the Confederation Caravan; both had exhibitions outlining Canada's history, with the Caravan designed for communities not on the railway lines. In all, 2.5 million Canadians in 63 communities came out for the train, and 6.5 million in 655 communities visited the Caravan. "For thousands of school children, unable to travel to Montreal for Expo 67 or too young to take part in the youth exchange program, this would be their most lasting impression of Centennial year," noted Helen Davies in her book *The Politics of Participation: Learning from Canada's Centennial Year.* Only in Quebec did the Centennial Train fail to impress—in fact, it got a few eggs tossed at it by separatists. "With 60 percent of the tour finished, only 5.5 percent of Quebeckers had visited the exhibit, compared with 38 percent of the population that went to see the Caravan display," observed Davies. "The discrepancy between the figures supported the findings of a survey conducted earlier by the government illustrating graphically the level of discontent among a growing number of educated, urban residents who were not satisfied with Quebec's position in the Confederation."[3]

Many people celebrated the centennial through personal projects or challenges. Rowing, biking, knitting, swimming—you name it and somebody probably took it on. There were plenty of communal endeavours as well. Nanaimo, B.C., hosted its bathtub race. In Bowsman, Manitoba, they burned the town privies with great pomp and ceremony. Secretary of State Judy LaMarsh considered the small, bilingual St. Paul, Alberta, as "the greatest centennial town in Canada" for its many individual centennial projects, of which the largest, certainly the most novel, was the development of a landing strip for UFOs.[4]

Because her government portfolio carried responsibility for federal centennial initiatives—which is to say, for the Canadian Centennial Commission—Judy LaMarsh found herself front and centre at many ceremonial occasions, none more conspicuous than the July 1 celebrations on Parliament Hill in Ottawa. The giant birthday cake was her brainchild. Though the cake was made from plywood, she insisted it be covered in "gorgeous squishy real icing."[5] LaMarsh wanted the celebrations for Canada's centenary to be a great big birthday party with as many children in attendance as possible, and everyone knew kids loved "gorgeous squishy real icing." Naturally, the principal focus of interest at this birthday party would be the presence of HRH Queen Elizabeth II and her consort, Prince Philip, Duke of Edinburgh. The occasion marked the royal couple's first trip to Canada since the visits to Charlottetown and Quebec City three years earlier and, besides Ottawa, the royal itinerary included a visit to Expo 67 aboard the Royal Yacht *Britannia*. The queen had recently established another milestone of sorts, this one domestic rather than geopolitical: a meeting with her uncle, the duke of Windsor, and his wife, a family rift that had taken years to mend. The duke and duchess of Windsor, incognito, visited Expo later in July.[6]

Everywhere one looked, the balloons, gold centennial pins and Canadian flags spoke to the specialness of that day, and the weather cooperated. Some forty thousand people jammed Parliament Hill under a cloudless sky in eighty-degree heat. Toronto composer Bobby Gimby kicked off the festivities by leading an Ottawa children's choir down the red carpet to the stage; the children sang Gimby's "Ca-na-da," a ditty that became the centennial anthem. The queen used the same knife her father, King George VI, used when he cut his own birthday cake in Canada in 1939. Fortunately, she did not attempt to slice into plywood. A layer of real fruitcake had been added to the four-tier, seven-metre-high edifice. The slice prompted a robust chorus of "Happy Birthday" as, on cue, a thousand coloured balloons ascended upwards, drifting over, and in some instances getting entangled with, the facade of the East Block of the Parliament Buildings.

"No one who was in Ottawa over that Dominion day weekend can ever forget that period," Judy LaMarsh wrote in her memoir. "Nor will we ever forget the wonder of the crying and laughing and singing and dancing, as thousands of Canadians thronged the Hill, joining together in their suddenly free-welling love for their country."[7]

LESTER PEARSON WOULD LATER SPEAK about his foreboding when, after the heady success of the centennial celebrations on Capital Hill, he and his wife joined the queen and Prince Philip in a drive to Kingston and then an overnight voyage on the Royal Yacht *Britannia* to Montreal in the pouring rain. Seeing the Canadian Guard of Honour soaked to skin in their new green uniforms, the prime minister thought to himself, "This isn't going to be much of a success."[8] Another casualty of the rain was the giant birthday cake, left out overnight on Parliament Hill. The squishy icing had run, revealing large patches of plywood. "From a distance," observed one spectator, "the mixture of white and brown had the look of chocolate sauce spread over a vast sea of vanilla ice cream."[9]

The prime minister's apprehension, however, had less to do with weather than recent history. The previous royal visit in 1964 unravelled into a public relations nightmare. Quebec separatists made their presence known in the Quebec City leg of the tour and the local police overreacted in their handling of demonstrators in what became known as "*Le samedi de la matraque*" or "Truncheon Saturday." Now the queen was once more in Canada and once more in Quebec—though, significantly, she never actually set foot on Quebec soil, save for Île Notre Dame in the middle of the St. Lawrence, a feat of diplomatic fine-tuning that led opposition leader John Diefenbaker to mischievously suggest Her Majesty "was being sent to Coventry."[10] Expo officials agreed to close off a portion of the site during her visit, resulting in a tour that included the pavilions of Great Britain, the Western Provinces, Quebec, Ontario, the Atlantic Provinces and the Indians of Canada.

The royal couple seemed to enjoy themselves. Instead of spending the allotted twenty-five minutes at the British Pavilion, they spent forty, before heading on to the Western Provinces Pavilion. That pavilion featured a simulated trip down a mineshaft, from which the passenger emerged to face a farm exhibit that included a row of fabricated cows' heads on sticks behind a scrim. "Aren't they awfully cramped in there?" inquired Prince Philip as he surveyed the cows' heads. He was being facetious, of course, though the pavilion did receive a visit from the Quebec Humane Society, following up on several complaints that cows were somehow being quartered in a mineshaft.[11] Later on, during a walk through the Canadian Pavilion, the prince, with a tally-ho philistinism that came to seem reflexive, expressed doubts about what press releases described as the "music of the future," by composer Otto Joachim of the Montreal Symphony Orchestra. "How do you stand it all day?" he inquired of one of the pavilion hostesses, a fourth-year McGill student, as he winced at this bombardment of futuristic sound. "You get used to it," she replied. "Anyone who likes bagpipes probably likes this," suggested the duke of Edinburgh.[12]

In the course of the queen's visit to the Ontario Pavilion, Ontario premier John Robarts escorted her to a special, abbreviated, screening of the hit film *A Place to Stand*. "The queen told Robarts afterwards it felt so marvellous to sit down and see that marvellous film and be able to take her feet out of her shoes," says James Ramsay, the pavilion's director.[13]

The highpoint of her Expo visit occurred when the queen took a forty-five-minute minirail tour through the exhibition grounds.

Evidently, discussion about a possible minirail tour had taken place—"Only three other people knew of this arrangement," says Andrew Kniewasser, who was in on that discussion[14]—though the prime minister, in his memoir, makes the decision sound a bit more spontaneous. He had wanted to take her on a ride about the grounds on the minirail, but her security people had frowned at the idea. Nonetheless, just before that day's luncheon, he decided to ask her on the spur of the moment. The queen was delighted, though some of her entourage were not. Off they went—and the minirail ride was a huge success. Mother Nature offered her own benediction. The rains stopped, the sun came out.[15] Word got around and spectators waited for her as she passed by on the minirail. Kniewasser still can't believe how close at times the crowds were to her. Pierre Dupuy, among those in the queen's minirail entourage, recalled *"une masse de visiteurs criant, saluant, chantant. Sa Majesté ne cachait pas son émotion. Même mon coeur de vieux diplomate se sentait tout remué."*[16]

The day of the royal visit, the separatist group Rassemblement pour l'indépendance nationale (RIN) decided to commemorate the 130th anniversary of the Rebellion of 1837 with a wreath-laying ceremony at the base of the monument to the patriots of 1837 at the corner of de Lorimier Avenue and Notre Dame Street. When asked why the ceremony had been scheduled the day of the queen's visit to Expo, a RIN spokesman feigned innocence: "Oh, the queen is here, is she?" The timing, said the RIN official, was "pure coincidence."[17]

Painter Charles Pachter was one of those who managed a glimpse of Her Majesty and he specifically remembers her hat. It was "like a bathing cap," he says, "with flowers on it."[18] In his later, post-Expo life, Pachter incorporated Elizabeth II into his drawings and paintings. In fact, she became one of the signature icons—along with the noble moose—in a lot of his work. Pachter retained a fascination with, as well as an evident affection for, the queen, an affection not unmixed with a born parodist's amusement at the whole royal phenomenon.

The Expo tour ended with a state dinner aboard the Royal Yacht *Britannia*. Though he knew protocol decreed that one never spoke first to the queen, Robert Shaw, Expo's deputy commissioner general, apparently couldn't contain himself. "You were magnificent today, Your Majesty," declared an exuberant Shaw. "We were so pleased you could see Expo and be seen by the visitors." Her Majesty is said to have then expressed pleasure at the success of the tour and that, indeed, it was important in her role as queen to get out and be seen. "I know that carries some risks but that's part of my job."[19] The prime minister recalled that when the royal party reached the Beauharnois lock, about thirty-five miles from Montreal, a cheering crowd of seven thousand was on hand to welcome the queen as she said goodnight to her guests. The Pearsons and the Micheners, who were to spend the night aboard the Royal Yacht, could congratulate themselves on a successful and enjoyable day. A day that began on a note of trepidation about the rainy weather concluded on one of triumph. A good night's sleep was in order.[20]

IN HIS ACCOUNT OF CANADA'S centennial celebrations entitled *The Anniversary Compulsion*, Peter Aykroyd observes how the Centennial Commission people often cast a covetous eye in the direction of their counterparts at Expo 67. "They felt like poor cousins," writes Aykroyd, director of public relations for the Centennial Commission. "Expo was so big, so appealing, so clearly headed for success that it discouraged those who were plodding away on the less focused, something-for-everyone program of the Commission."[21]

In her memoir, Judy LaMarsh offers this explanation for why Expo emerged from the starting gate with a stronger profile than the Centennial Commission: "Expo 67, an independent Corporation which had been under the responsibility of three succeeding ministers ... had, by virtue of its formal participation with the Province of Quebec and the City of Montreal, by its disturbing acceleration of costs, and by its physical cohesiveness attracted far more of the attention of the Cabinet and the public." LaMarsh, a workhorse minister of a combative disposition, never did warm up to the Expo group or its "posturing" commissioner general, Pierre Dupuy. She was particularly irked that provision had not been made to accommodate as guests at the opening ceremonies of the exhibition those who had laboured long and hard at the Centennial Commission—this snub despite entreaties to the minister of trade and commerce from both herself and the prime minister.[22]

Judy LaMarsh's irritation with Expo must be understood, at least in part, through the prism of the problematic Centennial Commission she inherited as secretary of state. The roots of its administrative difficulties began with the sour relationship between her predecessor as secretary of state, Maurice Lamontagne, and its commissioner, John Fisher. "An untidy looking man, he is warm, friendly and outgoing," LaMarsh observed of John Fisher. "He suffers from a lifetime of over-patted ego and a fear of the future."[23] Fisher had been a Diefenbaker appointee. As executive director of the Canadian Tourist Association in Toronto, Fisher hosted a three-times-a-week CBC radio program called *John Fisher Reports*. An unabashed Canada booster, he called his radio scripts "pride builders." In turn, fans of his show called him "Mr. Canada," a title he took to heart. But a title he held dearer, perhaps, was "Senator"—the inducement Diefenbaker employed to get him to agree to head the Centennial Commission. Diefenbaker, though, could be indecisive and never did make good on that promise of a seat in the Senate before the April 1963 federal election when the Liberals defeated the Tories to form a Liberal minority government.

Fisher was never much of an administrator, his principal strength being, as Peter Aykroyd noted, "his enthusiasm about the romantic ideal of Canada and his lyricism in describing various colourful Canadians and some Canadian historical events."[24] He tended to micromanage and, as Aykroyd says, when Fisher was out of the office, a kind of calm prevailed.[25]

Peter Aykroyd and his family were at Expo that September for the conclusion of the commission's canoe pageant, a 103-day journey by 90 modern-day voyageurs who had covered more than 4,500 kilometres of the old fur trade routes by land and water, starting at Rocky Mountain House, Alberta, and finishing at the Expo marina; these voyageurs, ranging in age from seventeen to fifty-one years, came from all walks of life. The Aykroyds stayed in an apartment at Habitat; a decade or so later, Dan Aykroyd, one of Peter Aykroyd's two sons, would become known to millions on the U.S. television program *Saturday Night Live*. Judy LaMarsh was on hand as well to welcome the voyageurs as they entered the marina. Their canoes made two circuits of the basin near the Quebec and Ontario Pavilions before the Manitoba crew was declared the winner. The Alberta team presented LaMarsh with a deer-hide case containing beaver pelts and a buffalo cape. But what moved LaMarsh particularly was the young Cree from the Saskatchewan team who presented her with a broken paddle. The occasion marked his first real taste, as LaMarsh put it, "of the vastness of the country."[26] Each of the ten canoes bore the name of an early trader or explorer associated with its particular region. Fraser, Mackenzie, Radisson, La Vérendrye, Champlain, Cabot ... a list of names that can, with a little sympathetic imagination, suddenly resonate with a modern sensibility and become touching and inspirational. Centuries earlier, intrepid individuals, for their own reasons, left their homelands for the curious and unknown place we know today as Canada. They brought a spirit of adventure, gritty natures, and an endurance that enabled them to carve out for themselves the significant places in our history they did. We owe them. The canoe race ending in the Expo marina that day in September of 1967—not to say the grit of the modern-day voyageurs who participated—helped bring that message home.

Asked if all the centennial-year hoopla would have an impact beyond being "just a big birthday party," John Fisher pointed to all the concert halls, sports arenas, schools and other community improvements that came about as special projects of that year. But, added Fisher, "It's also a spiritual thing. It's taking stock. It's looking back to say 'thanks.' It is looking at today and saying kindly to each other 'let's build' and it's looking ahead. It's an emotional investment."[27]

FOURTEEN

Vive le Québec Libre!

Québec libre, oui, oui, oui!
Québec libre, De Gaulle l'a dit!

—ANON. C. 1967

The French naval cruiser *Colbert*, carrying French president Charles de Gaulle, reached Quebec shores on July 23, 1967, following the same river pathway as Jacques Cartier 432 years before when he arrived to claim the territory for France. The *Colbert* docked at Wolfe's Cove, so named for General James Wolfe who, in 1759, landed there and took the French force by surprise at the Battle of the Plains of Abraham. The British conquest became the centrepiece of New France mythology. For many Quebecers, the conquest also came to represent the moment the mother country abandoned them. The symbolic significance of the landing site was not lost on General de Gaulle, nor the fact that the warship on which he travelled bore the name of Louis XVI's minister in charge of reorganizing France's colonial regime and the promotion of immigration to New France.[1] Ottawa officialdom awaited his arrival nervously. They knew this was a chess game, played opposite a proven master of the sudden and capricious move. Their fears were realized soon enough. Observers, for instance, noted the *Colbert* did not fly the Canadian flag, a courtesy expected under ordinary circumstances, but then "ordinary circumstances" and "Charles de Gaulle" never quite belonged in the same sentence.

The de Gaulle itinerary was to start off with a tour of Quebec City and a visit to the Citadel, to be followed the next day by a motorcade from Quebec City to Montreal on a stretch of Highway 138 along the northern shore of the St. Lawrence known as the Chemin du Roy, the King's Highway. The general was to attend France's national day at Expo on July 25, then leave for Ottawa on the afternoon of July 26. In Ottawa, de Gaulle would meet with Prime Minister Pearson and attend a state luncheon on July 27. This, at any rate, was the plan. The Fates had a good chuckle.

Protocol indicated that de Gaulle's visit ought properly to start in Ottawa. But beginning with Jean Lesage's Liberal government and continuing with the Union Nationale government of Lesage's gregarious and enigmatic successor Daniel Johnson, Quebec had moved to initiate direct ties with France in the cultural and educational arenas. To such overtures, unfiltered as they were by the federal minions in Ottawa, de Gaulle proved warmly receptive. Though Ottawa officials grumbled and worried, Pearson, intent on mollifying Quebec aspirations where he could, essentially ceded the travel arrangements (with stipulations) to Daniel Johnson, who earlier issued his own invitation to de Gaulle, and it was this provincial, not federal, invitation that the general accepted.[2]

The French president made it clear to associates that he had come to Canada "to make waves." Certainly, he had no intention at all of congratulating Canada on its centennial, declaring, "We need not celebrate the creation of a state founded on our historic defeat, and on the assimilation of a part of the French people into a British struc-ture. Besides, this structure has become quite precarious."[3] De Gaulle

entertained a romantic notion of a *francophonie* united under his benefi-
cent influence, with Quebec one of those French-speaking territories his
vision embraced. In this way, he believed, Quebec could free itself of an
oppressive American hegemony. De Gaulle wasn't notably fussy when
it came to conflating English-speaking Canada with the United States,
nor, for that matter, conflating all of French Canada with the province
of Quebec. These were mere details, in no way diminishing the cosmic
synchronicity of his grand plans.

"De Gaulle made it clear that he was in Quebec to celebrate 'the
advent of a people,'" wrote historian Robert Bothwell. Which is to
say, he hoped the French of North America would soon "become their
own masters" and work out their independent destiny with the English
Canadians. "But there was no doubt that the General regarded Quebec's
past as well as its present as something to be overcome, and discarded,
in favour of a new identity and a new relationship with the rest of
Canada."[4]

Paintings by French masters lined the walls of de Gaulle's presidential suite aboard the *Colbert*—Matisse, Bonnard, Dufy. And, right
up there, between the Matisse and Bonnard, was the work of French-
Canadian abstractionist Jean-Paul Riopelle.[5] A nice touch. The ties that
bind! Here was the general's theme. He tried it out when the *Colbert*
anchored briefly at Saint-Pierre et Miquelon, and embraced it ever more
fervently upon reaching Quebec.

At the welcoming ceremony, Governor General Roland Michener
gamely attempted to assert a federal presence onto the proceedings, but
his welcoming remarks were mostly drowned out by the two Quebec
government press and information helicopters hovering overhead.
Fortuitously, the racket had subsided by the time Premier Johnson and
de Gaulle made their speeches.[6] Johnson had already told the governor
general that Michener would not be part of the motorcade taking
de Gaulle through Quebec City to a reception in the Legislative Council
Chamber. Clearly, this was to be a *Quebec* greeting.

The next day, de Gaulle and Johnson made the 270-kilometre journey along the King's Highway to Montreal. The Union Nationale government declared a public holiday and ensured crowds lined the route waving the flags of Quebec and France. A number of separatists lined the highway as well, cheering the general on, waving placards that read *"Vive la France,"* *"Vive de Gaulle"* and *"Vive le Québec libre."* At certain stops along the route, de Gaulle led his listeners in renditions of "La Marseillaise," the French national anthem. Proclaimed the general in Trois-Rivières: *"Nous sommes maintenant á l'époque ou le Québec, le Canada français, devient maître de lui-même."* His selective vision applied in a literal as well as figurative sense. At one point along the way, he raised his arm to salute spectators, not realizing those spectators were, in fact, telephone poles. Alerted beforehand to the general's prideful refusal to wear glasses, Premier Johnson diplomatically chose to salute the telephone poles himself.[7]

The arrival in Montreal was a triumph, with tens of thousands lining Sherbrooke and St. Denis Streets to greet the general. Later it became a point of contention as to whether or not the English-language press played down the numbers in reporting the event.[8] By the time de Gaulle reached City Hall to be greeted by Mayor Drapeau and the fifteen thousand people gathered outside, he was raring to go. A journalist offered him a microphone. Sensing trouble perhaps, Drapeau informed the general the mic did not work, something he knew for a fact since he, himself, had ordered the sound system disconnected.[9] But a nearby technician offered to remedy the situation and, before long, de Gaulle stepped out onto the City Hall balcony overlooking Place Jacques Cartier to address the crowd. He told his listeners the journey from Quebec City reminded him of the joyful atmosphere as he made his way into Paris at the time of the liberation of France. Coming to the conclusion of his remarks, he started offering verbal salutes. *"Vive Montréal!"* he declared. *"Vive le Québec!"* More emphatic this time: *"Vive le Québec libre!"* Two remaining salutes—*"Vive le Canada français!"* and *"Vive la France!"*—got lost, and stayed lost, amid the din greeting *"Vive le Québec libre!"* In repeating the slogan of Quebec separatism, de Gaulle, some felt, simply got carried away by the mood of the occasion. But this suggestion is to underestimate the calculation in the man.[10]

Reaction to his City Hall performance was electric. Jean Riley, granddaughter of the former Liberal prime minister Louis St. Laurent, watched the proceedings on television as she worked on a dress. "I got so angry," she says, "I sewed the back on the front."[11] Gail Corbett, recently graduated from the University of Toronto and employed at the Expo 67 newspaper archive, recalls that most of her colleagues were young Québécois. "My three young French-Canadian co-workers were so excited," she says. "*We* were furious. They were thrilled!"[12] "In those days we all thought this was great," says Louise Arbour. "Rock the boat! Way to go, Charlie!"[13] "The reaction was one of complete aston-ishment but also *l'exaltation*," says Monique Simard. "It's kind of 'Oh, *Vive le Québec libre!*— from *him!*' In a way, it's a lot the reaction of the *colonisé*: 'The Big Man says that!'"[14] "He was heady," says Marianne McKenna, among those in the throng outside City Hall. "There was great cheering—it was only when you got home and the implications were explained to you. But you could also tell he was doddery."[15]

René Lévesque happened to be on the large terrace behind City Hall while the general was proclaiming. When de Gaulle started to speak "confidentially" about a particular climate of liberation, Lévesque and a political colleague moved instinctively nearer the television set up to transmit the live broadcast. When they came, the words *"Vive le Québec ... libre!"* absolutely transfixed him for several seconds. "Then, hearing the deathly silence that reigned behind us," recalled Lévesque, "we turned to face the rest of the guests. In a state of shock, frozen in a fury that as yet was only emitting a few anticipatory rumblings, stood the Anglophone city."[16]

Expo's general manager, Andrew Kniewasser, was standing beside French foreign minister Maurice Couve de Murville at City Hall. After de Gaulle's speech, Kniewasser turned to the senior diplomat. "*Voilà, monsieur,*" he said. "*C'est dommage,*" Couve de Murville replied.[17]

In Ottawa, Lester Pearson seethed, especially offended by de Gaulle's linking of the procession into Montreal with the march into Paris during the liberation of 1944. Moreover, he reasoned he could not allow the remarks to go unanswered. The next day, Pearson offered his reply: that Canadians were a free people and did not need to be liberated and that Canada would remain united and rebuff any attempts to destroy that unity. The next move would be the general's.[18]

THE VISIT OF CHARLES DE GAULLE to Expo 67 on July 25 started with the customary ceremonies at Place des Nations. The day was hot and humid, the skies sunny. The general arrived in a limousine accompanied by Lionel Chevrier, commissioner general for state visits to Expo 67. According to Lionel's son Bernard, de Gaulle did not ask his father questions about the passing scene. Instead he wanted to know Chevrier's thoughts about his City Hall peroration the day before. Lionel Chevrier is said to have replied something along the lines of, "If you think Quebec can be free within Confederation, it's fine; but if it's outside Confederation, we can't accept that." To which de Gaulle reportedly replied in lively, if ambiguous, fashion, "But sir, there cannot be a question about it."[19] Besides de Gaulle and Chevrier, the honour party on the dais at Place des Nations included Premier Johnson, Mayor Drapeau and Commissioner General Dupuy. The crowd of more than seven thousand erupted in cheers when the Royal Canadian Corps of Signals military band played "Vive la Canadienne," the march of the Royal 22nd Regiment. The general himself received a thunderous ovation. Shouts of "*Vive de Gaulle!*" echoed from all corners of the stadium. Dupuy spoke in glowing terms about France's prestige in the world and about his affection for the seventy-six-year-old French president, reiterating the theme of Expo—that "what unites peoples is more important than what divides them." In turn, de Gaulle complimented Expo and Montreal and expressed his satisfaction that the exhibition was being held on "the soil of Quebec—of French Canada." He closed his remarks with *"Vive le Canada!"* and *"Vive le Québec!"*[20]

As far as Pierre Dupuy was concerned, the general's visit was a great success. He would not involve himself in matters beyond his own, Expo-centric, purview. Dupuy later recorded that, from his point of view as commissioner general, the day with the general had gone beautifully—*"parfait en tous points."* True, the day's visit went off well enough, if not quite *"parfait en tous points."*[21]

Stops on de Gaulle's itinerary included the French, Quebec and Canada Pavilions, followed by luncheon at the Pavillon d'Honneur. Then it was on to the U.S. and U.S.S.R Pavilions, as well as those of West Germany, Italy and the African nations. A reception and dinner at the French Pavilion would cap the day. Lionel Chevrier kept Ottawa closely informed of the general's every move. Fifteen minutes at the French Pavilion. Two minutes at the Canadian Pavilion! (One at least imagines Chevrier implicitly, if not explicitly, noting this fact with an exclamation point.) *Forty-five minutes* at the Quebec Pavilion!!![22] Outside the French Pavilion, police arrested an Algerian who ran alongside the de Gaulle limousine shouting *"assassin."* Quebec nationalists clashed briefly with police from various constabularies at the bridge leading from the French and Quebec Pavilions to the Canadian Pavilion. Outside the Canadian Pavilion, the RCMP arrested a man speaking in what was described as "heavily continental English" after three times shouting *"assassin"* at de Gaulle and hurling a paper bag that landed within several feet of the French president. The bag contained garbage.[23]

Less threatening—though for a few seconds no doubt unnerving for the security force—was a publicity stunt orchestrated to coincide with the moment de Gaulle crossed Cosmos Walk, the bridge linking the U.S. Pavilion on Île Ste. Hélène to the U.S.S.R Pavilion on Île Notre Dame. To publicize the Maurice Chevalier–headlined revue *Flying Colours*, then playing at the Autostade, an enterprising PR man arranged matters so that one of the acts, a woman whose specialty included hanging by her teeth from a helicopter rope, performed this specialty as the general made his way across the bridge. The stunt paid off, attendance at the Autostade that night increasing by ten thousand.[24]

The luncheon for de Gaulle at the Pavillon d'Honneur turned into what was described as a "tense" and "subdued" affair.[25] Trepidation reigned before the event even began. The general's remarks of the day before raised such a hue and cry that the federal government leaned on Expo not to receive him. Both Dupuy and Shaw resisted the pressure on the premise that Expo was above such political considerations.[26] A number of the invited luncheon guests—including Dr. Wilder Penfield, one of the original Montebello planning group—cancelled in protest.[27] Krystyne Romer had counted on ninety people, what would have been the Pavillon's largest luncheon by far, with imperial caviar shipped in from Iran, swans carved out of meringues—the works. But the cancellations flooded in and her list shrank from ninety to fifty-five.[28]

Dupuy then threw Romer a curve when he informed her that de Gaulle's schedule had gone out of whack and she must entertain him and Mme de Gaulle for an hour before the start of the luncheon. "Don't worry," Dupuy told her, "he talks for three." Mme de Gaulle uttered not a word during that hour's entr'acte, but the general, as Dupuy promised, more than compensated. And while the young *maîtresse* babysat the de Gaulles in Montreal, in Ottawa, Lester Pearson stood poised to admonish the general for his interfering ways. Though he never explicitly uninvited de Gaulle to the capital, Pearson probably entertained few illusions about what de Gaulle's reaction might be to this stern rebuke.

"He was a very cultivated man," says Krystyne Griffin of de Gaulle. "He spoke like a literary person, he did not speak like an army person. He manipulated the language, you know?" The general craved gossip, and their conversation touched on a person of mutual acquaintance, the wife of a minor royal whose louche behaviour attracted the general's mischievous interest. He knew of Romer's diplomatic family and her

Polish heritage, and so they spoke about the history of Poland and the cultural links between Poland and France through literature and music. Griffin recalls that she was completely eye-to-eye with him. "He's got this enormous nose which he carries parallel to his shoulder, so it makes him seem taller," she says. They had tried to ensure they had a bed large enough for him. They expected someone around six feet, seven inches, whereas he seemed, in person, a bit shorter. (De Gaulle stood six feet, five inches.) "In a sofa, he's a big, bulky man—a bear of a man. His eyes are close together, like an elephant. He could look at you with his eyes and go right through you. He liked being with women. He felt good. He flattered you." When the time came to end the conversation and join the luncheon, the general whispered to Romer, *"Entre nous, mademoiselle, 'Vive la Pologne libre.'"*

When word filtered back about Pearson's rebuke, de Gaulle cancelled the Ottawa leg of his trip and decided to fly back to France the following evening. His decision left Governor General Michener and his wife with a lot of extra food on their hands. The one-hundred-person menu would be, according to a Government House spokesman, "sort of like the Thanksgiving turkey," to be used for leftover snacks.[29] One account had the chef who created the special *soufflés glaces* take a knife to some of his artful creations when news arrived of the guest of honour's no-show.[30] Pique was definitely on the menu that day.

By default, then, the centrepiece of the general's final day in Canada became the luncheon at City Hall given him by Mayor Drapeau, and many felt the luncheon a Drapeau triumph. Indeed, Jean Drapeau had laboured intensively over the speech he gave that afternoon. Without offering insult, he intended to reframe for de Gaulle the aspirations of French Canada within the context of the tumultuous welcome accorded the French president. Jean Drapeau intended to put things right. "The speech was vintage [Lionel] Groulx," wrote Brian McKenna and Susan Purcell, Drapeau's biographers, in reference to the mayor's philosophical mentor. In his speech, Drapeau harked back to the story of how sixty thousand Quebecers had been abandoned by France, yet had survived and flourished. Drapeau, acknowledging the warm reception offered de Gaulle by the citizens of Montreal, said that response should be interpreted as a tribute to the general's greatness but not as any nostalgia for France: "The existence of French-Canada ... has never been an issue of any interest to France until you appeared, Mr. President." Quebec quite naturally felt a large debt of gratitude for the mother country's heritage of language, culture and civilization, he noted, but Quebec had managed thus far nicely on its own and required no other help from France than its always welcome moral support. What Quebecers wanted, said Drapeau, was "an enlargement of our mastery of our own destiny to better serve the land of our ancestors."[31] The speech was televised with simultaneous translation across Canada, and people everywhere watched with rapt attention. A group of Expo public relations people became so engrossed, they failed to notice the eminently noticeable Liberace as he walked about the Expo site.[32]

To Jean-Louis Roux, de Gaulle resembled at one point a little boy just reprimanded by his master.[33] The speech thrilled Jean Riley, who, two days earlier, had mangled the dress she was making, so incensed had she become at de Gaulle's comments. "You felt so proud," she says. "We were not answering insult with insult but we were putting him back in his place. In fact, I hadn't really liked Jean Drapeau until then. Until then I had always assumed Jean Drapeau was a small 'p' politician. His speech showed considerable intellect and culture."[34] Pearson got in touch to express his appreciation and admiration for the speech: "You gave us yesterday a lesson in grace, wisdom and patriotism that will do much to heal the wounds inflicted on our country these last few days."[35]

Drapeau's speech won him widespread praise. He naturally received some boos from separatists—though at a Boston Pops concert at Place des Nations, while the audience offered Premier Johnson only polite applause, it gave the mayor a standing ovation.[36] Once more, a discrepancy existed between reactions in the French- and English-language press. Where the English press interpreted Drapeau's speech as a verbal birching, French-language commentators found the mayor not all that reproving and, indeed, the general himself, in a response praising Montreal and Expo 67, thanked Drapeau for his "truly moving and profound speech."[37]

Reactions varied on the prime minister's rebuke of de Gaulle. Some— John Diefenbaker for one[38]—felt Pearson had not been tough enough. Others believed Pearson had overreacted. "My impression was that the government's reaction had just gone too far," says Bernard Chevrier. "I was surprised for a diplomat like Pearson to have gone that far. He could have said we don't support what he said but we look forward to discussing it with him."[39] In fact, subsequent polls found that a majority of Quebecers said they did *not* interpret de Gaulle's outburst as a call for independence.[40] But then again, with Quebec, Pearson always seemed between a rock and a hard place. Regardless of how one interpreted his remarks, de Gaulle succeeded in what he set out to do—shake things up mightily.

Francois Aquin, a Quebec Liberal MNA, inspired by the comments of de Gaulle, bolted from his seat to sit in the assembly as an independent, his first words upon taking his seat in that new role: "*Vive le Québec libre.*" For René Lévesque, biding his time before he, too, left the provincial Liberals to sit as an independent and herald the creation of the separatist Parti Québécois, the general's comments proved more an annoying distraction than anything else. "*Québec libre,* by all means, but who wanted the liberty to seem an imported product?" observed Lévesque.[41]

Robert Bothwell noted that Canada survived the de Gaulle visit, though not without damage. "He may have accelerated the separatist timetable in Quebec, and he obviously contributed to ill feeling between French and English Canadians. The centennial was more of a mixed memory than it should have been, and the image of Montreal and Expo was slightly tarnished. As time passed, de Gaulle was remembered in

English-Canada more for his exploits as leader of Free France than as the architect of Quebec separation; in that role he was more sorcerer's apprentice than sorcerer."[42]

Canada's undersecretary of state for external affairs, Marcel Cadieux, deputed Lionel Chevrier to see the general off at the airport. Canada's ambassador to France, Jules Léger, also attended that farewell, as did Premier Johnson and Mayor Drapeau. Chevrier, according to his son, remembered Couve de Murville thanking him for coming and remembered the general as cordial but distant. Says Bernard Chevrier, recalling his father's memories of that evening, "That goodbye was very cold. Very, very cold."[43]

FIFTEEN

Winding Down

These were glory days to be sure, but Expo was not without its political hiccoughs and occasional misadventures. The furor over the de Gaulle visit rippled through the dog days of summer. "The odour from the abattoir greeting visitors on the Bonaventure Autoroute and Place d'Accueil these warm days is frightful," bemoaned a newspaper columnist in late July.[1] Early in August, an Expo hovercraft collided with a bridge pillar, slightly injuring four passengers.[2] Later that month, thousands of visitors found themselves stranded mid-river on a Saturday evening when the No. 4 Métro line to Île Ste. Hélène broke down. The trains ceased operation beneath the river at 10:05 p.m. and were out of commission for nearly an hour. Thousands of visitors at either end of the Expo site, at La Ronde or Place d'Accueil, then had to try and find alternative forms of transportation to get them back to Montreal. On Labour Day, Commissioner General Pierre Dupuy and several union leaders laid wreaths at a plaque in Place des Nations to commemorate the ten construction workers who died during the building of the Expo site:[3] dreams exact their toll. On the whole, though, administrators considered themselves lucky. Most accidents that occurred were not too serious; only one was considered major.[4] Yes, there were the threats and near misses, such as the firebomb that exploded at the U.S.S.R. Pavilion; the detonators were thought to be flashbulbs, the same modus operandi as those that had detonated a firebomb weeks earlier at the Man the Producer Pavilion, which, probably not coincidentally, happened to be next door to the Cuba Pavilion. Neither situation, though, reported extensive damage.[5]

By the conclusion of Expo 67, security personnel reported over 8,300 infractions, including:[6]

68 vehicle thefts
551 thefts of over $50
706 thefts of under $50
609 thefts by pickpocket
11 reported cases of gambling (in La Ronde)
13 cases of possession of offensive weapons
121 cases of disturbing the peace (mainly drunkenness)
474 counterfeit money
51 damage to property
1 death by accidental cause
20 deaths by heart attack
487 vehicle accidents
30 bomb threats
5 demonstrations
154 assistance in locating a lost person
23 illegal vending
175 illegal possession of a pass
426 fraudulent entry
2357 assistance to sick or injured persons
46 vandalism
2 attempted suicides

Then there were the snafus and glitches. Expo, like any operation of its magnitude, had its share. People complained about the hours spent standing in line, the food costs at certain restaurants and the relative absence of shelters during rainstorms. Besides picking pockets, thieves made off with valuable items from some of the pavilions, including a scarlet dress worn by actress Marilyn Monroe in one of her movies, an item stolen not once but twice from the U.S. Pavilion.[7] A good deal of the criticism, however, centred around a computer-run lodging service called Logexpo that the Expo corporation operated in tandem with the provincially run Quebec Lodging Service. Anecdotal evidence of that provincial service's inefficiency (and worse) became legion, and Expo itself was faulted for complacency. "Logexpo wasn't a failure," noted Robert Fulford; "it was a disaster."[8]

Newspaper columnist Charles Lazarus reported phoning Logexpo to ask whether the service could find him a room for two. Informed the request required a couple of hours to confirm, Lazarus next phoned the Queen Elizabeth and Windsor Hotels and received immediate confirmations, a circumstance he duly relayed to his readership.[9] An example of what could, and sometimes did, go wrong was provided by the Motel Poulin in the Montreal suburb of Brossard. A special commissioner appointed by the provincial government closed it down after it was discovered the "motel" was actually nothing more than a small trailer park. The proprietor, approved by Logexpo and permitted to charge twenty-two dollars a night, initially promised a two-hundred-unit establishment but instead ended up offering two units and fifteen trailers. The trailers had washbasins but no shower or bath facilities—though an employee later told a reporter that management *did* plan to install a shower in the wooden shack where they stored the sheets and towels.[10]

Philippe de Gaspé Beaubien maintains Logexpo was just a coordinating agency set up to pair those seeking accommodation with the lodgings approved by the provincial housing service and should not have been held accountable when things went awry. "I had seen the problems they had in Belgium [at the 1958 Brussels World's Fair] and we would devise a system that would eliminate those problems," he says. "But it was in the hands of the provincial government ... I said, this [arrangement] is a mistake. But the [Expo] board did not have authority over that, over the prices of accommodation and where people could go."[11] Logexpo gave the Expo people a public relations black eye, its lodging problems reaching the floor of the U.S. Senate, where one senator denounced the "shoddy housing accommodation for visitors to Expo 67."[12] It was "one of Philippe's nightmares," says Andrew Kniewasser of Beaubien. "Poor guy, got grey hairs I'm sure. Some of the people were very poorly accommodated. When you are running a thing as big as that thing, there's constant surveillance. 'Poor family from New York, no bathroom ...' Makes the front page."[13]

Another great idea that turned out not to be a great idea was Reservexpo. Intended as a method of allowing visitors to book tickets for events and thus avoid lineups, Reservexpo often frustrated as much as it facilitated. "It worked—but not half as well as it could because I didn't have the budget where people could go to separate booths and avoid those bottleneck events," says Beaubien. "So I had to do it at the *information* booths and when you went there that could take quite a bit of time."[14] One lineup replaced another. The booths were unpopular both with visitors and the booth hostesses left to deal with visitor hostility.

There was no letting down for Beaubien; he was always on the go. The "mayor of Expo" earned his grey hairs. Often, he could be seen manoeuvring his Cushman cart about the Expo site, armed with Bellboy beeper and portable dictaphone, checking things out. The *Montreal Star*'s Charles Lazarus accompanied him on one such tour and watched as, on that occasion, he stationed himself outside a women's washroom and inquired of the women, as they emerged, if everything was in order. "*Oui, c'est propre,*" one woman replied; "*pas comme chez moi, mais c'est propre.*" "*Merci, madame,*" responded Beaubien. One thing that gave Beaubien a considerable degree of satisfaction was that, with time, the Expo team had "learned to play with the site" and there was both surprise and pleasure in the way the visitors to Expo had respected the grounds. He was noting this point to Lazarus just as he spied a youth tossing a paper cup away. Beaubien at once admonished the youth to pick it up. "Pick it up, will you," he said, "please pick it up." And the youth did.[15]

Lazarus professed to sense a new cost-consciousness in the Expo administration: "One was made to feel guilty of extreme gaucherie with questions about the Habitat tab jumping from $14,000,000 to $23,000,000, when the prime concern should be with the product, rather than costs. Fair enough, I thought ... Now, it turns out, I really didn't understand what was happening, since panic buttons are being pressed all over the Expo site to cut costs, cut costs, cut costs, at no matter what cost."[16]

Certainly, the political masters in Ottawa were applying heat. In one instance, Minister of Trade and Commerce Robert Winters wrote to Expo deputy commissioner general Robert Shaw in July, pressuring him to watch out for increases in the cost of maintaining the site and additional staff requirements; of particular alarm to Winters were items in the area of administration and ticketing.[17] Asked many years later whether he noticed any new cost-consciousness in this latter half of Expo's run, Beaubien plays down the matter. Cost-consciousness, he says, had always been built into the operation. "I couldn't claim for a cab ride," he says, "if I didn't have a receipt."[18]

Bottom-line worries of a troubling nature, though, started to cloud Beaubien's horizon early in September. One heard rumblings about a strike by members of the Montreal Transportation Employees Union— rumblings that became reality at 12:01 a.m. on September 21, 1967, when six thousand bus and subway drivers walked off the job. Expo Express was not expected to be affected since its terms had been negotiated separately between the union and the Montreal Transit Commission and fell under a no-strike clause Expo demanded of its workers. Beaubien and the Expo people had had a couple of hours to warn visitors about the strike, though more than eighteen thousand of them decided to take their chances and remain on the site past the midnight deadline. Said one customer to a waitress at The Bulldog, a British pub at La Ronde, the Expo site that always closed last, "I'll have another pint, dear—and the bus drivers can strike forever."[19]

By the 2:30 closing time at La Ronde, necessity being the mother of invention, Beaubien and his colleagues mobilized various alternative modes of transport to get people off the site. The trackless trailer train La Balade provided one means, carrying passengers from the main gate at Place d'Accueil to the Victoria parking lot. Boats from the marina ferried those whose cars were at the Longueuil parking lot across the river. Expo's invaluable labour troubleshooter Jean Cournoyer said he saw Beaubien doing just about everything—organizing groups, securing boats to transport visitors from La Ronde to Longueuil, finding cars that could take them someplace else.[20] Beaubien later called the transit strike the low point of his Expo mayoralty. Yet he marvelled at the way the stranded visitors on that first night took the situation—literally—in stride. "People *walked* home," he says of the long procession emanating from La Ronde. "I thought Jacques Cartier Bridge would fall."[21]

As of September 12, Expo had total revenues of $106,592,955, coming close to the projected $111,781,297, with admission charges providing the lion's share of that sum. On the other hand, revenues from the performing arts programs and the games and rides at La Ronde fell below expectations. The attendance numbers were good; people simply didn't spend enough. With the transit strike, Beaubien predicted Expo could lose as much as two million dollars a week.[22] On September 22, 1967, Expo officially surpassed 42,073,561 visits, the previous record held by the 1958 Brussels World's Fair. (While the 1900 Paris exposition attracted fifty-one million visitors, its run lasted seven months and not the six of Brussels and Montreal, and the accuracy of its accounting methods left room for doubt. Both the 1939 and 1964–65 New York fairs drew bigger numbers—forty-five million and fifty million respectively—but they both ran for two six-month periods each.) Plans initially called for a ceremony to celebrate this milestone. Then came a change of heart. They did not wish to appear ungracious toward Brussels' achievement. Accordingly, Expo exceeded the Brussels number without fanfare. But by then, with the transit strike in full swing, they felt in no mood to gloat.

When attendance continued to rise throughout the summer, the Expo managers began confidently to predict as many as fifty million visits by the closing day of October 29. But by the end of September, such confidence had evaporated. They might, or they might not, reach that magic fifty million number. But now, thanks to the transit strike, all bets were off.

A STRIKE by transit workers. A French president with an agenda. Wars in Vietnam and the Middle East. The outside world insinuated itself into the bubble that was Expo in any number of ways, like the bizarre case of the project engineer at the West German Pavilion, found to be a Missouri prison escapee on the FBI's "10 Most Wanted" list and deported back to the United States. (It was noted, not without admiration, that this individual, travelling under the alias "Alex Bormann," performed his engineering duties without benefit of any university degree.)[23] In the final weeks of the exhibition, several celebrated foreign visitors, trailing with them their own particular geopolitical and historical associations, arrived in Montreal to catch the fair of fairs before it closed.

One of these was the twenty-seven-year-old King Constantine of Greece, who came with the Danish-born, twenty-one-year-old Queen Anne-Marie. Constantine's appearance for the Greek national day on September 6 had not, at first, been a certainty. There was that business before Expo opened in late April about the offending photograph in the *Camera as Witness* exhibition that showed a weeping Turkish Cypriot woman whose husband was killed in a Greek raid on her village. The affronted Greek delegation demanded the photograph's removal and there were mutterings that Constantine's attendance might depend on Expo officialdom's response. A practised hand at smoothing ruffled feathers, Commissioner General Pierre Dupuy swung into action and, *voilà, voilà*, the picture disappeared. Now, with Constantine's arrival, came the payoff for such toadying.

Since April of that year, however, the king had other matters to preoccupy him. A military junta had taken control of the Greek government and some felt Constantine was sympathetic to the colonels, as witness a small swastika someone pencilled onto the exterior of the Greek Pavilion.[24] A celebration by the Greek-Canadian Committee for Freedom and Democracy became an occasion to protest the dictatorship that had suspended that country's constitution. The event program included recorded messages from Greek actress Melina Mercouri, who won an Academy Award for playing an Athens prostitute in the 1960 film *Never on Sunday*, and composer Mikis Theodorakis (*Zorba the Greek*), both of whose work was on the banned list in their native country. A number of the protestors subsequently turned their attentions to Constantine, booing him outside the Chateau Champlain Hotel, and carrying signs that read "The king must go" and "Constantine Assassin."[25] When the Greek National Theatre came to Expo as part of its World Festival, the company's star, Oscar-winning Katina Paxinou (the fiery Pilar in Hollywood's adaptation of Ernest Hemingway's *For Whom the Bell Tolls*), was questioned about Mercouri's criticism of her for remaining in Greece after the coup. "Who is Melina Mercouri anyway?" hissed Paxinou. "She's no actress. She doesn't play in our company."[26]

During a luncheon at the Pavillon d'Honneur, Constantine asked Krystyne Romer to help him locate an old girlfriend who lived in Montreal. Indeed, Romer knew the former girlfriend well. But perhaps not wishing to cross a delicate line here—he had, after all, arrived with his wife, who had given birth to their second child a few months earlier—Romer played dumb and pretended not to know how to contact her. "Of course, I have to accept that," replied the king, "though I don't have to believe it."[27] Late in 1967, Constantine attempted to launch a counter-coup against the junta, but the effort ended in failure and he, with his family and prime minister, fled Greece never to return again as monarch; later, following the overthrow of the colonels, a referendum vote in 1974 formally abolished the monarchy.

Back at Expo, Yugoslav premier Mika Špiljak could, once in a while, be glimpsed behind a massive cordon of RCMP and plainclothes officers.[28] United Nations Secretary General U Thant, who called Expo the "most successful exhibition in human history," was a more visible presence, but security issues marked his visit as well. A bazooka shell attached to a clock and battery was discovered near the Africa Place complex and defused shortly before he was to visit there. Later, Thant had to evacuate the Habitat apartment where he was staying because of another bomb scare.[29] Moshe Safdie recalls leading a group of RCMP and Navy bomb experts to several critical points in Habitat's structure where a bomb might be strategically placed, but they found nothing. The note had said the bomb would go off at nine. It did not. U Thant checked out the next morning for New York. And meanwhile, for the Safdie children, horrified they had had to leave the goldfish behind in the race to evacuate the building, life could return to normal.[30]

That October brought Jacqueline Kennedy, widow of the slain U.S. President John F. Kennedy, as well as Rose Kennedy, the late president's mother. Lynda Bird Johnson, elder daughter of Lyndon and Lady Bird Johnson, also arrived; she had recently become engaged to Vietnam-bound Marine captain Charles Robb (her dates with bon vivant actor George Hamilton now a distant memory). Then came royalty: Princess Margaret, sister of Queen Elizabeth II, and her commoner husband Lord Snowdon, the erstwhile Antony Armstrong-Jones, an accomplished photographer, whose work was featured in Expo's *Camera as Witness* exhibition.

The royals "didn't have the star power you would expect," says Deirdre McIlwraith, Krystyne Romer's assistant at the Pavillon d'Honneur, where a small luncheon was arranged for Princess Margaret and her consort. Besides their tour of Expo, the couple attended several private dinners and cocktail parties. One party featured seventy-five guests in their thirties and forties, because, it was said, the princess and her husband had expressed an interest in meeting people their own age. Not a few of the thirty- and forty-somethings on the guest list—who included Paul Desmarais and Charles Bronfman—would still be social forces more than forty years on. "Most women will be fascinated to learn the princess wears seamed stockings," noted the *Montreal Star*'s society reporter. At one of the dinners, the princess re-met John Turner,[31] Liberal MP for the Montreal riding of St. Lawrence-St. George from 1962 to 1968, who had once, famously, been the princess's dancing partner. That was in 1959 and a photograph of the handsome couple on the dance floor prompted a momentary flutter of romantic speculation in the press.

"They were not happy," says Deirdre McIlwraith of Princess Margaret and her husband. "I don't know whether they were having a fight. *He* had shocking red hair."[32] Philippe de Gaspé Beaubien and his wife, Nan-b, dined with them one evening and grew distressed at the marital sniping. "It was an unpleasant experience," says Beaubien of that dinner.[33]

Jacqueline Kennedy and Indian prime minister Indira Gandhi topped that year's United Press International editors' poll of most influential women. (Others on the list included Lady Bird Johnson, Queen Elizabeth II, actress Elizabeth Taylor, and Jiang Qing, wife of Mao Zedong.) Jackie Kennedy was a magnet for the curious wherever she went, and crowd control at Expo at times bordered on chaos.[34] Spectators offered her warm greetings, though when she arrived late at the Czech Pavilion, which had been closed in anticipation of her visit, she drew scattered boos from the regular folk lined up waiting to get in.[35] Actually, the booing of VIPs at the Czech Pavilion, because of the delays they caused the average fair-goer, became a commonplace. Similar reactions awaited Princess Margaret and Lord Snowdon, the shah of Iran, and Lynda Bird Johnson.

Jackie Kennedy won over most of the Expo people, but not all. At Expo, officials were bemused when she called a press conference to announce her arrival after earlier informing them she planned to travel incognito. At the behest of the U.S.A. Pavilion's commissioner general, Robert Shaw, though very busy, made a point of going over to pay her his respects. He found the celebrated visitor engrossed in a book of press clippings. She rose, held his hand in hers, offered him a smile later described as "plastic," and then sat down again without uttering a word.[36] But Kennedy did charm Krystyne Romer. "She was sweet, with that little nasal voice, impeccable, very polite," she says. "So *sweet* compared to Mrs. Johnson, who I think was rude."[37]

As Expo approached its close, another world figure arrived to demand acknowledgment, this time in spectral form—an icon of martyrdom who became immediately the catalyst for a cottage industry in T-shirts and posters for the emerging counterculture. Cuban prime minister Fidel Castro's revolutionary colleague, Ernesto "Che" Guevara, had been slain in a guerrilla campaign in Bolivia in October 1967. In death, Che arguably acquired much greater value than in life, and Castro well understood the dead revolutionary's propaganda value to the cause. At the Cuba Pavilion at Expo 67, they quickly mounted a memorial.

EXPO, DECLARED PIERRE BOURGAULT, promoted the illusion that Quebec was better off than it really was and, in doing so, damaged the cause of Quebec independence. As founder of the Rassemblement pour l'indépendance nationale (RIN), that cause was dear to the former journalist's heart. Yet, as he told his listeners at the Youth Pavilion at Expo, "there is a lesson at Expo that Quebecers may be missing. Here we can see the pavilions of many peoples, who, although they are less numerous and less wealthy than Quebecers, have made themselves into sovereign nations." Quebec, he believed, could achieve nationhood through democratic means rather than violence: "But if in the last resort we find violence is the only answer, I will adopt it at once."[38] Bourgault had earlier been in the news for leading a separatist demonstration against the Confederation Train at Jean-Talon CPR station. Demonstrators chanted slogans like *"Maudit Canada"* and *"Le Train de la Confédération, Non. Quebec, Oui,"* and a few hurled yellow and black paint bombs at the train.[39] The following year, Bourgault would be all over the news, when he was arrested for his role in a Saint-Jean-Baptiste Day celebration that turned violent. The same year, he folded the RIN into René Lévesque's newly minted Parti Québécois.

One place where Expo now appears to have been ahead of the curve was in the Indians of Canada Pavilion. That pavilion amounted to a kind of breakthrough. Situated in a forest setting near a lake on Île Notre Dame, this pavilion was a stylized thirty-metre teepee funded by the Department of Indian Affairs and Northern Development. The First Nations peoples chose the exhibits themselves, and one of the significant aspects of the pavilion was that it brought together the various First Nations to work together from a common point of view—a point of view that often registered a strong sense of grievance. The exhibits included testimonials from street interviews taken in nine provinces and two northern territories, testimonials full of recrimination and tales of betrayal and abuse by white society: "The welfare of the Indian was regarded as proper work for retired soldiers, many of whom were kindly and well-intentioned, but treated their charges like amiable backward children"; "An Indian child begins school by learning a foreign tongue ..."; "Give us the right to manage our own affairs ..."

Arthur Laing, minister of Indian affairs, had urged the Native leaders to favour an upbeat narrative line. When he previewed the Native pavilion storyline that took white churches to task for attempting to wipe out Native culture, Laing had misgivings. But, as historian Bryan D. Palmer noted, it was the reference to his own department as "historically treating 'the welfare of the Indian … as proper work for retired soldiers' who regarded indigenous peoples as 'amiable backward children' that, in the words of one DIA official, caused Laing to 'just about shit.'" Laing threatened to close down the pavilion but backed off when cooler heads persuaded him the resulting political scandal would be much worse than some critical signage.[40]

In 1960, it was estimated that the average Native person lived only to thirty-four years of age; Native infant mortality and suicide rates far exceeded the national average. When former prime minister John Diefenbaker visited the pavilion, he signed its guest book with his several Indian names—Chief Walking Buffalo, Chief Many Spotted Horse, Chief Great Eagle—and reminded his listeners it was he who first gave Indians the right to vote federally, and that was only as recently as 1960.[41] The folksinger Buffy Sainte-Marie, a Cree Indian, applauded the pavilion. "It's more serious than most pavilions; it's like a classroom, but that's what's needed."[42] For many who visited, the Indians of Canada Pavilion proved an eye-opener.

In his speech at the Indians of Canada Day at Place des Nations, Governor General Michener reminded listeners, "None of us should ever forget that Canada cannot expect to achieve true greatness while any of its earliest people still live in the shadows."[43] Ceremonial Native headdresses were presented to Expo officials, among them Pierre Dupuy, who graced the pages of the next day's newspapers wearing his. The governor general is said to have donned his headdress and joked with visiting chiefs from across Canada at that evening's dinner at the Hélène de Champlain restaurant; the planned buffalo roast for six hundred on Île Notre Dame had to be cancelled because of the rain.[44] In his Expo memoir, Dupuy's own summation of the First Nations and their impact seems weirdly maladroit: The *"Peau-Rouge"* today was simply another Canadian, *"qui semble hâlé par le soleil des vacances,"* which was to say, he was like anyone else but with a better tan. He dresses like you and me, wrote Dupuy, and now works in the city. No doubt well intentioned, the brief summary comes across as odd, to say the least.[45] Obviously, the question of First Nations identity was a more problematic and complex subject than these curious brotherhood-of-man sentiments might suggest, and the First Nations' relationship to Canada, and Canada's to them, are being re-examined and reworked to this day. Translating the concept of "separate and equal" into practicable and equitable terms continues to be a work in progress.

FOR ALL THE EMPHASIS it laid upon a vision of the future, Expo, like world's fairs before it, reflected present-day attitudes and realities. Historian Eva-Marie Kröller complained, "While Calder's Man and Saint-Exupéry's Terre des hommes nominally included both men and women, the emphasis was clearly on the male portion of humanity, and Saint-Exupéry's vision of a legendary race of supermen contained a strong tinge of misogyny." She specifically deplored what she saw as the "stylization" of Expo hostesses into miniskirted versions of the traditional teacher-and-nurse stereotype.[46] Actually, the stereotype often seemed closer to flight attendant—or stewardesses, as they then were known—than teacher or nurse.

When Expo celebrated International Women's Day at Place des Nations in early June, the centrepiece of these celebrations was a variety show entitled *It's a Woman's World*, which included a pageant called *Women through the Centuries*, where, according to a dutifully breathless reporter, "bare-footed young ladies, glamorously costumed to represent an assortment of women who made their mark on history, cavorted about behind the grandstand while designer Yvan Duhaime adjusted their flowing, felt robes." Flowing felt robes—under a blazing sun in early June! Poor Eve. Poor Cleopatra. Poor Joan of Arc with her "proud Mia Farrow haircut." The media then, as now, mirrored the biases of their times.[47]

The broadcaster Gloria Bishop recalls how she and a woman friend discussed the issue of feminism on a Montreal bus sometime in the early sixties and how a male passenger approached them and admonished, "Would you please stop talking like that—my wife is *quite* happy with the situation she's in right now."[48] When not hostile, reactions tended to the oblivious. A reporter asked Judy LaMarsh whether she was a parliamentarian or a woman first, and, not surprisingly, he received an indignant reply. Would a *man* be asked such a question?[49] Novelist Susan Swan points to the time an uncle of a friend of hers visited the McGill *Daily*'s offices and "seeing me working there, [said], 'Why, you're taking this more seriously than I thought!' I didn't say anything then, but I thought, 'Why *wouldn't* I take it seriously?'"[50]

When Governor General and Mrs. Michener took their own informal tour of Expo, they had the press in tow. In a newspaper photograph, a debonair Roland Michener is shown in his brown summer suit, holding a cigarette in one hand. Is that a look of resignation on his face? Well, consider the cutline accompanying the photograph: "A HUSBAND GOES SHOPPING: Mrs. Roland Michener is buying presents and souvenirs and her husband, the Governor General, takes the role familiar to most men—the patient waiter, enjoying a smoke in the open air, watching the Expo world go by." As a snapshot of certain social attitudes in the middle sixties, that cutline serves nicely.[51]

The baby boom generation did not erase the gendered double standard, but it put a large dent in it,[52] thanks to the sexual revolution and the introduction of the Pill (which came later to Canada than it did to the U.S., and the dissemination of birth control information did not become legal here until 1969). Canada never had an equivalent for *Cosmopolitan* magazine, nor for its editor, the flinty, buoyantly determined Helen Gurley Brown. Brown was a kind of Dr. Pangloss with big hair, ever flashing her vulpine smile. "We're still womanly, we have babies, and men fall in love with us," Brown told a reporter. "And in addition to these traditional functions, we have this whole other thing—the career world. I think we've got it all."[53] Brown had no desire to overthrow the patriarchy; she sought to burrow from within and reap the rewards of conquest through seduction and guile.

Canada did have, on the other hand, Doris Anderson, editor of the women's magazine *Chatelaine* (French Canada had its own version under an equally formidable editor, Fernande Saint-Martin). Anderson was earnest and dourly plain-spoken, her approach antithetical to the cutie-pie scenarios of Helen Gurley Brown. Anderson's *Chatelaine* mixed staples like homemaking tips, recipes, and fashion ideas with more substantive articles that pursued an avowedly feminist agenda—a folksy-serious combination of elements that gave *Chatelaine* a pride of place in the cultural life of the country and helped account for it being represented at Expo by a "showcase of the century" model home many found as conventional and underwhelming as the *Chatelaine* design ideas for the model units at Moshe Safdie's Habitat. Women's rights, like Native rights, were on the cultural radar in 1967, but the true dawning of the age of identity politics and political correctness did not occur until the following decade.

As for the gay rights movement, you would not expect to see much evidence of it at Expo, mainly because in the society at large, on any significant level, it didn't exist. Out of sight, out of mind, and in the closet. "Gay" as a term to describe homosexuals had yet to come into common usage—and would not do so in the grammatically staid *New York Times* until 1987.[54] In his novel of the period, *The Red Notebook*, Michel Tremblay offers a poignant metaphor for society's tolerance of gays: The madam of the bordello for transvestite hookers, established specifically to cater to the tastes of the worldly clients Expo 67 was expected to attract to Montreal, decides to treat her "girls" by taking them on a visit to Expo. The madam is celebrating her sixtieth birthday and is in an expansive mood. The young woman who is the novel's narrator observes the reaction of fair-goers as their little group makes its way about La Ronde. At first she is rather thrilled by the accepting reaction of their fellow sightseers. After a while, though, the mood changes and a crushing realization sets in. Like La Ronde, concludes the narrator, drag queens are not at their best in the sunlight; the spectators and passersby begin to regard the group less sympathetically and the occasional contemptuous comment could now be heard.[55]

When the gay and transvestite demimonde turned out in force for the opening of Marlene Dietrich's Expo show,[56] this was okay, fun, glamorous even. This was showbiz. Exotic creatures they were, these birds in all their plumage, non-threatening and easily compartmentalized and dismissed out of mind. But social and legal changes were occurring that would create a challenge—or a threat—for those who could so easily compartmentalize and dismiss. In July 1967, the British House of Commons gave "overwhelming" approval to a bill that legalized homosexual acts between consenting males in England and Wales. "This is not a vote of confidence in, or congratulation for, homosexuality," announced Labour home secretary Roy Jenkins. "Those who suffer from this disability carry a great weight of loneliness, guilt, shame and other difficulties. The crucial question we have to answer is whether, in addition to these other disadvantages, they should also be made subject to the full rigour of the criminal law." Rear-Admiral Morgan Giles weighed in with the Tory opinion: "[The bill] will only encourage our enemies and those who disparage us, and it can only dismay our friends."[57] But in December of 1967, Canada's minister of justice, Pierre Trudeau, would introduce into the House of Commons his omnibus crime bill, a bill with far-reaching consequences in its proposed decriminalization of homosexual acts and abortion.

The year 1967 also saw the publication of Scott Symons's *Place d'Armes*. A Toronto blueblood who made a name for himself in Montreal journalism, Symons created a scandal when he walked out on his marriage and took up with a young male lover. *Place d'Armes* tells of an uptight anglo who finds spiritual as well as physical redemption in the arms of the French-Canadian male prostitutes he encounters at that eponymous Montreal location. His autobiographical novel acquired an immediate notoriety, though probably very few readers actually got through it. Symons became a gadfly of note, perversely but proudly steering his own singular course. "I'm homosexual," he'd say, "but not gay." Not for him identity politics. He was his own movement, a movement battling against the "Blandmen" and "gliblibs" of his background, whom he blamed for repressing the vital energies in himself and the country as a whole. Symons loathed Canada's new flag because "it didn't come out of battle, or passion, or love, or fervour. It came out of Committee." He loathed Expo 67, too, damning it as "the biggest plastic hurdy-gurdy side-show in history." [58]

While there were no "gay" pavilions at Expo (contrary to the opinion of one affronted visitor to the U.S. Pavilion, with its pop art and photographs of movie stars, who called it "a blatant victory of the homosexual"),[59] Expo's design czar, Norman Hay, would nowadays be considered a gay man. Furthermore, Hay's mentor and one-time lover was Alan Jarvis, part of that illustrious panel of thinkers at the Montebello conference in May 1963. One discerning critic, while touring the Expo grounds, strongly detected Jarvis's presence and influence throughout.[60] Jarvis had been Canada's cultural boy wonder, his most celebrated post being director of the National Gallery in Ottawa. During his tenure there, his disciple Norman Hay served as head of the gallery's design centre. A conflict with the Diefenbaker government over disputed art acquisitions forced Jarvis out, and Hay left his own job shortly afterward. Jarvis would take on a variety of arts-related appointments, but the downward spiral had begun. He died in the early 1970s at the age of fifty-seven, overwhelmed by, as one writer put it, "a mess of booze." Norman Hay died at the age of sixty-three in 1988. A friend recalled bumping into him at a Toronto gay bar named Katrina's in 1980. Hay was then fifty-six years old and down on his luck, dishing out food to the "disco bunnies" because it made him feel "grandfatherly."[61] Hay, by this account, faced his hard times with gallantry and humour. Moreover, his legacy is remembered. "Whatever Expo had in a visual sense," says the filmmaker Graeme Ferguson, "Norman supervised."[62]

SIXTEEN

Goodbye and *au Revoir*

To All Users:
This is OPS Control.
If anyone has anything in particular
to send on the Expocom please advise.
If not we are saying goodbye and au revoir.
Good luck and thanks for your cooperation.
Toodles.

—FROM OPS CONTROL, OCT. 29, 2130 HRS

They did it.

Expo crossed the fifty million visits mark the managers had set for themselves, which, for the better part of its final month, appeared increasingly in doubt. The transit strike cut attendance by one-third and rainy weather and gale force winds did not help. Expo management could scarcely conceal its panic when mutterings began about a strike by trainmen who carried out maintenance on the semi-automatic

Expo Express system. Had such a strike occurred, it might have dealt a crippling blow.[1] (Never mind that these employees had committed to a no-strike clause.) The transit strike ended after a month, leaving the Expo people a bit of time for catch-up. Montrealers, particularly, sensing the curtain about to fall on this epochal event that so transformed their city, decided to go the limit in reaching for that fifty million mark.

Premier Johnson declared a provincial school holiday for the final Friday before closing so children could attend the exhibition in case they already had not. Corinne Sévigny worked at Expo as a guide for the Texas company that built the escalator in the U.S. Pavilion. She, too, felt this sense of urgency. "The last three days of Expo I took off," she says. "I told them, 'Don't pay me! I have seventy-six more things I want to see.'"[2]

On Saturday evening, October 28, the day before closing, Martha Racine from Repentigny, Quebec, became visitor number fifty million to pass through the turnstiles at Place d'Acceuil. This was the twenty-fifth time she and her husband had come to Expo. Their prizes for being the landmark visitors included a pair of watches, a colour television set and a two-week, all expenses paid trip to Osaka, Japan, to see Expo 70. A reporter asked Mme Racine if she had ever flown before. She nodded yes, "We once took a trip from Bagotville to Montreal." Earlier that evening, a woman gave birth to a seven-pound girl at Clinic Number One on Île Ste. Hélène.[3] A night of milestones, then. Later calculations revealed that about 51 percent of the 50 million visits came from the host country (half of that number from Montreal) and 45 percent from the United States. Of the remainder, one of the larger segments, about 120,000 visitors, came from France.[4]

To commemorate the end of Expo 67 and to observe United Nations Week, a Bal des Nations was held at the Bonaventure Hotel the evening of October 28; the gala marked the Bonaventure's official opening. More than eight hundred people attended the event, held under the patronage of Governor General and Mrs. Michener. A guard of honour composed of the national pavilion hostesses accompanied the entry of the head table, which included the usual suspects: Pierre Dupuy, the Shaws, the Beaubiens and the Churchills. In Dupuy's honour, the assembled rose and sang "*Il a gagné ses épaulettes*" and "For He's a Jolly Good Fellow." "People raised their arms to form the Expo emblem and sang lustily," noted a reporter covering the event.[5] Later on, the soon to be ex–commissioner general of Expo 67 wandered over to Place des Nations to watch the dancing; the nightly dances organized for the Youth Pavilion had had to be moved there because of the large numbers. Some in the throng recognized Dupuy and came over to offer congratulations. A few even embraced him. The Youth Pavilion—the youth—had always been close to his heart. He recorded in his memoir that, because of their long hair, he sometimes found it hard to tell whether it was a young woman or young man giving him a hug. It was a supremely happy moment for him.[6]

Unlike the VIPs-only inauguration of six months earlier, the public was allowed onto the Expo site on closing day, Sunday, October 29. The gates opened, as usual, at 9:30 a.m. Planners went through a number of drafts of possible closing event ceremonies before settling on a scenario pleasing to both Expo management and government authorities.[7] Closing ceremonies took place at Place des Nations at 10 a.m. The governor general inspected a guard of honour and bestowed souvenirs on the commissioners general of the national pavilions. Prime Minister Pearson presented souvenirs to the commissioners of Expo's private pavilions. Each participating pavilion's flag was then lowered. The fifteen thousand guests and spectators who jammed Place des Nations shivered under a grey autumn sky. Speeches were meant to be no more than five minutes each, though Mayor Drapeau could not restrain himself and spoke for twelve, concluding with a ringing "Expo is over! Long live Man and His World!"

Everyone knew by now that this was not empty talk: Drapeau had already announced that the spirit of Expo would live on with a Man and

The Canada Pavilion, designed by a group of Toronto and Ottawa architects headed by Rod Robbie, was called Katimavik, the Inuktitut name for "gathering place." *(LAC/Canadian Corp. for the 1967 World Exhibition fonds/ e001096693)*

A steel band performs on the lagoon in front of the Trinidad-Tobago and Grenada Pavilion, while looming in the background is the very popular British Pavilion. *(LAC/Canadian Corp. for the 1967 World Exhibition fonds/e000990896)*

The Ontario Pavilion, designed by architect Macy DuBois, was a series of open-ended, tent-like shapes attached to steel poles and arrayed over granite blocks. The Academy Award–winning film *A Place to Stand* made its debut here. *(LAC/ Canadian Corp. for the 1967 World Exhibition fonds/e000996019)*

The Quebec Pavilion (top), ultra-sophisticated and austere, showcased a new image of Quebec in line with the modern strides the province had made during its Quiet Revolution of the early sixties. *(LAC/Canadian Corp. for the 1967 World Exhibition fonds/e000990969)*

French President General Charles de Gaulle's notorious *"Vive le Québec libre!"* became a centrepiece of the Expo narrative. *(LAC/Canadian Corp. for the 1967 World Exhibition fonds/e000996503)*

France's pavilion drew criticism from architecture critics but impressed visitors with its exhibits. It survives today as the Montreal Casino. *(LAC/Canadian Corp. for the 1967 World Exhibition fonds/e000990848)*

The great entertainer Harry Belafonte brought his family along when he came to perform at Expo with Miriam Makeba. Here he visits the Indians of Canada Pavilion. *(LAC/Canadian Corp. for the 1967 World Exhibition fonds/ e000996519)*

Walking Woman, by mixed-media artist Michael Snow and featured at the Ontario Pavilion, became one of the iconic images in Canadian art of the 1960s. *(LAC/Canadian Corp. for the 1967 World Exhibition fonds/ e000996028)*

The Man the Producer Pavilion on Île Notre Dame was one of the major theme pavilions at Expo; another was the Man the Explorer Pavilion on Île Ste. Hélène. *(LAC/Canadian Corp. for the 1967 World Exhibition fonds/e000990891)*

The Western Provinces Pavilion attracted plenty of attention for its ingenious features such as a logging exhibit and a simulated mine-shaft journey. *(LAC/ Canadian Corp. for the 1967 World Exhibition fonds/e000990962)*

Buckminster Fuller's visionary design for the geodesic dome, which served as the U.S. Pavilion, became one of his more spectacular accomplishments. *(The Montreal Star, April 24, 1967)*

The Czech Pavilion appealed to both connoisseurs and the masses, and lineups to get in were long. The vitality of its exhibits spoke to a Czech renaissance later known as the Prague Spring. *(LAC/Canadian Corp. for the 1967 World Exhibition fonds/e000996560)*

The Jackie Kennedy mystique transfixed the public. People swarmed around her wherever she went at Expo. *(LAC/ Canadian Corp. for the 1967 World Exhibition fonds/ e000996531)*

Senator Robert F. Kennedy came to Expo's La Ronde with an extensive entourage of family and friends, including the writer/bon vivant George Plimpton (rear) in this shot of them on the roller coaster. *(LAC/ Canadian Corp. for the 1967 World Exhibition fonds/e000996599)*

Thailand's King Bhunibol Abulyadej and Queen Sirikit, proclaimed by some as the most beautiful woman at the exhibition, were among a host of foreign dignitaries who arrived at Expo to honour their country's national day. *(LAC/Canadian Corp. for the 1967 World Exhibition fonds/e000990927)*

The amusement park La Ronde offered a contrast to the high-toned cultural attractions of Man and His World. One of its popular rides was the Gyrotron, which took travellers from outer space deep into the earth's core. *(LAC/Canadian Corp. for the 1967 World Exhibition fonds/e000995981*

His World theme park, about which he had been in talks with federal and provincial governments. Actually, Quebec Premier Daniel Johnson had told the mayor he was, in effect, on his own in the matter. For its part, the federal government agreed to defer by two years Montreal's share of Expo 67 costs and to purchase most of the buildings, including Habitat and the Autostade, on the federally owned Cité du Havre site. It also picked up half the operating deficit on La Ronde, the City of Montreal and the province of Quebec picking up the other half; after two years, La Ronde was to be sold to the city for a price to be agreed upon. And then there were the pavilions themselves, including those of the United States and France, donated to Montreal by the participating nations. Success, at least in the mind of Jean Drapeau, seemed a foregone conclusion. People had doubted his predictions before—yet look how things turned out. Long live Man and His World! He was on a roll and everyone knew it. Had he not just declared Montreal would seek the 1976 Summer Olympic Games?

"To me," said Lester Pearson in his speech that final morning, "[Expo's] lasting impact is: That the genius and fate of man know no boundaries but are universal; That the future peace and well-being of the world community of men depend on achieving the kind of unity of purpose within the great diversity of national effort which has been achieved here at this greatest of all Canada's Centennial achievements. It has also shown that Canada and Canadians, if we work together, can achieve any objective and reach any goal. Expo was such a goal and now it is a glorious page in our history."

Premier Johnson voiced similar sentiments, though sentiments filtered through the specific prism of Quebec history. Expo, noted Daniel Johnson, had "shown to those who surround us that, far from wanting to isolate ourselves, we take the chance offered to us to open our hearts to others, to converse and cooperate with others. And by its immense success, it has shown us that we are capable of doing great things."

Then it was the turn of Pierre Dupuy, who received several standing ovations in the course of these closing ceremonies. Dupuy declared that he drew three main lessons from Expo 67. First: Canadians ought to have more confidence in themselves. Second: in the eyes of the world, and particularly of its neighbour to the south, "Canada has acquired a new stature as a great nation." Third (and here was the grandiloquent uplift typical of the man): "We can therefore believe in our gifts to build a happier world together." Then, bringing to a close what he referred to as his "report" to the International Bureau of Exhibitions, he pronounced, "Mission completed. *Mission accomplie.*"[8]

It was noted that at these closing ceremonies "God Save the Queen" was not played as a national anthem but only "O Canada" was. This was a change from the opening ceremonies six months earlier. Moreover, the royal salute to the governor general had been "Canadianized." Rather than "God Save the Queen" and the royal salute on behalf of the queen, the new format consisted of the first half of "God Save the Queen" and the first half of "O Canada."[9] In deference to his listeners, shivering in the frigid weather, Governor General Michener cut short his own comments before declaring, at 12:15 p.m., Expo 67 officially over. No doubt, his listeners welcomed this gallant and sensible gesture. Yet Roland Michener's speech *not* given suggests a depth of feeling that can still strike a chord many years later:

> When I was a small boy, my mother used to tell me about the wonders of the Chicago World's Fair. She had gone there, from Ontario, with her parents when travel was not easy, and it had been one of the highlights of her youth.
>
> Doubtless it is too early to say how long Expo 67 will live in our minds and hearts. Only time will give the answer. Wonders do not have the same durability in this age of rapid change as they had in Victorian days.
>
> However, I am prepared now to predict with more preciseness than is usually expected of a Governor-General, that those who have visited the Universal and International Exhibition in Canada will be telling their children and grandchildren about it for many years to come, and

that the effects of this great and successful enterprise of Canadians and their foreign friends will be profound, upon Canadians at home in their domestic affairs, and upon Canada's international status.

Expo has been no mere world's fair, no seven-day, modern wonder, to be seen and heard and touched, and then forgotten.

For Canadians, from every part, it has been a deeply emotional experience of what they are and who they are at this notable point of time in their history. It has given them a sense of their collective achievement as a great composite community of various peoples and regions, all working together for a common good.

More than that, Expo with its participants from 60 countries, and visitors from every part of the world, has given Canadians a pride of place in the family of nations, and an appreciation of the deep friendship and regard which are accorded to them by other peoples.

These feelings, these sentiments are surely no mirage which will fade with the setting of the sun. No! Something of value has been added to the personality of each of us Canadians, and to the corporate personality of Canada as a whole. It augurs well for our future, no matter what problems we may have to face ...[10]

At 2:00 p.m., the Expo site was closed to further visitors. At 3:30 P.M., they stopped the sale of liquor, while the minirails and boat rides closed up shop. A hundred-gun salute announced the closing of the pavilions. At 4:00 p.m., there was a twenty-five-minute fireworks display and, at 4:30 p.m., those visitors who remained were ushered off the site.

Mission accomplished.

Goodbye and *au revoir*.

René Lévesque, who by this time represented another form of national vision, arrived late for the closing ceremonies. Andrew Kniewasser happened to be in the vicinity, and photographers suggested a picture of the two men together. Lévesque, recalling perhaps some of the unpleasant wrangles they had in the years before Expo opened, demurred. "Andrew, you don't really want your picture taken with me," said Lévesque. "And I said," says Kniewasser, "'Minister, we all make mistakes.'" "Thank you for saying that," replied Lévesque. "He didn't apologize," says Kniewasser, "but he said that."[11]

In those final days, there was apprehension about theft and vandalism. The histories of other fairs and exhibitions in their final days offered a trove of horror stories. People were pleasantly surprised, then, when those fears proved unfounded at Expo. "It just didn't happen that way in Montreal," says Andrew Kniewasser. "On the final day, October 29, 430,000 people crowded the site, and when the closing ceremonies ended they left quietly—strangers hugging one another, holding hands, and crying."[12]

Author and journalist Peter Desbarats expressed in verse the feelings of many:

> ... We knew it right away
> As the real image of ourselves.
> We danced with it
> All through the summer
> In the phoney French-Canadian village
> We embraced it
> In the imitation gondolas
> On the temporary canals
> We hugged it
> In the ersatz beer gardens
> And kissed it
> Over borscht
> Brewed by some Lebanese chef
> From the Bronx.
> Somehow, in this unreal world,
> We discovered our first true love
> For ourselves.[13]

The night Expo 67 closed, a gratified Philippe de Gaspé Beaubien hosted a reception for staff and directors and their spouses at the Hélène de Champlain restaurant. "I remember the great weight off my shoulders the night I gave the Bellboy to my secretary," says Beaubien about that final day. "What *relief* I had. For me it was three years of slavery."[14]

"Everybody was exhausted," says Diana Thébaud Nicholson. "One felt drained, and sad that it was over."[15]

They had beaten the odds, defied the naysayers and put on a great show—something ephemeral that might one day, perhaps, grow into something more, something durable and lasting. Not in the tangible sense—not in the sense of Mayor Drapeau's plan for a Man and His World theme park. But that more mysterious alchemy, when particular moments or events lodge themselves in the collective psyche and become personal touchstones.

The World Festival's redoubtable communications chief, Mary Jolliffe, looks back at those days and her role in them and shakes her head and smiles. "Jesus, what a ride," she says.[16]

That it was.

SEVENTEEN

The Best Place to Be

April 2012 marks the forty-fifth anniversary of Expo 67. If anything, the Expo mystique may have gained in power over the years. Even those too young to recall the hoopla of the period are intrigued. "It was like an old *Star Trek* movie," Jason Stockl, born in 1977, told *The Globe and Mail* on the exhibition's fortieth anniversary. "People thought we'd all end up living in domes and riding monorails."[1] It is likely, however, that as one generation succeeds another, Expo 67 will eventually seem more historical moment and less emotional touchstone. Such is the way of things. But that, even now, Expo continues to exert a hold on the imaginations of so many Canadians is testimony to the way it encapsulated a spirit of optimism so particular to its time.

That spirit of optimism spoke to a fundamental demographic shift. In 1967, half the country's population was under the age of twenty-five, and many baby boomers came of age during Expo. Doug Owram describes the older cohorts as simply being overwhelmed because, for a period of some twenty to twenty-five years, there existed not just a demographic imbalance but an imbalance that shifted values and politics in Canada to the values and politics of the country's youth. The fifties flirtation with gadgets and technology as nifty evidence of the future had ceded to a more earnest and searching spirit that, in Owram's words, "sought to tie technology to personal growth."[2] Expo 67's thematic linking of humanity's potential for personal growth with advances in technology spoke to this new attitude.

Yet crucial to Expo's mystique is its position on the cusp of the social tumult engulfing the remainder of the decade. A sense of the elegiac hovers about the idea of Expo. "Expo 67: Canada's Camelot?" is the title of a scholarly article written not long ago, in which the author does her best to puncture any such simplistic notion. But the rhetorical question is raised and, looking back, it is easy to understand how this best of times/worst of times dichotomy so entrenched itself and why Pierre Berton, for a book he wrote on Canada in the year 1967, employed the subtitle "The Last Good Year."

The assassinations of civil rights leader Martin Luther King, Jr., and Senator Robert Kennedy occurred in the spring and summer of 1968. Then there were the troubling images of police clashing with demonstrators at the Democratic Party convention in Chicago and the eventual ascension of Republican candidate Richard Nixon on the law-and-order ticket. The advent of Nixonian politics meant that we started to hear a lot about a certain "Silent Majority." Part of Nixon's pandering appeal to those citizens who felt cowed by and resentful of the radical left, this idea poisoned the U.S. political bloodstream for generations. Soviet tanks rolled through the streets of Prague, crushing the Czech experiment with greater freedoms—an experiment that, one year earlier, had delighted so many at Expo. Vietnam became more of a quagmire; student riots accelerated. The first violent student protest in Canada occurred at Sir George Williams University (now Concordia University) in Montreal in February 1969. The savagery of the Manson family murders in Los Angeles cast a pall over the peace-and-love vibe emerging from Woodstock. The excesses of sixties radicalism soon ceded to the excesses of seventies reaction. The sense of optimism bearing us aloft through much of the sixties began to fade.

Perhaps we in Canada held on to that optimism a little longer than did our American neighbours. Lester Pearson, having fought the good fight for national unity, and plainly exhausted by his labours, announced his retirement in December 1967. "Well, goodbye," he said at that press conference, "*c'est la vie*"—parting words that, in their determined congeniality and matter-of-factness, seemed somehow characteristic of the man. Pearson's successor as Liberal leader and then, in April 1968, as prime minister, was his justice minister, Pierre Elliott Trudeau. Trudeau had youth, vitality, a nonconforming edge, progressive convictions, glamour—and he was French-Canadian and an outspoken federalist. In many ways, the tide of pan-Canadian confidence that captured so many in the wake of Expo 67 abetted Trudeau's meteoric rise. "You could argue that Expo made it possible for Trudeau not to seem like a visitor from Mars, that he personified the kind of style that Expo displayed," says Graham Fraser.[3] The historian Ramsay Cook adds, "I don't think Expo 'created' Mr. Trudeau—but it sure helped."[4]

Canada became swept up by "Trudeaumania," and Parti Québécois leader René Lévesque could barely conceal his contempt. He saw Trudeau as the "elegant receptacle into which Canada could pour all its hidden hopes, among them the sneaking wish to see French Canada put in its place. The unspoken but fiercely eloquent slogan that floated in the air everywhere was 'Keep Quebec Quiet!'"[5] Trudeau's landslide victory followed the rowdy Saint-Jean-Baptiste Day celebrations in Montreal, where protestors pelted those on the reviewing dais with beer bottles. The reviewing party, which included Mayor Drapeau, quickly sought cover. Trudeau stood firm and defiant, an image seared into voters' minds as they ventured to polling booths the next day. It was a Canadian pastime—and in certain ways, still is—to compare and contrast ourselves with our American neighbours and invariably come up short. Expo went some ways to mitigate this inferiority complex. So did the pride many felt in their new prime minister. "They" had that crafty old retread "Tricky Dick" Nixon. "We" had a philosopher king who spoke about a just society and dated Barbra Streisand. For one brief, shining moment, some of us felt almost smug.

But if we did, the moment quickly passed. October 1970 brought a national trauma—the October Crisis—when members of the FLQ kidnapped British high commissioner James Cross from his Montreal home, demanding the release of twenty-three of their members from prison. They issued a manifesto designed to draw the world's attention to the plight of the Québécois, shackled by a Canadian federal system and oppressed economically by American capitalism. An FLQ group called the Chénier cell kidnapped the provincial labour minister Pierre Laporte.

Trudeau responded with the War Measures Act, a suspension of civil rights that saw the arrest and jailing of nearly five hundred people— most, as it turned out, having little or no connection with the FLQ, among them singer Pauline Julien, labour leader Michel Chartrand and journalist/provocateur Nick Auf der Maur. A number of people, and not just separatist sympathizers, felt that Trudeau overreacted, but, in the main, public opinion backed him. Pierre Laporte's death, while in captivity, cast a darkness over Montreal and, in fact, the country as a whole. James Cross was eventually released and, in return, the kidnappers received passage to Cuba, but the political calculus changed forever in terms of Quebec's relationship with the rest of Canada. Anglo-Canadians, whose knowledge of French Canada consisted mainly of *The Plouffe Family* on television and the Canadiens hockey team, realized with a jolt that the relationship was more complicated than they had imagined, if they had ever much thought about it at all.

Moreover, the trauma of the October Crisis could not check the newfound confidence among Quebecers ushered in by the Quiet

Revolution. "It is not surprising that in Quebec, where the will to survive has characterized three centuries of history, intense nationalism became a new faith to replace old beliefs in a society undergoing rapid change," observed Ramsay Cook.[6] By 1976, René Lévesque and his plans for "sovereignty-association" with the rest of Canada led the nationalist Parti Québécois to victory at the provincial polls. Expo 67 played its transformational role in this confidence-building process in Quebec. If the separatists scoffed, many Quebecers—and certainly many Montrealers, who visited Expo as much as ten times or more each—had been impressed. "There was a national renaissance," says Mark Starowicz. "There was a Quebec revolution. It was intoxicating. Expo was one of the turning points in it. You didn't have to be a separatist to celebrate the shedding of the Church, the celebration of an indigenous culture. It was there before—but Expo certainly accelerated it."[7]

Says Louise Arbour: "It gave French Canadians the sense that they existed in the eyes of the world."[8] Adds Monique Simard: "It was a very strong catalyzer, especially for francophones who had a 'shy' relationship to the world. Suddenly they felt they *were* a part of the world."[9] Quebecers felt a distinct sense of ownership. When speaking with foreign dignitaries, Quebec representatives often played down the centennial aspect. Canada may have turned one hundred, but Montreal was celebrating its 325th birthday! As one observer remarked, Expo 67 offered many Quebecers the chance to have a party and not have to celebrate Canada.[10] Subsequent studies reveal the exhibition as a kind of demarcation point. There was Before Expo and there was After Expo. And it was After Expo—and, more specifically, after a special meeting of the Quebec Estates General in November 1967—when, for many Québécois, French Canada (which in their minds had come to mean the province of Quebec) did constitute a nation, with its own territory and its own right to act as it saw fit.

In 2008, Professors David Anderson and Viviane Gosselin published *Private and Public Memories of Expo 67: A Case Study of Recollections of Montreal's World's Fair, 40 Years after the Event.* They canvassed fifty visitors to Expo—thirty-one women and nineteen men; twenty-five were from British Columbia and twenty-five from Quebec. One thing they discovered was that not one of the Québécois francophones associated Expo 67 with Canada's centennial. For the francophone participants in their study, Expo 67's triumph was because of Quebec. On the other hand, the anglophone participants regarded it as a Canadian accomplishment and no special mention was made of its importance for Quebec.

Anderson and Gosselin found a second divide between the two groups of respondents. While some of the anglophone respondents situated Expo within a context of cultural tensions between English and French Canadians—all-French-language laws, for example, or the October Crisis—none of the francophones did. Instead, they spoke to what they saw as Quebec's backwardness and how Expo was part of a continuum that began with the Quiet Revolution—was a catalyst, a key event that helped Quebec to "wake up." Even though two of the anglophone participants had been long-time Quebec residents, they shared the same views as the other anglophones in the study. "This affirms an argument that linguistic/cultural affinities, within the sample at least, took precedence over geographic ones when discussing questions of collective identities." Anderson and Gosselin conclude: "What is remarkable is the clear appropriation of the same event by two different collectives, for two different national narratives. Clearly, Expo 67 was part of a modern epic for two nations: Canada's and Quebec's."[11]

Cathy Fauquier, now a senior vice-president at BMO Nesbitt Burns in Toronto, worked as a hostess at the Kodak Pavilion at Expo 67 and had a great time. The Kodak Pavilion was situated near the Jamaica and Iran Pavilions and she remembers "the 'Yellow Canary' drink at the Jamaica Pavilion and those huge bowls of caviar at the Iranian Pavilion. It was an international party." Fauquier had such a good time at Expo, she volunteered for hostess duty at the Ontario Pavilion at Expo 70 in

Osaka. Osaka, though, fell a bit flat. "There was a Quebec Pavilion there," she says, "and they didn't feel like Quebec-Canada, they felt like Quebec-Quebec." Nonetheless, the experience proved fulfilling enough to convince her to apply for a job at the Montreal Summer Olympics in 1976. She worked in the public relations department, one of two anglophones there. And while she enjoyed her visits to the Royal Yacht *Britannia*, other aspects of the job disappointed her. "Even though I was supposedly bilingual," she says, "they used to stop the meeting and speak English for me even though I could understand. They made me feel so uncomfortable, as if I was a pariah. As if I was in *their* nation."[12] That may indeed have been the general idea. As far as some of Fauquier's francophone co-workers were concerned, this *was* their nation now.

HE DID NOT LIVE in the past—he made it a point to say this on more than one occasion. And, as he spoke, I thought, looking southward from his thirty-third floor Place Ville Marie office toward the waterfront and, just beyond, toward the site of Expo 67 itself, maybe he *didn't* live in the past, but the past was certainly always out there gazing back at him.

Philippe de Gaspé Beaubien was eighty when we first met on a gloomy October day in 2008. His manner courtly, his voice soft-spoken, he wore a charcoal-grey jacket whose lapels were of a slightly darker charcoal. Affixed to the left lapel was an Order of Canada pin. Beaubien sported a light tan. In *The Great Gatsby*, F. Scott Fitzgerald wrote of Daisy Buchanan's voice as having the sound of money. So it is with the look of certain tans. Such tans possess a burnished understatement, a glow, suggesting refinements of a life well, and probably expensively, lived.

Indeed, in the decades following Expo 67, Philippe de Gaspé Beaubien became a media titan and legendary figure in Canadian business, thanks in good part to fortuitous discussions with Power Corporation chair Paul Desmarais and Jean Parisien, a Desmarais business associate. Over time, those meetings led to Beaubien acquiring control of Quebec Telemedia, a company whose nucleus was formed of a group of Quebec radio stations but whose scope and market Beaubien considerably enlarged to include *TV Guide Canada*, *Canadian Living*, and *Homemakers* magazines, reaching well beyond Quebec borders. Later, his children became involved in the leadership of the company and, later still, the family sold the Telemedia broadcasting and magazine assets in the early 2000s. Nowadays, he devotes much of his considerable energy to the de Gaspé Beaubien Foundation set up to help and encourage those individuals and entrepreneurial families who are seeking to improve their communities. Life has been kind to the former "mayor of Expo," though the same qualities serving him well in that capacity—discipline, stamina, attention to detail, the smooth charm and conviction of the born salesman—also enabled him to be ready when opportunity knocked. "I don't think I would have had the Telemedia," he says, "without Expo."

At both our meetings, we were eventually joined by his wife, Nan-b, who occupied an office nearby. Eight years his junior and still quite youthful in appearance, Nan-b has been his life partner in the full sense of that term. Plainly, he dotes on her, and relies heavily on her opinions. As we neared the end of that second meeting, and as Beaubien attempted to summarize certain key lessons from his Expo experience, a comment of Nan-b's floated back to me. "Most of the time it's ego that gets in the way," she said. "Whereas in this instance there was little room for ego because there was such a close deadline. And there was such a determination that Canadians were *not* going to fail. I think that people *knew* that Canada was on the line. That was the thing about Expo—what incredible things we can achieve if we park our egos at the door."[13] That *was* the thing about Expo—the teamwork, how disparate personalities knitted together in pursuit of a common goal. Their example, in and of itself, amounts to quite a legacy.

Pierre Dupuy began to have health problems shortly after Expo closed. In May 1968, he experienced a heart attack in Paris and his condition compelled him to decline Mayor Drapeau's invitation to attend the opening of Drapeau's Man and His World exhibition in Montreal. The exertions of his role as Expo's commissioner general doubtless contributed to his subsequent problems. He was not a young man when he took that role on. On the other hand, it is reasonable to assume he would not have traded away a second of it. In May of 1969, while on the French Riviera for the Cannes Film Festival, he suffered a fatal heart attack. He was seventy-two. "He died penniless," says Beaubien. "Just breaks your heart. He was a great guy."[14] Jean Drapeau's office took over the funeral arrangements. The service was held in Montreal, Dupuy's coffin draped with the Expo flag and attended by an honour guard of Expo hostesses in their Expo uniforms. Diana Thébaud Nicholson remembers that some of the hostesses' uniforms did not fit too well. "They'd had a baby or two—the poor embarrassed hostesses were falling out of their uniforms," she says. "It was *tacky*."[15]

Robert Shaw, Expo's deputy commissioner general, died in 2001 at the age of ninety-one. Following Expo, Shaw became vice-principal of McGill University and, early into that tenure, called on Mayor Drapeau for police support in the face of a massive demonstration demanding the institution become bilingual. Mark Starowicz, then editor of the McGill *Daily*, was among the minority of anglo voices on campus that supported the bilingual initiative, a stand that cost him dearly when he tried to get a job at *The Gazette*. The anglo press would not touch him, nor did he feel confident enough about his written French to pursue a career with the francophone press. He became another Montreal exile headed for Toronto, though not for the usual reason. "Out of the quarter million who left," he says, referring to the non-francophone diaspora that occurred in the years following the triumph of René Lévesque and the Parti Québécois, "I'm proud of saying I had to leave because of the *English* and not the French."[16]

Shaw later went to Ottawa as Canada's first deputy minister of the environment; in 1975, he became president of the Engineering Institute of Canada. Asked once what he regarded as his greatest accomplishment,

Shaw replied: "I don't think I could name any one particular event. What did I achieve? God, I had a lot of fun."[17]

Colonel Edward Churchill collapsed and died on a golf course near his home in Sarasota, Florida, in August 1978 at the age of sixty-five. He had twice been hospitalized for exhaustion during the run-up to the Expo opening. If Expo produced its share of heroes, most agree Edward Churchill was a hero among heroes, seeing to it the site was built and ready to go by the April deadline—though it was close. "We were building the exhibition ten minutes before the exhibition opened," says Andrew Kniewasser.[18] Churchill later remarked that the Expo job spoiled him for everything else. "I'm no longer satisfied just to put one brick on top of another," said Churchill. "I want to build things that have meaning."[19] His many admirers include architect Moshe Safdie, who credits Churchill for essentially saving, albeit in modified form, his Habitat project. "When I got the Massey Medal, I gave it to him," says Safdie. "He was very moved and he took it—and when he died, he willed it back to me." But Safdie has not received the medal and has no intention of pursuing the matter. "The kids should have it," he says.[20]

Expo survivors whom I met included the redoubtable PR man Yves Jasmin, who, more than anyone, appears determined to keep the history of Expo 67 alive and in the forefront; that vigorous octogenarian Andrew Kniewasser, Expo's general manager, whose post-Expo resumé counted many years as president of the Investment Dealers Association of Canada; Jean Cournoyer, labour troubleshooter for Expo's secretary and general counsel, Jean-Claude Delorme, who entered politics, replacing the slain Pierre Laporte as labour minister in the provincial government of his friend Robert Bourassa, and later still became a public affairs commentator; and Krystyne Romer, who became a successful business-woman and is now Krystyne Griffin after her marriage to Scott Griffin, a nephew of Walter Gordon and the philanthropist who underwrote the Griffin Poetry Prize.

I met Sandy van Ginkel in his last months. He had suffered a series of strokes. His eyes were alert, but they betrayed the considerable effort required for our meeting; his wife and partner Blanche did much of the talking. He died in July 2009 at the age of eighty-nine. After his frustrating time at Expo, he continued to consult and invent. In the seventies, he devised the Ginkelvan, a hybrid electric vehicle for transporting shoppers along streets closed to vehicular traffic in New York City. When Mayor John Lindsay decided not to run again, the project was mothballed, though Vail, Colorado, purchased the Ginkelvan prototype. Also in the seventies, van Ginkel created the first atlas of the communities of the Mackenzie River as part of the study into the proposed Mackenzie Valley gas pipeline. The van Ginkels moved from Montreal to Toronto in 1977, when Blanche became dean of the Faculty of Architecture and Landscape Architecture at the University of Toronto, the first woman to hold such a position at a Canadian university. By the eighties, Sandy van Ginkel was working mainly as a sculptor and printmaker.[21]

Pierre de Bellefeuille, Expo 67's director of exhibitions, agreed to speak with me over the phone. He had scandalized some of his Expo colleagues when he became a separatist. De Bellefeuille sat for nine years in the National Assembly as a member of the Parti Québécois. His relationship with René Lévesque, the PQ leader, however, remained tenuous. "We got along all right," he says of Lévesque, "but he did not have a thorough trust in me. I'm not sure why. One possible reason was the fact that I was an Ontarian. I was born and brought up and went to school in Ottawa. Another factor was my connection with [Toronto-headquartered magazine publisher] Maclean-Hunter."[22]

The young people who worked in various jobs at Expo make up an illustrious honour roll: a Montreal mayor, Pierre Bourque; a Supreme Court justice (and currently president and CEO of the International Crisis Group in Brussels), Louise Arbour; an eco-warrior, Paul Watson; a newspaper publisher, Roger D. Landry; a National Film Board executive, Monique Simard; a cultural consultant, Barry Lord; a film producer,

Lionel Chetwynd, who, in addition to his duties as coordinator in charge of reproduction rights at Expo's World Festival was also finishing up law school at McGill (the exertions made him lose forty pounds);[23] a newspaper editor and museum director, William Thorsell; a painter, Charles Pachter; an HIV/AIDS activist, Ron Rosenes ... The list goes on and on, these many journeys that looped in and out of Montreal at that time and then spun off in their manifold and particular—sometimes strange, sometimes triumphant, sometimes tragic—ways over the next forty-plus years.

And I think of someone on that list no longer with us. Robert McDonald, if you'll remember, was the press aide who received that cogent bit of life wisdom from Laurence Olivier. Bob's VIP-escort role at Expo also introduced him to the actor Jack Lemmon, whose son he ended up tutoring after he moved to Los Angeles to attend film school there. I knew Bob—known to his friends as McD—only slightly from school days. But I later found him to be fun and funny, a true pleasure. He ended up in the film business in New York, though he later left films to help his great friend, designer Perry Ellis, then gravely ill, run the latter's clothing empire. I last spoke to Bob when he had become very ill. That was autumn 1989. Bob joked over the phone that he had become like his elderly, and quite blind, dog Josh: now both of them, he said, with that sardonic lilt uniquely his, were bumping into the apartment furniture. He died of AIDS complications in January 1990. He was in his mid-forties, a blithe spirit to the end, one of Expo's bright lights extinguished far, far too soon.

And, lest we forget—But how could we? He wouldn't let us!—mention must be made of that dynamo Jean Drapeau, the mayor of Montreal who bet big, and won big, on the realization of the Expo dream. In the exhibition's final days, Drapeau held a press conference at which a reporter had the temerity to ask him whether he thought a $250 million deficit for Expo, a figure contained in an Ottawa document, seemed rather a high number; that figure was five times the estimate predicted four years earlier.[25] ("Did anyone ever calculate what accrued to us in tourism and employment?" Philippe de Gaspé Beaubien asked, when that figure was raised during our conversation. "The balance of payment numbers *far* outweigh our deficit."[26]) Drapeau, who at several points during the press conference kept stressing the value of Expo to Canada as a whole and not just to Montreal, refused to countenance any talk about deficits. "Is the cost too high for what Expo has done?" he asked. "No true Canadian would say the cost was too high." History backs him up. Expo was a good investment, for Canada and for Montreal, though the rhetorical bombast is strictly Drapeau.

History also suggests Expo as the crowning glory of an often tumultuous career. Drapeau's plan for a permanent Man and His World theme park withered quickly. While a number decided to let him take over their pavilions, certain foreign pavilions were beyond his reach. The Russians dismantled theirs almost at once and shipped it back to Moscow. Premier Joey Smallwood scooped up the Czech and Yugoslav Pavilions to be used as cultural centres back in Newfoundland. For a time, Drapeau had the Canadian Pavilion, but Rod Robbie and his partners eventually took the federal and Montreal governments to court in order to shut it down. "It turned into a Coney Island," says Robbie of the mayor's Man and His World theme park. Robbie's grievance, however, had more to do with issues of legal liability than aesthetics. "These were temporary buildings," says Robbie. "They were not intended to last. We were horrified at this."[27] Man and His World limped along, a pale echo of its former self. "He started to compromise," says Andrew Hoffman, the planner for La Ronde. "Keep this, scrap that. Things became smaller and smaller."[28] What had once been a place of exuberance and wonder now appeared rather forlorn. In winter, it became positively bleak and American filmmaker Robert Altman used it precisely for this bleakness in his dystopic yarn *Quintet*.

In 1976, fire destroyed the transparent acrylic covering Buckminster Fuller's "Skybreak Bubble" and the U.S. Pavilion remained closed until

1990, when it reopened as a teaching centre under the auspices of Environment Canada. Today, the French Pavilion serves as the Montreal casino and the neighbouring Quebec Pavilion is also part of the casino complex. The amusement park La Ronde likewise endures.

Though not a big baseball fan, Jean Drapeau understood that a world-class city had to have its own major-league baseball team and, following years of back-and-forth negotiations, he got one: the Montreal Expos (1969–2004). He also opened his own restaurant, the Vaisseau d'Or, located in the Windsor Hotel, inspired by a visit the mayor had made to a restaurant in Paris, where diners at the appointed time put down their knives and forks and listened to a string quartet. Somehow, Montrealers resisted this Drapeauian vision of "quality." The trappings were fine, but the food and service never measured up. Opening night was chaos, the dessert arriving before the soup.[29] The Vaisseau d'Or opened its doors in September 1969 and closed them in January 1971.

Of course, what was meant to be Drapeau's crowning glory—bigger even than Expo 67—was the Summer Olympics of 1976. Having tried, and failed, to secure the 1972 Olympics (which went to Munich), he redoubled his efforts and, with the assistance of Georges Marchais, his invaluable European fixer, concentrated on those diplomatic back channels he had so assiduously cultivated in the cause of Expo. When the mayor set out for Amsterdam in 1970, he felt confident Montreal could seal the deal—and he was right. But when journalist Bill Bantey encountered Drapeau not long after this triumph, he found him looking morose. What was wrong? he asked Drapeau. "Life is going to be boring now," Drapeau replied. Why? asked Bantey. "Well, there's nothing left to do. We've done Expo and now [we've done] the Olympics."

Drapeau often tried to have a say in the running of Expo 67. After all, everyone knew it really was *his* show, did they not? Fortunately, Shaw and Beaubien, among others, stood guard at the gate. Drapeau did manage, though, to get his fingerprints all over the Montreal Olympics, and this time without the aid and good sense of Lucien

Saulnier, his right-hand man at City Hall. They had drifted apart. "Different views of how the city should be run," explained Bill Bantey. Thinking big, as was his wont, Drapeau spent big. Fiscal restraint went out the window. He would famously declare that an Olympic Games could no more lose money than a man could have a baby—a line that eventually offered at least one editorial cartoonist a field day with his drawing of a pregnant Jean Drapeau. "He was a visionary," says Philippe de Gaspé Beaubien, "but not a very good administrator."[30] Drapeau's favoured French architect, Roger Taillibert (Drapeau had wanted him to create a special tower for Expo, but that plan was quickly shot down), designed an Olympic velodrome meant to cost $16.8 million but that cost instead $74.5 million—and the roof *still* leaked. This was symptomatic: the games saddled the city with a massive debt and it took decades for Montreal to pay it down. "Without the Olympics, the city would be paved in gold," rued a Canadian Bond Rating Service managing director in 1992. "It has had a devastating impact on Montreal."[31]

Something else that had a devastating impact followed the political victory of René Lévesque and the Parti Québécois in 1976. Over the next decade, Montreal, the city that had embraced the world during Expo 67, saw many of its non-francophone citizens pack up and leave, many moving to Toronto, then undergoing its own metamorphosis into one of the most multicultural cities anywhere on the planet. "The lesson of Expo is that things are more fragile than they seem. Nothing is certain," says William Thorsell, the young man from Alberta who once had fallen hard for Montreal's special allure. "The recessive move into parochialism was a shocker. It just goes to show, you can make a lot of progress—and fall off a cliff."[32] The mayor, as always, preferred to look on the bright side, though he could be defensive on the matter. The developer Jack Rabinovitch, whose company Trizec relocated to Toronto in 1985, recalls a meeting with Drapeau soon after Lévesque's election victory. "I said Montreal could become Vienna—a city with an illustrious past and a dismal future," says Rabinovitch. "He almost threw me out of his office."[33]

Jean Drapeau's extraordinary tenure as mayor finally ran out of steam in 1986. A CROP poll in April that year indicated that challenger Jean Doré could expect 56 percent of the potential vote, to Drapeau's 44 percent. In June, Drapeau called it quits, announcing he would not contest the autumn election. He had been in office twenty-six years since his re-election in 1960, not counting those three years as mayor prior to 1957. "*Quand c'est fini, c'est fini,*" he told reporters at City Hall—though Drapeau was not quite *fini* with public life. Prime Minister Brian Mulroney named him Canada's ambassador to UNESCO in Paris, a position he held for nearly five years. Health problems dogged him in these later years and, according to a friend, his mind went "to some extent."[34] He died in 1999 at the age of eighty-three.

Whatever his foibles and flaws, whatever his tyrannical and—said some—megalomaniacal ways, Drapeau left a deep imprint on the city he loved. We remember him as the man who campaigned relentlessly to bring Expo 67 to Montreal and then, with equal tirelessness, made certain the rest of the world knew about it when it was there. Both then, and in retrospect, the six months of Expo still seem in many respects a golden time. Thus do we offer a heartfelt *merci, Monsieur le Maire, merci beaucoup*. Montreal. Expo 67. Definitely the best place to be.

THE SETTING was a cocktail party at Moshe Safdie's penthouse apartment at Habitat in the fall of 2009. The apartment originally belonged to Pierre Dupuy; in commemoration of the late commissioner general of Expo 67, Habitat's address became 2600 Avenue Pierre Dupuy. Safdie and his wife, Nina, had moved out of their first Habitat apartment because Nina "felt totally overwhelmed being in Habitat after Expo," says Safdie. "She had to have her privacy and I respected that. We bought a house in Westmount, but the house burned down. We knew the family who had taken over the Dupuy apartment and when they decided to move, we said, okay, let's move back in. Later, we divorced and my wife moved to a new apartment and I stayed there."[35]

That evening's cocktail party was under the auspices of an architectural conservancy group; Habitat's exterior and the Safdie apartment had been granted historic monument status that March by Quebec's minister of culture. Prominent in attendance was Madame Architecture herself, Phyllis Lambert, founder of the Canadian Centre for Architecture in Montreal. Safdie did not attend, but Yves Jasmin, the sultan of Expo public relations, did and received an honour from the group in the form of a framed copy of a 1967 *New Yorker* cartoon. The captionless cartoon showed a little boy building a sandcastle on the beach. The sandcastle was a replica in miniature of Habitat. Even then, Habitat had become a kind of byword, requiring no captions.

Yet if Habitat made Safdie famous, it never guaranteed him job offers. The project may have attracted international interest and the promise of future Habitats in places like New York and Puerto Rico, but the New York and Puerto Rico projects failed to materialize, and in Canada no one was nibbling. "Ironically," he says, "the next fourteen years were completely dry for me." Safdie blames Quebec nationalism for the absence of any offers for the Montreal Olympics. And that no one asked him to enter the initial competition to design Ottawa's National Gallery especially galled him. Toronto architect John C. Parkin won that initial competition, but the plan was abandoned. When in 1982, Prime Minister Trudeau reactivated plans for a National Gallery, Safdie applied for the job and got it. By then he had left Canada to headquarter himself just outside Boston. "All of my Canadian projects," he says, "came after I became a resident of the United States."[36]

Safdie considers the National Gallery project a career highlight, but so are the United States Institute of Peace Headquarters on the Mall in Washington, D.C.; the Holocaust History Museum Building and the Children's Memorial at Yad Vashem in Israel; the Skirball Cultural Center and Museum in Los Angeles; as well as the more recent Marina

Bay Sands, a massive resort–commercial complex in Singapore. Also along the way, the disappointments. He cites the Columbus Center project in New York and the Ballet Opera House in Toronto as two of the latter. "Somehow when these things occur," he says, "I turn around and immerse myself in the next thing."[37]

As for the legacy of Habitat, more than forty years on, Safdie is still uncertain such a determination can be definitively made. "I think it's too early to say," he says. "I think [Habitat's] an idea that has still to come. I see it everywhere in the next generation of architects. At the public level it has always been a desirable idea, but the question was how to deliver it in a way that's affordable. It's a humane way of planning housing. I think it's still there to be worked out." He defends the complex's grey concrete colour on the grounds that "the colour of the building comes from the life within it," yet does concede those who questioned whether certain features of Habitat were appropriate for a northern climate may have had a point. "It was a prototype, it had to be refined, fine-tuned," he says. "That's *why* we built it as a prototype."[38]

Walking about the decks of Safdie's Habitat penthouse, feeling the chill breeze off the St. Lawrence, surveying its surroundings—the harbour and Cité du Havre and, out beyond, in the middle of the river, the islands where it all began—encourages thoughts about Expo and how it helped define the Canada we know today. In certain respects, Expo seems like only yesterday. But, of course, it wasn't only yesterday and so much has happened in the intervening years. "The period from the mid-sixties to the mid-eighties will be seen by Canadian historians as the period of one of the most radical reinventions in the history of a country, from Expo 67 to the Charter of Rights and Freedoms," Michael Ignatieff told the *New Yorker*'s Adam Gopnik (whose family once lived in Habitat). "We reinvented ourselves as a multicultural bilingual nation."[39] That process of reinvention expressed itself in a number of ways, notably in a boomlet of Canadian literature, and inevitably through our relationship with the United States. Expo had helped temper a reflexive inferiority complex toward our southern neighbour. Paradoxically, it did so in part because *Life* and *Time* and *Look* and Ed Sullivan—America!!—gazed so approvingly on the fruits of our efforts. Still, the sea change was real. "It was a defining moment for me professionally and in my creative life," says artist Charles Pachter. "People would say, 'Why did you go back to Canada after graduate school in the U.S.?' And I'd say, I love my country and I want to try and raise the bar. Part of what helped me to solidify that feeling was being at Expo."[40] Noted Robert Fulford: "My favourite personal symbol of how things changed after Expo was a comparatively modest one: a cartoon, in the *New Yorker* magazine of November 18, 1967, in which a man in a business suit says to another man in a business suit, 'You don't look like a Canadian.' That was, in my opinion, a post-Expo joke. It couldn't have been made the year before. It suggested that a Canadian might somehow be different, be recognizable. It suggested that, finally, a Canadian was something to *be*."[41]

As this reflexive compare-and-contrast with the United States continued after Expo, a stronger sense of national identity emerged, the comparative weighting of national values no longer automatically favouring America. Vietnam played its role in this shift and, later, a new war provided a further line of demarcation. In fact, on his return to Canada from Harvard University (and before that, there had been the illustrious sojourn in London, England), Michael Ignatieff's political fortunes encountered a bump in the road because of his prior (later recanted) endorsement of an unpopular American war in Iraq—not to mention skepticism and resentment toward an authorial "we" that appeared to identify him as American while writing about this war for American publications. No one could be more eloquent on the subject of "blood and belonging," and yet Ignatieff found himself blindsided by this pricklier and more assertive sense of nationalism that materialized in the thirty years he was gaining renown for himself outside Canada.

"The crowning glory of the decade was undoubtedly Expo 67," wrote Gretta Chambers. "The event itself—the buildings, the site, its very existence—was a most powerful symbol of Quebec's energy, momentum and potential. One cannot exaggerate the effect of Expo on people of my generation [Chambers turned forty in 1967]. We were as though reborn." With hindsight, of course, those expectations seemed too lofty. Chambers remembers how designers from all over the globe came to Montreal, which they saw as a new hotbed of innovation. Alas, most did not stick around long. "We were not ready to follow the Expo star in any concerted way. Our euphoria denoted a frame of mind more than a state of affairs. When the world moved on, we were once more left to face the inward-looking social, economic, and cultural habits alone. They proved more difficult to transcend on our own without the impetus of a grand, overriding design."[42]

I asked journalist Bill Bantey what Expo 67 meant to him. "Moments of great pride," he replied. "Beyond that, I'd say very little."[43] Yet for others, Expo ran deep. It meant the memory of a time and place—a memory, as well, perhaps, of one's own hopes and expectations *in* that time and place—that remains as vivid today as it did then. When I spoke about Expo with lawyer and art critic Harry Malcolmson and his wife, Ann, Harry started to describe their first visit there and he had to stop in mid-sentence. Early May, cloudless sky, a nip in the air ... He started to tear up. "I still am emotional to this day ..." His eyes glistened, he offered an apologetic snuffle. "I still am emotional *to this minute* about it," he says. "You just wanted to envelop yourself in the totality of it. Each new thing led you forward. The magic, too, was of all the different countries. One thing they were extremely successful with was the individuality of the different pavilions. A great deal of it was the interchange of experiences between people—especially in the early days. We felt like pioneers. We felt special. We had got there and seen it!"[44]

To walk the grounds about Habitat is to be drawn irresistibly to the river. On a sunny autumn late afternoon, I stood at the top of the embankment and watched as men and women in wetsuits, surfboards under their arms, dutifully lined up on the shore below, awaiting their turn to bob and weave in the swirling currents marking this spot in the St. Lawrence. The rapids that enable the reverse flow below the Habitat embankment are a legacy of diking around that area in order to dredge fill for the riverbank at Cité du Havre that went on a half-century earlier.[45] This scene, the surfers with their polite rituals and the cold, indifferent beauty of the river, was to me quite powerful. Who knows how many untold stories, over who knows how many centuries, lie immersed in these waters? The past has left its imprint on the river and the future lies ahead, a mystery. And everything in between, which is to say, right now, will be what we make of it—will lie in how we decide, or not, to find our particular joy. How much time do these men and women have to ride their wave? Five minutes at most? Does it matter? For them, the joy in those five minutes makes the effort worthwhile. The river beckons them as it has beckoned so many others. There is magic in its spell.

NOTES

PROLOGUE: ISLAND DAYS

1. Peter Desbarats, "It Sang What Was Hidden in Our Hearts," *The Montreal Star*, October 30, 1967, p. 34.

2. See Don Foley, "Black Ink Blots Press Dupuy Says," *The Montreal Star*, May 5/67, p. 5; in a speech, Expo commissioner general Pierre Dupuy calls the Canadian press the most pessimistic in the world. "Expo never fully succeeded in selling itself to the Canadian business community," observed Robert Fulford in *This Was Expo* (1968), p. 192. See also, along these lines, Pierre Berton, *1967: Canada's Turning Point* (1997), p. 283.

3. See Gary Miedema, *For Canada's Sake: Public Religion, Centennial Celebrations, and The Re-making of Canada in the 1960s* (2005), pp. 161, 200.

4. Peter C. Newman, "It Could Change the Whole Direction of Canada's History," *Toronto Star*, April 28/67, p. 1.

5. Pierre Berton, op. cit., p. 288.

6. Mordecai Richler, "Notes on Expo," *The New York Review of Books*, vol. 9, no. 4, Sept. 14/67, p. 18.

7. Only two other Expos after Expo 67 would meet that status in the twentieth century: Osaka in 1970 and Seville in 1992. The BIE sanctioned an extension of Expo 67's duration by an extra two days, so that it could end on Sunday, October 29 rather than the originally planned Friday, October 27.

8. New York had antagonized the BIE by making it clear that it would follow its own rules; the consequence was that the BIE requested that its member states not participate and hence the Soviets and Western Europe declined (Spain excepted); the Middle East, Africa and Latin America did show up. See John and Margaret Gold, *Cities of Culture, Staging International Festivals and the Urban Agenda, 1851–2005* (2005), p. 111. Robert Moses, president of the New York fair, visited Expo 67 in August and elected to remain largely noncommittal—though he did

pointedly note that Expo had nothing to compare with Michelangelo's *Pietà*, on view in the New York Vatican Pavilion (see John Gray, "Moses Cool about Expo," *Montreal Star*, Aug. 11/67, p. 25).

9. See "Ikar 1964," "The Keeper of the Purple Twilight on Expo 67: 40th Anniversary," blog, Nov. 2/07, p. 1.

10. Cited in Samy Mesli, "L'Expo 67 dans la presse française : la vision du Québec dans l'Hexagone," in Denis Monière and Robert Comeau (Eds.), *Expo 67: quarante ans plus tard*, special edition of *Bulletin d'histoire politique*, vol. 17, no. 1, Autumn 2008, p. 67.

11. Ada Louise Huxtable, "A Fair with Flair," *The New York Times*, April 28/67, p. 18.

12. Doug Owram, *Born at the Right Time: A History of the Baby Boom Generation* (1996), pp. 179, 228–229, 276.

13. "Bond declared Indonesia menace," *The Montreal Star*, May 16/67, p. 33.

14. Zoe Bieler, "Any length of hem all right if it is 12 inches above the knee," *The Montreal Star*, July 17/67, p. 8.

15. "Expo Called Psychedelic Experience," *The Montreal Star*, July 4/67, p. 32.

16. Doug Owram, op. cit., p. 188.

17. Lester Pearson proposed a royal commission to examine the question of bilingualism in the public service and education, a recommendation leading eventually to the establishment of the Royal Commission on Bilingualism and Biculturalism, known as the Bi and Bi Commission.

18. See Wendy Michener, "Expo 67 to the Rescue: A Pause to Conflict. It's Boom, not Bombs, in Montreal," *Saturday Night*, January 1967, p. 29.

19. René Lévesque, *Memoirs* (1981), p. 80.

20. See Pierre Dupuy, *Expo 67 ou la découverte de la fierté* (1972), p. 110; in a piece for *Tamarack Review* (Summer 1967), author Hugh Hood found Dupuy's rationale for the preview opening "among the most charmless public statements I can remember" (Hugh Hood, "It's a Small World," pp. 77–78). "The subtle note of condescension keeps on making itself heard, probably without the Commissioner-General's being at all aware of it. Everybody says he's a pretty nice man."

21. Author telephone interview with Roger D. Landry, April 15/09.

22. John Gray, "Gates Ready for Friday Rush," *The Montreal Star*, April 27, p. 1.

ONE: IN AT THE CREATION

1. Robert Prévost, *Montréal: A History* (1993), p. 49.

2. Donald Creighton cited in Ramsay Cook, *The Maple Leaf Forever* (1971), p. 154.

3. Hugh Hood, *Around the Mountain: The Collected Stories IV* (1994), p. 150.

4. Robert Prévost, op. cit., p. 361.

5. See Bryan MacDonald, "La participation canadienne aux expositions universelles et internationales (1958–2000)," in Denis Monière and Robert Comeau (Eds.), op. cit., p. 38.

6. See Yves Jasmin, *La petite histoire d'Expo 67: l'Exposition Universelle et Internationale de Montréal comme vous ne l'avez jamais vue* (1997), p. 15.

7. Author interview with Corinne Sévigny, Montreal, Feb. 11/09; see also Bruno Paul Stenson's Master's thesis, *(A) Man and His (Expanding) World: Jean Drapeau's Evolving Enthusiasm for Expo 67* (2003), p. 29.

8. Corinne Sévigny, op cit.; officialdom was slow to warm to any notions about a world's fair in Montreal. See Cabinet Meeting Minutes 1962/02/26, "Suggested World Fair Canada—Policy to be followed." Cabinet agreed "that the federal officials on the committee should be instructed in confidence that, based on the information available, the Federal Government regarded the proposal [i.e., the renewal of Canada's application to the BIE] as impractical ..." (RG2 PCO Series A-5-a, V. 6192); "Cabinet Conclusions." Library and Archives Canada, www.collections canada.gc.ca/databases/conclusions/index-e_html.

9. Bruno Paul Stenson, op. cit., p. 30.

10. Corinne Sévigny, op. cit.

11. See Raymond Grenier, *Inside Expo 67* (1965), pp. 12–13.

12. The term "world's fair" was first used, with its connotation of trade and commerce, at the New York fair in 1939. See Blanche Lemco van Ginkel, *International Universal Exhibition 1967: "A Concept,"* lecture delivered to the Province of Quebec Association of Architects Convention, Jan. 1/63, p. 12 (courtesy of Blanche Lemco van Ginkel).

13. Robert Prévost, op. cit., p. 271.

14. See Bruno Paul Stenson, op. cit., p. 8.

15. See Erik Larson, *The Devil in the White City* (2004), p. 247; see also Erik Larson re. the first electric chair sighting and, for many, the first real encounter with electricity (p. 267). According to Manny Fernandez in *The New York Times,* Aug. 8/10, p. 3 WR ("Let Us Now Praise the Great Man of Junk Food"), the Cracker Jack recipe was not perfected until 1896, though a popcorn, molasses and peanut confection was sold at the 1893 Chicago fair.

16. See John Allwood, *The Great Exhibitions* (1977), p. 114.

17. Ibid, pp. 128–129.

18. Eva-Marie Kröller, "Expo 67: Canada's Camelot?" *Canadian Literature,* Spring-Summer 1997, p. 37.

19. See Raymond Grenier, op. cit., p. 23.

20. Author interview with Yves Jasmin, Montreal, Oct. 2/08; see also Jasmin, *La petite histoire,* p. 17.

21. Corinne Sévigny, op. cit.

22. See Bruno Paul Stenson, op. cit., p. 33: "*Les Russes ne veulent pas avoir a surveillé 20 millions d'étrangers, et ils ne veulent pas montrer au monde entier la misère du systeme socialiste. Ils vont se désister.*"

23. Ibid; the Soviets were also concerned about "spiralling costs," and cited that as the reason for their withdrawal in April 1962 (see John and Margaret Gold, op. cit., p. 114.)

24. Raymond Grenier, op. cit., p. 27.

25. Cited in Bruno Paul Stenson, op. cit., p. 34.

26. Raymond Grenier, op. cit., p. 26.

27. Yves Jasmin, Oct. 2/08.

28. Bruno Paul Stenson, op. cit., p. 36; Yves Jasmin, *La petite histoire*, p. 21; Toronto's attitude tended to shift the nearer a world's fair became a reality. In the beginning, the assumption was that there might be a contest between Toronto and Montreal and, per a Cabinet Minute of 1958, a recommendation was made that "the government should take every precaution to avoid being involved in this kind of dispute," Oct. 29/58 (RG2 Series A-5-a,V.1899). Several years later, Mayor Phillips of Toronto, having backed away from the idea, started to offer objections, voicing concerns that a Montreal fair could have an adverse effect on the Canadian National Exhibition held each summer in Toronto. In a Cabinet Minute of 1962/09/26, it was stated, "The Prime Minister had reminded Mayor Phillips that two years ago the City of Toronto had not been interested in the subject and that at that time the Federal Government had agreed to apply for the designation of Montreal as the site of a world fair" (RG2 PCO Series A-5-a,V. 6193). Subsequently, a new federal government sought to make it clear (Cabinet Minute 1964/01/05) that Toronto had had its chance: "In any further statements on the Montreal World's Fair, the point should be emphasized that Toronto had been offered the opportunity but had decided in the end not to compete for the fair" (RG2 PCO Series A-5-a,V. 6264; op. cit.).

29. Raymond Grenier, op. cit., p. 27.

30. Ibid, p. 43; the advantages of an islands site for Expo are summarized in John and Margaret Gold, *Cities of Culture*, p. 115: sequestration and compensation would be less of an issue; opposition would be less likely, except for from wildlife groups opposed to the destruction of bird habitats and the residents of St. Lambert, who lived nearby; the location aligned with Montreal's "'linguistic geography'," being situated as it was between the English- and French-speaking areas of the city; and it met Mayor Drapeau's objective to be near the city's transportation system. Last, but hardly least, the island settings were dramatic and spectacular, "magical" even.

    Though the original act creating the Expo corporation required any site to be situated on the island of Montreal itself, a Cabinet Minute of 1963/03/05 indicated that no one felt changing that act would be a serious problem. See also Raymond Grenier, op cit., pp. 44–47.

31. Yves Jasmin, Oct. 28/09.

32. Corinne Sévigny, op cit.

33. Author interview with Jean-Louis Roux, Montreal, Feb. 10/09.

34. Cited in Raymond Grenier, op. cit., p. 48.

35. Author interview with Tom Kent, Kingston, Ontario, April 22/09.

36. See Andrew Cohen, *Lester B. Pearson* (2008), p. 165.

37. Author interview with Alan Hustak, Montreal, Oct. 21/08.

38. See Raymond Grenier, op. cit., p. 58; Lester Pearson was trying in those early days to get a handle on costs: according to a Cabinet Minute of 1963/08/14, he outlined

a fifty-million-dollar federal commitment, which included twenty million dollars to capital cost and twenty-one million to the Canadian Pavilion, with the remainder to be allocated to an ice boom to protect the site from the vicissitudes of the St. Lawrence (RG2 PCO Series A-5-a, op. cit.).

39. Raymond Grenier, op. cit., p. 59.

TWO: DRAPEAU

1. See Brian McKenna and Susan Purcell, *Drapeau* (1980), p. 156.
2. Lester B. Pearson, *Mike: The Memoirs of the Rt. Hon. Lester B. Pearson, Volume Three* (1975), p. 306.
3. Brian McKenna and Susan Purcell, op. cit., pp. 21, 29.
4. See *Derniere Heure, Édition Spéciale: Hommage à Jean Drapeau 1916–1999*, project manager Annie-France Charbonneau (1999), p. 11.
5. Brian McKenna and Susan Purcell, op. cit., p. 158.
6. Yves Jasmin, *La petite histoire,* op. cit., p. 23.
7. Corinne Sévigny, op. cit.
8. Raymond Grenier, op. cit., pp. 46–47.
9. Email to author from Yves Jasmin, July 9/09; see also Raymond Grenier, op. cit., p. 50; St. Lambert challenged Montreal, claiming that Île Notre Dame would be within its boundary and it should thus receive revenues.
10. Yves Jasmin, email to author, July 9/09.
11. Author interview with Yves Jasmin, Montreal, Feb. 11/09.
12. Author interview with Steven Staples, Toronto, March 24/09; the French architect in question, Taillibert, would later be engaged by Drapeau to design the velodrome for the Montreal Olympic Games of 1976.
13. Jean-Louis Roux, op. cit.
14. Attachment to letter from Lucien Piché to Paul Bienvenu, 31/05/63: *Le thème "Terre des Hommes" et son developpement à l'Exposition Universelle Canadienne de Montréal en 1967* (i.e., The report from the Montebello Group), p. 3. (RG71, V.155, Sommaries No.10 1963)
15. Moshe Safdie, *Beyond Habitat by 20 Years* (1987), p. 89.
16. Yves Jasmin, *La petite histoire,* p. 144.
17. Author interview with Krystyne Griffin, Toronto, Sept. 23/08.
18. Corinne Sévigny, op. cit.

THREE: *LES DURS*

1. Author interview with Gloria Bishop, Toronto, Sept. 24/08.
2. Charles Ritchie, *The Siren Years: A Canadian Diplomat Abroad 1937–1945* (2001), p. 156.

3. Cited in "Expo 67 Top Man, Pierre Dupuy, Dies in France," *The Gazette* (Montreal), May 22/69, p. 25.

4. See Brian McKenna and Susan Purcell, op. cit., p. 149.

5. Author interview with Diana Thébaud Nicholson, Montreal, Oct. 1/08.

6. Ibid.

7. From Robert Shaw obituary in *The Gazette* (Montreal), by Alan Hustak, March 24/01, p. A4.

8. Ibid.; person cited is Yves Jasmin.

9. Author interview with Gretta Chambers, Montreal, April 30/09.

10. Diana Thébaud Nicholson, op. cit.

11. Author interview with Jean Cournoyer, Montreal, Feb. 10/09.

12. Author interview with Jerry Miller, Montreal, April 30/09.

13. Diana Thébaud Nicholson, op. cit.

14. Pierre Dupuy, *Expo 67*, pp. 31–32; Writing as Marshall Delaney (*Saturday Night,* May 1967, p. 23), Robert Fulford noted that while Fiset "in theory" had the right to veto any building whose design he did not approve, this did not always happen. "In most cases" where there were fights, Fiset and the Expo design people had their way.

15. Author interview with Andrew Kniewasser, Nepean, Ontario, Aug. 27/08.

16. Author telephone interview with Yves Jasmin, Sept. 12/08.

17. Andrew Kniewasser, op. cit.

18. Roger D. Landry, op. cit.

19. Diana Thébaud Nicholson, op. cit.

20. Author interview with Philippe de Gaspé Beaubien, Montreal, Oct. 22/08.

21. Gretta Chambers, op. cit.

22. Author interview with Philippe de Gaspé Beaubien, Montreal, Oct. 27/09.

23. Philippe de Gaspé Beaubien, Oct. 22/08.

24. Ibid.

25. Author telephone interview with Pierre de Bellefeuille, March 16/09.

26. Yves Jasmin, *La petite histoire*, p. 46.

27. Diana Thébaud Nicholson, op. cit.

28. Yves Jasmin, Oct. 2/08.

29. Pierre de Bellefeuille, op. cit.

30. Yves Jasmin, *La petite histoire*, p. 297; Philippe de Gaspé Beaubien, Oct. 22/08.

31. Andrew Kniewasser, op. cit.; according to Kniewasser, spouses likewise formed an unofficial club. His wife, Jacqueline, was a great friend of Mme Drapeau, and they and the wives of Drapeau's right-hand man Lucien Saulnier and Quebec Minister of Trade Gerard D. Lévesque would frequently meet for lunch.

32. Ibid.

33. Author interview with Charles Oberdorf, Toronto, Feb. 16/09.

34. Andrew Kniewasser, op. cit.

35. Pierre de Bellefeuille, Mar. 16/09.

36. Peter Kohl cited in *Maclean's* June 1967, found on the internet as part of *The Expo 67 in Montreal: Using the Critical Path Method (CPM) to Build Expo 67*, http://expo67.ncf.ca/expo67_critical_path_method_p5.html.

37. Andrew Kniewasser, op. cit.

38. Author interview with Blanche Lemco van Ginkel and Daniel "Sandy" van Ginkel, Toronto, Jan. 14/09; Claude Robillard had been committed to the restoration of Old Montreal and the South Shore. He died at the age of fifty-six after a long illness in May 1968. Robillard and the initial Expo commissioners, Bienvenu and Carsley, were "the upper crust," says Diana Thébaud Nicholson, "they really weren't used to getting their hands dirty" (Diana Thébaud Nicholson, op. cit.)

39. Blanche Lemco van Ginkel, Jan. 14/09.

40. Pierre Berton, op cit., p. 305; Author telephone interview with Moshe Safdie, Dec. 30/09; Safdie says that he came up with the "spines" concept, but his colleague planner Adèle Naudé (later Adèle Naudé Santos) developed it.

41. Author interview with Steven Staples, Toronto, April 2/09.

42. Steven Staples, March 24/09; Moshe Safdie would write: "Beaudoin arrived with a scheme that displayed such a lack of understanding of the city, in terms of where people came in and where people left, where the subway alignment was and other such mundane facts, that it just came to a natural end" (*Beyond Habitat by 20 Years,* p. 70).

43. Ibid.

44. Letter from Sandy van Ginkel to Edward Churchill, Oct. 26/63 (courtesy of Steven Staples).

45. Letter from Pierre Dupuy to Steven Staples, Oct. 29/63 (courtesy of Steven Staples).

46. Raymond Grenier, op. cit., p. 82.

47. Andrew Kniewasser, op. cit.

48. René Lévesque, op. cit., p. 184.

49. See "Premier Calls Expo Terrific," *The Montreal Star,* April 17/67, p. 3.

50. Philippe de Gaspé Beaubien, Oct. 22/08.

51. See Michel Dumas, Master's thesis, *Public Relations at Montreal's Expo 67 as Seen in the Light of a Model of Quality for World Exhibitions* (1972), p. 60.

52. Andrew Kniewasser, op. cit.

53. Michel Dumas, op. cit., pp. 73–78.

54. Author interview with Larry Schachter, Toronto, May 6/09.

55. Raymond Grenier, op. cit., p. 58: The design was adopted March 13, 1964, but not without great controversy (a number of politicians did not warm to these "stick men").

56. Raymond Grenier, op. cit., p. 96.

57. See Michel Dumas, op. cit., p. 83.

58. Larry Schachter, op. cit.

59. Author telephone interview with Jane Pequegnat Burns, Jan. 2/09.

60. Author interview with Alan Hustak, Montreal, Oct. 21/08.

61. Charles Oberdorf, op. cit.

62. See Yves Jasmin, *La petite histoire,* p. 84.

FOUR: THE OTHER MAYOR

1. *The Montreal Star,* April 28/67; see Don Foley, "Expo 'First' to be his last," p. 3; Harold Poitras, "All-night visit to be first," p. 3.

2. Andrew Kniewasser, op. cit.

3. Yves Jasmin, *La petite histoire,* p. 137.

4. Philippe de Gaspé Beaubien, Oct. 22/08.

5. Yves Jasmin, *La petite histoire,* pp. 83–84.

6. Author telephone interview with Philippe de Gaspé Beaubien, Sept. 4/08.

7. Charles Friend et al. (Eds.) (Expo Public Relations Department, Oct. 1967), *The Expo 67 Story,* vol. 1, *April 27–July 31,* p. 44. The person collecting these figures might have gotten a little carried away, since they add up to 105 percent.

8. Philippe de Gaspé Beaubien, Oct. 22/08.

9. "Ban taxis from La Ronde," *The Montreal Star,* June 1/67, p. 2.

10. See Walter Poronovich, "Control Room is all Nerves," *The Montreal Star,* April 13/67, p. 10.

11. Executive Central Registry correspondence, daily OPS logs from the Canadian Corporation for the 1967 World Exhibition Fonds (LAC-BAC), RG 71 series; date of entry: May 24/67.

12. Philippe de Gaspé Beaubien, Oct. 22/08.

13. Ibid.

14. Ibid.; see Yves Jasmin, *La petite histoire,* pp. 249–250: From October 14, 1965, to July 13, 1966, thirteen million passports had been sold in advance at the $20 level; from August 1, 1966, until February 28, 1967, they sold at $22.50, then were upped to $25 for the period from March 1, 1967, to April 27, 1967. Around ten million passports were sold after the April 28, 1967, opening for $35. Daily admission to the Expo site was $2.50.

15. Philippe de Gaspé Beaubien, Oct. 22/08.

16. Steven Staples, March 24/09.

17. Steven Staples, April 2/09; Expo Express could carry thirty thousand persons an hour from one end of the exhibition to the other (Michel Dumas, op. cit., p. 43).

18. Ibid.; the Blue Minirail cost fifty cents and the two Yellow Minirails cost twenty-five cents each. All three systems were approximately six miles each in length.

19. Ibid.; see also Wikipedia biography of Josef Kates http://en.wikipedia.org/wiki/Josef_Kates.

20. Canadian Corporation for the World Exhibition, *Rules for the Calculation of Building Areas and Volumes,* January 1965; buildings could cover a minimum of 40 percent up to a maximum of 60 percent of their assigned lot.

21. Rhona Richman Kenneally and Johanne Sloan (Eds.), *Expo 67: Not Just a Souvenir,* p. 17.

22. Robert Fulford, *This Was Expo,* pp. 21–23.

23. Paul Arthur's key link between the Canadian design community and the modernist design of Europe was recognized in an award he received from the Society of Graphic Designers in 1996.

24. Author interview with William Thorsell, Toronto, Dec. 4/08.

25. Yves Jasmin, *La petite histoire,* p. 69.

26. Author interview with Arlene Perly Rae, Toronto, Jan. 9/09.

27. Author interview with Louise Arbour, Toronto, May 13/09.

28. Robert Shaw quoted by Alan Hustak, *The Gazette* (Montreal), April 28/97.

29. Eva-Marie Kröller, op. cit., p. 48.

30. Author interview with Graham Fraser, Ottawa, June 17/09.

31. Author interview with Bruce Kidd, Toronto, April 9/09.

32. Author interview with Ann Malcolmson, Toronto, Jan. 28/09.

33. Alfred Heller, *World's Fairs and the End of Progress: An Insider's View* (1999), pp. 97–98.

34. Author interview with Nan-b de Gaspé Beaubien, Montreal, Oct. 22/08.

35. Author interview with Deirdre McIlwraith, Montreal, April 30/09.

36. Philippe de Gaspé Beaubien, Oct. 27/09.

37. Author interview with Nan-b de Gaspé Beaubien, Montreal, Oct. 27/09.

38. Gretta Chambers, op. cit.

39. Philippe de Gaspé Beaubien, Oct. 22/08.

40. Pierre de Bellefeuille, op. cit.

41. Diana Thébaud Nicholson, op. cit.

42. Gretta Chambers, op. cit.

43. Philippe de Gaspé Beaubien, Oct. 27/09.

44. Erik Larson, op. cit., p. 153.

45. John Allwood, op. cit., p. 162.

46. Author interview with Andrew Hoffman, Montreal, May 1/09.

47. Philippe de Gaspé Beaubien, Oct. 27/09.

48. Sean C. Kelly and Ronald S. Wareham (Eds.), *Expo Inside Out!* (1967), p. 16.

49. See John Gray "Gyrotron Box Office Is Riding High, Too," *The Montreal Star,* Sept. 28/67, p. 12.

50. Christopher Plummer, *In Spite of Myself: A Memoir* (Toronto: Alfred A. Knopf, 2008), p. 459.

51. Andrew Hoffman, op. cit.

52. Philippe de Gaspé Beaubien, Oct. 27/09.

FIVE: AT THE PAVILLON

1. Author interview with Krystyne Griffin, Toronto, Sept. 16/08.
2. Roger D. Landry, op. cit.
3. Author interview with Krystyne Griffin, Toronto, Sept. 23/08.
4. Andrew Kniewasser, op. cit.
5. Yves Jasmin, *La petite histoire*, p. 17.
6. Ibid., p. 15.
7. Krystyne Griffin, Sept. 16/08.
8. Ibid.; according to author Peter Stursberg, Governor General Roland Michener concluded Lulu was actually a "he" after hearing that "somebody saw it cock its leg against a piece of furniture" (Peter Stursberg, *Roland Michener: The Last Viceroy*, 1989, p. 175).
9. Lionel Chevrier, *The Montreal Star*, May 23/67.
10. Andrew Kniewasser, op. cit.

SIX: WONDERS OF THE WORLD: PART ONE

1. Moshe Safdie, *Beyond Habitat by 20 Years*, p. 66; according to Steven Staples (March 24/09), Dupuy wanted the key nations on Île Ste. Hélène, with France and Britain immediately in front, Ontario on one side, Quebec on the other. The planning group blocked him: "They had ideas much more related to how things operate."
2. Aude Hendrick, "Les pays africains à l'Expo 67: symboles du changement," in Denis Monière and Robert Comeau (Eds.), op. cit., p. 85.
3. Ibid., p. 86; see "No Racial Bias, Expo Chiefs Agree," *The Montreal Star*, April 5/67, p. 5.
4. Charles Friend et al. (Eds.), op. cit., vol. 1, p. 87.
5. Ibid., p. 59.
6. See Pierre Dupuy, *Expo 67*, p. 61.
7. See Bruce Taylor, "Montreal days and nights" (column), *The Montreal Star*, June 23/67, p. 4.
8. See "Arab Pavilion Unruffled, Police Remove Expo Hecklers," *The Montreal Star*, June 9/67, p. 22.
9. Pierre de Bellefeuille, op. cit.
10. Pierre Dupuy, *Expo 67*, p. 49.
11. Ibid., p. 64.
12. Yves Jasmin, *La petite histoire*, p. 63.
13. Charles Friend et al. (Eds.), op cit., vol. 2, *Aug. 1–Oct. 29, 1967*, p. 2.
14. Bruno Paul Stenson, "Some Expo 67 Pavilions That Were Never Built." http://expo67.ncf.ca/never_built_index.html

15. Charles Friend et al. (Eds.), op. cit., vol. 1, p. 18.
16. Pierre Dupuy, *Expo 67*, p. 47.
17. Pierre de Bellefeuille, op. cit.
18. Robert Fulford, op. cit., p. 192.
19. James Acland, "Expo: The Space Frame Fair," *artscanada*, May 1967, p. 4.
20. Charles Friend et al. (Eds.), op. cit., vol. 2, p. 16.
21. Tony Burman, "Haiti Marks National Day in Tight Web of Security," *The Montreal Star*, Aug. 21/67, p. 23.
22. Pierre Dupuy, *Expo 67*, p. 43, French orig: *"Quel meilleur endroit pour faire une démonstration de civilisation?"*
23. Ibid., p. 45.
24. John M. Lee, "Again the U.S. and U.S.S.R Are Rivals," *The New York Times*, April 23/67, p. 185.
25. See John Allwood, op. cit., pp. 154–155 for the contrast in 1958 between the United States and Soviet Union.
26. "U.S. Show Disappoints Romney," *The Montreal Star*, May 18/67, p. 12; see Virginia Anderson, "Locating the Map: Jasper Johns, Buckminster Fuller and the 1967 Expo Lecture" (2006), p. 4.
27. *Expocheck Report,* http://jdpecon.com/expo/expo67.html.
28. Mark Robson, cited in Charles Friend et al. (Eds.), op. cit., vol. 1, p. 44.
29. Charles Oberdorf, op. cit.
30. Alan Hustak, Oct. 21/08.
31. Alfred Heller, op. cit., p. 99.
32. Author interview with Harry Malcolmson, Toronto, Jan. 28/09.
33. Charles Friend et al. (Eds.), op. cit., vol. 1, p. 40.
34. John Allwood, op. cit., p. 169.
35. Charles Oberdorf, op. cit.
36. Ada Louise Huxtable, op. cit.
37. Charles Friend et al. (Eds.), op. cit., vol. 1, p. 34.
38. James Acland, op. cit., p. 6.
39. Robert Stall, "Beatles Out, But UK Swings," *The Montreal Star*, April 22/67, p. 12.
40. Aurora Wallace, "Girl Watching at Expo 67," in Richman Kenneally and Johanne Sloan (Eds.), op. cit., p. 118.
41. "Mini-skirts banned in St. Peter's," *The Montreal Star*, Sept. 15/67, p. 1.
42. James Acland, op. cit.
43. Ada Louise Huxtable, op. cit.
44. Samy Mesli, op. cit., p. 66.
45. John Allwood, op. cit., p. 169.
46. Author interview with Jean Thérèse Riley, Toronto, Jan. 12/09.
47. Yves Jasmin, Oct. 2/08.
48. Author interview with Rod Robbie, Toronto, April 17/09.

49. John Allwood, op. cit., pp. 141, 156.

50. Mordecai Richler, op. cit.

51. Rod Robbie, op. cit. One of Robbie's partners, Australian-born Colin Vaughan, would suggest turning the Expo site into an urban development for 75,000 to 100,000 persons, a "laboratory [that can] determine the ideal future forms of the city, and the … housing units could be the means of underwriting a program for the industrialization of housing, thus helping to solve the housing crisis in all cities of Canada" and "Says Expo could house 100,000," *The Montreal Star*, Oct. 3/67, p. 15. Colin Vaughan went on to become a familiar figure in Toronto, as both politician and television pundit.

52. Author interview with James Ramsay, Toronto, Jan. 21/09.

53. William Thorsell, op. cit.

54. Don O'Hearn, "'Expo Model Is 'Superlative,'" *Cornwall Standard-Freeholder*, March 3/65, p. 4 (courtesy of Helga Plumb).

55. Robert Fulford, "Two Images at Expo: Ontario and Quebec," *Toronto Star*, April 26/67, p. 43.

56. Randal Arthur Rogers, Master's thesis, *Man and His World: An Indian, A Secretary and a Queer Child, Expo 67 and the Nation in Canada* (1999), p. 62, http://spectrum.library.concordia.ca/923/1/MQ43681.pdf.

57. Author interview with Helga Plumb, Toronto, June 9/09.

58. Robert Fulford, "Two Images at Expo."

59. Ray Timson, "Ontario's a Winner Hands Down over Quebec in Expo Pavilion," *Toronto Star*, April 19/67, p. 1.

60. Audrey Stankiewicz, "The Last Word," *Canadian Architect*, Dec. 1967, p. 50.

61. Charles Friend et al. (Eds.), op. cit., vol. 1, p. 50.

62. Ada Louise Huxtable, op. cit.

63. Author telephone interview with Moshe Safdie, Jan. 26/10.

64. Author interview with John Hillier, Toronto, Sept. 29/11.

SEVEN: NEIGHBOURS

1. According to Lester Pearson in his memoirs, the Canadians did not learn of President Johnson's impending arrival until the day before (Lester Pearson, op. cit. p. 307).

2. "Dorothy Parker, Humorist, Dies at 73," *The Montreal Star*, June 8/67, p. 28; see "Mrs. Luce Delighted by Expo," *The Montreal Star*, May 29/67, p. 7.

3. Author interview with Barry Lord, Toronto, Dec. 1/08.

4. Author interview with Donna Mergler, Montreal, April 30/09.

5. William Thorsell, op. cit.

6. "Montreal Sees Little of LBJ," *The Montreal Star*, May 25/67, p. 1.

7. Pierre Dupuy, *Expo 67*, p. 161.

8. Gretta Chambers, op. cit.

9. Lester Pearson, op. cit., pp. 126–128.

10. Tom Kent, op. cit.

11. Robert Bothwell, *Alliance and Illusion: Canada and the World, 1945–1984* (2007), p. 234.

12. Graham Fraser, op. cit.

13. Lester Pearson, op. cit., p. 145.

14. See "Mrs. Johnson to be with Luci for first grandchild's birth," *The Montreal Star*, June 15/67, p. 56.

15. See Tony Burman, "Inveterate Sightseer Carries Texas Drawl," *The Montreal Star*, Aug. 21/67, p. 16; Joyce Douglas, "Lady Bird Praises Montreal for Its Good Housekeeping," *The Montreal Star*, Aug. 22/67, p. 38.

16. Charles Friend et al. (Eds.), op. cit., vol. 2, p. 14; see also John Gray, "So Lady Bird Really Looked," *The Montreal Star*, Aug. 22/67, p. 8.

17. Bruce Taylor, op. cit., Aug. 24/67.

18. Krystyne Griffin, Sept. 23/08.

EIGHT: WONDERS OF THE WORLD: PART TWO

1. Barry Lord, op. cit.

2. Eva-Marie Kröller, op. cit., p. 47.

3. James Acland, op. cit.

4. Author interview with Mark Starowicz, Toronto, Dec. 2/09; *The Gazette* reporter Nick auf der Maur did his best to create the tempest in this particular teapot.

5. Audrey Stankiewicz, op. cit., p. 49.

6. See Charles Friend et al. (Eds.), op. cit., vol. 1, p. 39.

7. Charles Oberdorf, op. cit.

8. E. J. Kahn, Jr., "Our Far-Flung Correspondents: Expo," *The New Yorker*, June 10/67, p. 132.

9. Mark Starowicz, op. cit.

10. See John M. Lee, "Cuban Goods Pose Expo 67 Problem," *The New York Times*, April 23/67, p. 30.

11. See Frank Moritsugu, "Expo Pavilion Disappoints: Japan Hits, But Misses," *The Montreal Star*, May 15/67, p. 10.

12. E. J. Kahn, Jr., op. cit., p. 135.

13. Audrey Stankiewicz, op. cit., p. 50.

14. Barry Lord, op. cit.

15. E. J. Kahn, Jr., op. cit., p.137.

16. Blanche Lemco van Ginkel, *International Universal Exhibition 1967*, p. 15; see Letter from Lucien Piché to Paul Bienvenu, May 31/63, op. cit.

17. Fred Bruemmer, "Expo 67: Man in the Community," *Canadian Geographical Journal*, June 1967, p. 181.

18. See Michel Dumas, op. cit., p. 39.

19. Robert Fulford, *This Was Expo*, p. 148.

20. Andrew Kniewasser, op. cit. According to Michel Dumas (op. cit., p. 52), the first economic and market research program done for the CCWE was from Southern California Laboratories of the Stanford Research Institute and submitted in March 1964. It projected potential attendance to be forty-five million, but probable attendance at twenty-six million. Steven Staples noted: "My recollection is that the mid-range forecast was for 26 million attendance. As for saying we should design for 12 year olds—no it [the SRI] did not. Andy was being Andy in saying that. We settled on 30 million as the planning figure for facilities and bore in mind that the Master Plan should be flexible to accommodate any eventuality: lower or higher attendance than planned for." Staples estimates that the actual number of individuals attending (many returning numerous times) was between 18.5 and 20 million (Steven Staples, December 11, 2011).

21. Michel Dumas, op. cit., p. 59.

22. Gary Miedema, op. cit., p. 142–145.

23. Ibid., pp. 162, 169.

24. Ibid, p. 164. See also, Monika Kin Gagnon, "The Christian Pavilion at Expo 67: Notes from Charles Gagnon's archive," in Richman Kenneally and Johanne Sloan (Eds.), op. cit.

25. Gary Miedema, op. cit., p. 177.

26. Ibid., p. 174.

27. Ibid., pp. 148, 152.

28. Ibid., pp. 157, 158, 194, 196–197.

29. See Ivan Carel, "L'Expo 67 et la jeunesse," in Denis Monière and Robert Comeau (Eds.), op. cit., p. 105.

30. Author interview with Monique Simard, Montreal, April 30/09.

NINE: ICONS

1. Moshe Safdie, *Beyond Habitat by 20 Years*, p. 87.

2. Nicolai Ouroussoff, "Fixing Earth One Dome at a Time," *The New York Times*, July 4/08, p. B21.

3. James Sterngold, "The Love Song of R. Buckminster Fuller," *The New York Times*, June 15/08, p. 26 AR.

4. Nicolai Ouroussoff, op. cit., p. B24.

5. Robert Fulford, *This Was Expo*, p. 56.

6. Nicolai Ouroussoff, op. cit.

7. Robert Fulford, *This Was Expo*, p. 39.

8. Author interview with Peter Hamilton, Toronto, June 30/09.

9. Author interview with Adrienne Clarkson, Toronto, March 27/09.

10. Patrick Watson, *This Hour Has Seven Decades* (2004), p. 298.

11. Author interview with Patrick Watson, Toronto, March 30/09.

12. Moshe Safdie, *Beyond Habitat by 20 Years*, pp. 53, 57, 58.

13. Ibid., pp. 62, 65, 76.

14. Ibid., pp. 80, 95.

15. Author telephone interview with Moshe Safdie, Dec. 3/09.

16. Moshe Safdie, *Beyond Habitat by 20 Years*, p. 91.

17. Author telephone interview with Moshe Safdie, Jan. 26/10.

18. Moshe Safdie, *Beyond Habitat by 20 Years*, pp. 93, 98.

19. Ibid., pp. 89, 92.

20. See Robert Fulford, *This Was Expo*, pp. 114–115.

21. Moshe Safdie, *Beyond Habitat by 20 Years*, p. 127.

22. Ibid., p. 129.

23. Ibid., pp. 89, 130.

24. Ibid., p. 132.

25. Ibid., p. 136.

26. Ibid., pp. 137, 138.

27. Ibid., p. 141.

28. Charles Friend et al. (Eds.), op. cit., vol. 1, p. 42.

29. Myrna Gopnik and Irwin Gopnik, "Generative Architecture: Moshe Safdie," *artscanada,* August/September 1971, p. 39.

30. Moshe Safdie, *Beyond Habitat by 20 Years*, p. 118.

TEN: SCREENINGS

1. Joseph Morgenstern, "Expo: The Point Is Pictures," *Newsweek,* July 17/67, p. 88.

2. See Alfred Heller, op. cit., p. 40.

3. John Allwood, op. cit., pp. 122, 144.

4. Alfred Heller, op cit., pp. 98–99.

5. Wendy Michener, "Where's It All Happening This Year? In Film, Baby," *Maclean's,* June 1963, p. 93.

6. Judith Shatnoff, "Expo 67: A Multiple Vision," *Film Quarterly*, Autumn 1967, p. 3.

7. Author interview with Graeme Ferguson, Toronto, June 10/09.

8. Judith Shatnoff, op. cit., p. 11.

9. Joseph Morgenstern, op. cit., p. 88.

10. Mordecai Richler, op. cit., p. 18.

11. "Shot while filming in U.S.: Montreal movie producer slain," *The Montreal Star,* Sept. 21/67, p. 3.

12. Author interview with Graeme Ferguson, Toronto, Oct. 22/09.

13. Author interview with Gar MacInnis, Toronto, May 26/09.

14. Nan-b de Gaspé Beaubien, Oct. 22/08.

15. "PM wants Disney film for Canada," *The Montreal Star*, Oct. 5/67, p. 19.

16. Jeremy Ferguson in email to author, Jan. 18/12.

17. Author interview with Beverly Hargraft, Toronto, Dec. 17/08.

18. James Ramsay, op. cit.

19. Author interview with Charles Pachter, Toronto, Dec. 5/08.

20. Leslie Scrivener, "Forty Years On, a Song Retains Its Standing," *Toronto Star*, April 22/07, p. D4.

21. Ibid.

22. Graeme Ferguson, op. cit. Chapman shot fifty-six kilometres of film over a period of two years, then had the film mounted with as many as fifteen images to a single frame on one 70 mm master print—what would have run some two and a half hours was condensed into seventeen and a half minutes (see Robert Fulford, *This Was Expo*, p.105).

23. Leslie Scrivener, op. cit.

24. "Expo Film Stirs Row in Ontario," *The Montreal Star*, Sept. 21/67, p. 9.

25. Ian Willoughby, "Kinoautomat," *Facsimile Magazine*, July 2008. www.facsimile magazine.com/2008/07/index.html

26. Author interview with Fred Langan, Toronto, April 29/10.

27. Author interview with Graeme Ferguson, Toronto, June 10/09.

28. Author interview with Roger Blais, Montreal, Feb. 11/09.

29. Patrick Watson, op. cit.

30. Robert Prévost, op. cit., p. 294.

31. André Loiselle, *Cinema as History: Michel Brault and Modern Quebec* (2007), p. 98.

32. Judith Shatnoff, op. cit., p. 2.

33. Moshe Safdie, *Beyond Habitat by 20 Years*, p. 100.

34. "Censors Ban Film at Festival," *The Montreal Star*, Aug. 8/67, p. 1.

35. Sandra Martin, "Allan King Made Empathetic Documentaries That Spoke Directly to the Human Condition," *The Globe and Mail*, June 16/09, p. S9.

36. Joan Irwin, "Canadian Film Festival Ends with Prize-Giving," *The Montreal Star*, Aug. 14/67, p. 14.

37. Moses Znaimer, email to author, Aug. 23/09.

38. Patrick Watson, op. cit.

39. Ibid.

40. Alan Hustak, Oct. 21/08.

41. See Mark Harris, *Pictures at a Revolution: Five Movies and the Birth of the New Hollywood* (2008), pp. 135–138, 148–154.

42. "Rap Brown Urges More Race Riots," *The Montreal Star*, July 28/67, p. 2.

43. Sydney Johnson, "Odd Choice From U.S. Opens Eighth Film Festival," *The Montreal Star*, Aug. 5/67, p. 26.

ELEVEN: ALTERED STATES

1. Author interview with Marianne McKenna, Toronto, Jan. 9/09.
2. Mordecai Richler, op. cit., p. 17.
3. Robert Prévost, op. cit., p. 389.
4. Brian McKenna and Susan Purcell, op. cit., p. 138.
5. Author interview with Jack Rabinovitch, Toronto, Oct. 15/08.
6. Fred Langan, op. cit.
7. Yves Jasmin, Oct. 2/08.
8. Author interview with Bill Bantey, Montreal, Oct. 28/09.
9. Charles Friend et al. (Eds.), op. cit., vol. 1, p. 23.
10. See Jean Paré, Editorial, *L'actualité*, May 1986, pp. 8–9, reprinted as "The Legacy of Jean Drapeau" in Geoffrey Simmins, *Documents in Canadian Architecture* (1992), pp. 290–293.
11. Bill Bantey, op. cit.
12. William Thorsell, op. cit.
13. Charles Oberdorf, op. cit.
14. Marianne McKenna, op. cit.
15. Louise Arbour, op. cit.
16. Mark Starowicz, op. cit.
17. Donna Mergler, op. cit.
18. André Loiselle, op. cit., p. 68: "By the late sixties and early seventies, a large number of Quebeckers, especially baby boomers, had come to call themselves *Québécois* rather than *Canadiens français*…"
19. "Fleur-de-lys to Be Flown at Government Buildings," *The Montreal Star*, June 26/67, p. 33.
20. "City Taxi Drivers Must Be Bilingual," *The Montreal Star*, May 4/67, p. 5.
21. In 1956, Jean Drapeau had demonstrated against the decision to name the new CNR hotel the Queen Elizabeth rather than Chateau Maisonneuve (Brian McKenna and Susan Purcell, op. cit., p. 106).
22. On the other hand, the times were not moving quickly enough. See René Lévesque, op. cit., p. 288: "We weren't told to 'Speak White!' any more, but we were still obliged to do so in many cases, right here in our own home."
23. See Richman Kenneally and Sloan, op. cit., p.17.
24. Jay Walz, "A 'Sin City' No More: Mayor Acclaims Montreal, the Home of Expo, as Great and Respectable," *The New York Times*, April 29/67, p. 16.
25. Bruce Taylor, op. cit., Sept. 1/67.
26. Michel Tremblay, *The Red Notebook* (2004), pp. 64–65.
27. Gratien Gélinas cited in "Gélinas donates prize to defend dancers," *The Montreal Star*, Oct. 27/67, p. 3.
28. Author interview with Judy Rebick, Toronto, June 11/09. The term "counter-culture" is credited to Theodore Roszak, whose *The Making of a Counter Culture:*

Reflections on the Technocratic Society appeared in 1969 after the Woodstock Festival (see obituary for Theodore Roszak in *The New York Times*, July 13/11, p. A24.

29. "Rolling Stones Sentenced to Prison," *The Montreal Star*, June 29, 1967, p. 41; Mick Jagger waged a successful appeal and proclaimed, "What I do with my consciousness is my own business"; see Anthony Lincoln, "Debate Reopened: Privacy and the Law," *The Montreal Star*, Aug. 12/67, p. 7.

30. "Fonteyn, Nureyev Arrested," *The Montreal Star*, July 11/67 , p. 1; "Fonteyn, Nureyev Cleared," *The Montreal Star*, July 12/67, p. 39.

31. "MPs, Beatles, plead for 'pot' smoker," *The Montreal Star*, July 24/67, p. 15.

32. Judy Rebick, op. cit.

33. Author interview with Susan Swan, Toronto, July 1/09.

34. Tony Burman, "Draft Card Burning Upsets U.S. Officials," *The Montreal Star*, Aug. 8/67; Charles Friend et al. (Eds.), op. cit., vol. 2, p. 5.

35. Alan Hustak, op. cit.

36. Ibid.

37. Mark Starowicz, op. cit.

38. Alan Hustak, op. cit.

39. William Thorsell, op. cit.

40. Rod Robbie, op. cit.

41. Author interview with Prudence Emery, Toronto, Sept. 22/09; "The carousing at the Beaver Club and the curious rituals engaged in by the members became legendary" (Robert Prévost, op. cit., p. 186).

42. Charles Oberdorf, op. cit.

43. Adrienne Clarkson, op. cit.

44. Author telephone interview with John Uren, May 14/09.

45. Mark Starowicz, op. cit.

46. Bill Bantey, op. cit.

TWELVE: SPECTACLES

1. David P. Silcox, "Art," *Canadian Annual Review* (1967), p. 480.

2. Andrew Hudson, "World Masterpieces at Superb Expo Show," *The Washington Post*, April 30/67, p. F8.

3. Frank Moritsugu, "Expo Photo Angers Greeks," *The Montreal Star*, April 11/67, p. 1.

4. Barry Lord, "Photography at Expo: The Camera as Witness," *artscanada*, June–July 1967, pp. 6–7.

5. Dusty Vineberg, "Guarding Sculptures Proving No Picnic," *The Montreal Star*, June 3/67, p. 10.

6. Charles Pachter, op. cit.: Calder's forty-one-tonne stainless steel sculpture, *Man*, was the largest single item at Expo aside from the buildings.

7. Robert Fulford, *This Was Expo*, p. 189.

8. David P. Silcox, op. cit., p. 482

9. Harry Malcolmson, "Sculpture: Disappointments at Expo," *Saturday Night*, July 1967, p. 43.

10. Ibid.

11. Author interview with Michael Snow, Toronto, Feb. 18/09.

12. Virginia Anderson, op. cit., p. 6.

13. John Canaday, "Exorcism in Montreal," *The New York Times*, April 30/67, p. D23.

14. Andrew Hudson, op. cit.

15. Barry Lord, Dec. 1/08.

16. Robert Helpmann, cited in "Expo Impresses Australian," *The Montreal Star*, May 23/67, p. 29.

17. Author interview with Mary Jolliffe, Toronto, Nov. 28/08.

18. Sir William Tyrone "Tony" Guthrie (1900–71) was an esteemed English theatre director who played a key role in the establishment of the Stratford Festival of Canada in 1953; a theatre was named after him in Minneapolis.

19. Pierre Dupuy, *Expo 67*, p. 122.

20. Mary Jolliffe, op. cit.

21. John Uren, op. cit.

22. Ibid.

23. Ibid; see also Helen Rochester, "The Duke Wows Them with Jazz," *The Montreal Star,* Sept. 6/67, p. 14.

24. Charles Friend et al. (Eds.), op. cit., vol. 2, p. 31.

25. John Uren, op. cit.

26. Sydney Johnson, "Marlene Dietrich Flies into a Problem: She'll Sing, Minus $100,000 Wardrobe," *The Montreal Star*, June 11/67, p. 4.

27. Mary Jolliffe, op. cit.

28. Krystyne Griffin, Sept. 23/08.

29. Author interview with John McGreevy, Toronto, April 15/09.

30. Bruno Paul Stenson, *(A) Man and His (Evolving) World*, p. 57.

31. Charles Oberdorf, op. cit.

32. Author interview with Ralph Heintzman, Toronto, Oct. 16/08.

33. Prudence Emery, op. cit.

34. Charles Friend et al. (Eds.), op. cit., vol. 1, pp. 43, 50.

35. Beverley Mitchell, "McLuhan May Have to Eat His Words," *The Montreal Star*, May 11/67, p. 21.

36. Monique Simard, op. cit.

37. Charles Friend et al. (Eds.), op. cit., vol. 1, p. 47.

38. "Dief Was Unofficial But Not Quite Incognito," *The Montreal Star*, July 19/67.

39. Bruce Taylor, op. cit., Aug. 4/67.

40. Ibid., July 7/67.

41. John McGreevy, op. cit.

42. Charles Friend et al. (Eds.), op. cit., vol. 2, p. 24.

43. Larry Schachter, op. cit.

44. Bruce Taylor, op. cit., Sept. 8/67.

45. Larry Schachter, op. cit.; Judith Thurman, "Helenism: The Birth of the Cosmo Girl," *The New Yorker*, May 11/09, p. 98.

46. Cynthia Gunn, "Glittering Party Ends Monaco Day," *The Montreal Star*, July 19/67, p. 53.

47. Yves Jasmin, *La petite histoire,* p. 109.

48. Author interview with Bernard Chevrier, Ottawa, June 17/09.

THIRTEEN: SIGNIFICANT BIRTHDAYS

1. John Fisher cited in Charles Friend et al. (Eds.), op. cit., vol. 1, p. 36.

2. See Helen Davies, *The Politics of Participation: Learning from Canada's Centennial Year* (2010), pp. 52, 53, 54.

3. Ibid., p. 97.

4. Ibid., p. 64; see also Stewart MacLeod, "The Time We'll Never Forget," *Weekend Magazine*, no. 43, 1967, p. 3, which mentions the burning of the privies in Bowsman, Man.

5. Judy LaMarsh, *Memoirs of a Bird in a Gilded Cage* (1969), p. 219.

6. Charles Friend et al. (Eds.), op. cit., vol. 1, p. 59.

7. Judy LaMarsh, op. cit., p. 224.

8. Lester Pearson, *Memoirs,* op. cit., p. 308.

9. "Rain Makes Icing on Cake Run," *The Montreal Star*, July 3/67, p. 5.

10. Charles Friend et al. (Eds.), op cit., vol. 1, p. 40.

11. William Thorsell, op. cit.

12. Dusty Vineberg, "'Futuristic' Music Puzzles Philip," *The Montreal Star*, July 4/67, p. 31. Otto Joachim's atonal music for Katimavik is thought to be the first score in Canada composed exclusively of electronically generated sound (see Alan Hustak, "Composer 'Laid Down Cultural Tracks,'" *The Globe and Mail*, Aug. 16/10, p. S10.

13. James Ramsay, op. cit.

14. Andrew Kniewasser, op. cit.

15. Lester Pearson, op. cit.

16. Pierre Dupuy, *Expo 67*, p. 152.

17. "RIN Recalls 1837 Rebellion," *The Montreal Star*, July 4/67, p. 30.

18. Charles Pachter, op. cit.

19. Yves Jasmin, *La petite histoire*, p. 109.

20. Lester Pearson, op. cit.

21. Peter Aykroyd, *The Anniversary Compulsion: Canada's Centennial Celebrations, A Model Mega-Anniversary* (1992), p. 169.

22. Judy LaMarsh, op. cit., pp. 181, 320.

23. Ibid., p. 180.

24. Peter Aykroyd, op. cit., p. 52.

25. Author interview with Peter Aykroyd, Kingston, Ontario, April 23/09.

26. Judy LaMarsh, op. cit., p. 194.

27. John Fisher cited in L. B. Kuffert, *A Great Duty: Canadian Responses to Modern Life and Mass Culture, 1939–1967* (2003), p. 226.

FOURTEEN: *VIVE LE QUÉBEC LIBRE!*

1. See Olivier Courteaux, "Foul-Weather Friend: How the War Disguised de Gaulle's Design," in Dimitry Anastakis (Ed.), *The Sixties: Passion, Politics, and Style* (2008), p. 121.

2. Pierre Godin, *Daniel Johnson: 1964–1968, la difficile recherche de l'égalité* (1980), pp. 195–196.

3. Olivier Courteaux, op. cit., p. 117.

4. Robert Bothwell, op. cit., p. 253.

5. Pierre Godin, op. cit, p. 213.

6. Ibid., p. 215.

7. Ibid., pp. 222, 223.

8. Ibid, p. 225.

9. Robert Bothwell, op. cit., p. 254.

10. See Pierre Godin, op. cit, p. 227; Olivier Courteaux, op. cit., pp. 116–125.

11. Jean Thérèse Riley, op. cit.

12. Author interview with Gail Corbett, Toronto, Sept. 18/08.

13. Louise Arbour, op. cit.

14. Monique Simard, op. cit.

15. Marianne McKenna, op cit.

16. René Lévesque, op. cit., p. 206.

17. Andrew Kniewasser, op. cit. Couve de Murville later described the general's actions as *"une connerie"* or major screw-up (Robert Bothwell, op. cit, p. 255).

18. Lester Pearson, op. cit., p. 268.

19. Bernard Chevrier, *Lionel Chevrier—un homme de combat* (1997), p. 177. Couve de Murville reassured Canadian foreign minister Paul Martin that the fuss over the speech would blow over and advised him to stay calm. Both Martin and Canada's ambassador to France, Jules Léger, accepted this view. But de Gaulle is reported to have spoken openly about Quebec independence with Lionel Chevrier during his Expo visit, and French officials had teased Chevrier (John English, *The Worldly Years: The Life of Lester Pearson, 1949–1972* (1992), p. 278).

20. "Place des Nations Display Non-political," *The Montreal Star*, July 25/67.

21. Pierre Dupuy, *Expo 67*, p. 157.

22. Michel Sarra-Bournet, "Les retombées politiques d'Expo 67 à travers le triangle Paris-Ottawa-Québec," in Denis Monière and Robert Comeau (Eds.), op. cit., p. 140.

23. Tim Burke, "Violence Erupts at Expo," *The Montreal Star*, July 25/67, p. 32.

24. John Uren, email to author, May 19/09.

25. Deirdre McIlwraith, op. cit.

26. Author interview with Yves Jasmin, Montreal, July 25/09.

27. "Penfield Declined Meal with de Gaulle," *The Montreal Star*, July 26/67.

28. Krystyne Griffin, Sept. 16/08.

29. "De Gaulle Debacle Leaves Micheners' Pantry Jammed," *The Montreal Star*, July 28/67.

30. Peter Stursberg, op. cit., p. 181.

31. Brian McKenna and Susan Purcell, op. cit., p. 166.

32. "Liberace Praises Habitat," *The Montreal Star*, July 27/67, p. 10.

33. Jean-Louis Roux, op. cit.

34. Jean Thérèse Riley, op. cit.

35. Lester Pearson, op. cit., p. 269.

36. See "Now Separatists Boo Drapeau," *The Montreal Star*, Aug. 14/67, p. 5; Bruce Taylor, op. cit., Aug. 23/67: "There was only polite applause when Premier Johnson joined the Place des Nations audience for the Boston Pops concert, but for Mayor Drapeau, a standing ovation ..."

37. "Text of de Gaulle's reply," *The Montreal Star*, July 27/67, p. 6.

38. "Dief's Reaction: Pearson Pussy-Footing," *The Montreal Star*, July 26/67.

39. Bernard Chevrier, June 17/09.

40. See "De Gaulle Talk Not Separatist," *The Montreal Star*, Aug.12/67; In the first public opinion poll since the speech, nearly 72 percent of French-speaking Quebeckers did not believe de Gaulle supported the separatist cause when he uttered "*Vive le Québec libre.*"

41. René Lévesque, op. cit., p. 208.

42. Robert Bothwell, op. cit., p. 258.

43. Bernard Chevrier, op. cit.

FIFTEEN: WINDING DOWN

1. Bruce Taylor, op. cit., July 28/67.

2. OPS Control Room Activity Log, op. cit., Aug. 3/67.

3. Brian McKenna, "Workers Chose to Sleep," *The Montreal Star*, Sept. 5/67, p. 10.

4. Canadian Corporation for 1967 World Exhibition (CCWE), *General Report on the World Exhibition*, volume 4, p. 1972.

5. See Larry Conroy, "Bomb Believed 'Inside Job,'" *The Montreal Star*, Sept. 19/67, p. 3.

6. CCWE, op. cit., pp. 1964–1965.

7. "Marilyn's Gown Vanishes," *The Montreal Star*, Oct. 4/67, p. 12.

8. Robert Fulford, *This Was Expo*, p. 188.

9. Charles Lazarus, "Logexpo in Trouble," *The Montreal Star*, July 10/67, p. 9.

10. "Quebec Closes Expo 'Motel,'" *The Montreal Star*, June 10/67, p. 3.

11. Philippe de Gaspé Beaubien, Oct. 27/09.

12. Raymond Heard, "Logexpo Reaches U.S. Senate," *The Montreal Star*, Aug. 17/67, p. 1.

13. Andrew Kniewasser, op. cit.

14. Philippe de Gaspé Beaubien, Oct. 27/09.

15. Charles Lazarus, "Beaubien Sees for Himself If Everything Is Shipshape," *The Montreal Star,* Sept. 14/67, p. 28.

16. Ibid.

17. Letter from Robert Winters to Robert Shaw, July 13/67 (MG 32, Series B 24, vol. 71, LAC-BAC).

18. Philippe de Gaspé Beaubien, Oct. 27/09.

19. Charles Friend et al. (Eds.), op. cit., vol. 2, p. 32.

20. Jean Cournoyer, op. cit.

21. Author telephone interview with Philippe de Gaspé Beaubien, Sept. 4/08.

22. See "Earnings total $106 million," *The Montreal Star*, Sept. 22/67, p. 23; see Ibid., "Expo Appeals for Service at Fair Site," Sept. 21/67, p. 1. The decision not to celebrate passing the Brussels fair's attendance figure is noted in John Gray, "Expo Scraps Celebration," *The Montreal Star*, Sept. 12/67, p. 10.

23. "His Alias Was Daily Warning," *The Montreal Star*, Aug.11/67, p. 17; see also Charles Friend et al. (Eds.), op. cit., vol. 2, p. 10.

24. OPS Control Room Activity Log, op. cit., Sept. 5/67.

25. Don Foley, "One Crowd Boos King, Another Cheers Him," *The Montreal Star*, Sept. 7/67, p. 3.

26. Sheila Arnopoulos, "Doyenne of Greek Theatre Plays Clytemnestra Tonight," *The Montreal Star*, Oct. 2/67, p. 11.

27. Krystyne Griffin, op. cit.

28. "Heavy Guard for Yugoslav," *The Montreal Star*, Sept. 2/67, p. 10.

29. Victor Steinberg, "Thant Cancels 'Africa' Tour After Bazooka Shell Found," *The Montreal Star*, Sept. 25/67, p. 14.

30. Moshe Safdie, *Beyond Habitat by 20 Years*, p. 175.

31. Doris Giller, "The Snowdons Enjoy Gay Social Whirl," *The Montreal Star*, Oct. 10/67, p. 40. The reporter in this instance was Doris Giller, who would eventually marry the developer-philanthropist Jack Rabinovitch. After her death, Jack Rabinovitch memorialized his late wife with what became one of Canada's premier literary awards, now called the Scotiabank Giller Prize.

32. Deirdre McIlwraith, op. cit.

33. Philippe de Gaspé Beaubien, Oct. 27/09.

34. John Gray, "'Mobs' Follow Jackie," *The Montreal Star*, Oct. 10/67, p. 47.

35. John Gray, "Boos Turn to Cheers," *The Montreal Star*, Oct. 7/67, p. 1.

36. Yves Jasmin, *La petite histoire,* p. 113.

37. Krystyne Griffin, op. cit.

38. "Bourgault Says Expo Has Hurt Separatism," *The Montreal Star*, July 10/67, p. 9.

39. Don Foley, "Noisy Separatist Mob Turns Fury on 'Train,'" *The Montreal Star*, Sept. 8/67, p. 1.

40. Bryan D. Palmer, *Canada's 1960s: The Ironies of Identity in a Rebellious Era* (2009), pp. 391–392.

41. Douglas Cardinal cited in Alanna Mitchell, "When the Good Times Rolled," *The Globe and Mail*, June 29/96, p. D1.

42. Helen Rochester, "Singer Seeks Self," *The Montreal Star*, June 13/67, p. 8.

43. John Gray, "Rain was bitter blow," *The Montreal Star*, Aug. 5/67, p. 10.

44. "Pow-Wow Washed Out by Rainfall," *The Montreal Star*, Aug. 5/67, p. 10.

45. Pierre Dupuy, *Expo 67,* p. 142.

46. Eva-Marie Kröller, op. cit., p. 42

47. Sheila Arnopoulos, "Variety Show Commemorates International Women's Day," *The Montreal Star*, June 6/67, p. 14.

48. Gloria Bishop, op. cit.

49. Judy LaMarsh, op. cit., p. 303.

50. Susan Swan, op. cit.

51. John Gray, "Visiting Micheners Go Almost Unnoticed," *The Montreal Star*, June 9/67, p. 21.

52. Doug Owram, op. cit., p. 271.

53. "Today's Women in Clover, Says Helen Gurley Brown," *The Montreal Star*, July 13/67, p. 6.

54. Frank Rich, "40 Years Later, Still Second-Class Americans," *The New York Times,* June 28/09, p. 8 WK.

55. Michel Tremblay, op. cit., p. 214.

56. John Uren, op. cit.

57. "UK House Votes 99 to 14 Homosexuality Bill Approved," *The Montreal Star*, July 4/67, p. 10.

58. The best essay on Scott Symons is by his friend Charles Taylor in the latter's *Six Journeys: A Canadian Pattern* (1977), pp. 189–243.

59. According to a Binghamton, New York, newspaper cited in Robert Fulford, *This Was Expo*, p. 59.

60. The discerning critic was Robert Fulford; as noted by Andrew Horrall, *Bringing Art to Life: A Biography of Alan Jarvis* (2009), p. 335.

61. Rick Bébout, *Promiscuous Affections: A Life in The Bar, 1969–2000*, www.rbebout.com/bar/1980.htm.

62. Graeme Ferguson, op. cit.

SIXTEEN: GOODBYE AND *AU REVOIR*

1. "Strikers Threaten to Close Expo Express Late Tonight ..." *The Montreal Star*, Oct. 13/67, p. 1.

2. Corinne Sévigny, op. cit.

3. Brian McKenna, "50 millionth visitor hailed," *The Montreal Star*, Oct. 30/67, p. 3.

4. Samy Mesli, op. cit., p. 69.

5. "Gala Ball Marks End of Expo," *The Montreal Star*, Oct. 30/67, p. 13.

6. Pierre Dupuy, *Expo 67*, p. 69.

7. John Gray, "Huge Parade May End Expo," *The Montreal Star*, Sept. 13/67, p. 3: At one point the thought was to have a parade through the site, up the Bonaventure Autoroute, and into the city—where it would end atop Mount Royal with a display of fireworks. The powers that be, who evidently had security concerns, decided to err on the side of caution and moderation.

8. John Yorston, "'Greatest of All Canada's Centennial Achievements,'" *The Montreal Star*, Oct. 30/67, p. 31.

9. "God Save the Queen Demoted," *The Montreal Star*, Oct. 30/67, p. 32.

10. "Michener's speech that wasn't given," *The Montreal Star*, Oct. 30/67, p. 33.

11. Andrew Kniewasser, op. cit.; Steven Staples (email to author Dec. 20/11) tells me that the actual number that last day was 221,554; the second-last day's attendance was 419,220.

12. Andrew Kniewasser, op. cit.

13. Peter Desbarats, op. cit.

14. Philippe de Gaspé Beaubien, Oct. 27/09.

15. Diana Thébaud Nicholson, op. cit.

16. Mary Jolliffe, op. cit.

SEVENTEEN: THE BEST PLACE TO BE

1. Tu Thanh Ha, "It Was the World Coming to Us, in a Joyous Fashion," *The Globe and Mail*, April 27/07, p. A3.

2. Doug Owram, op. cit., p. 311.

3. Graham Fraser, op. cit.

4. Author interview with Ramsay Cook, Toronto, March 31/09.

5. René Lévesque, op. cit., p. 229.

6. Ramsay Cook, *The Maple Leaf Forever*, p. 85.

7. Mark Starowicz, op. cit.

8. Louise Arbour, op. cit.

9. Monique Simard, op. cit.

10. Michel Sarra-Bournet, op. cit., p. 144; the average Montrealer probably visited Expo more than ten times (Ibid., p. 138).

11. David Anderson and Viviane Gosselin, "Private and Public Memories of Expo 67: A Case Study of Recollections of Montreal's World's Fair, 40 Years After the Event," (2008), pp. 11 and 14.

12. Author interview with Cathy Fauquier, Toronto, April 8/09.

13. Nan-b de Gaspé Beaubien, Oct. 22/08.

14. Philippe de Gaspé Beaubien, Oct. 27/09.

15. Diana Thébaud Nicholson, op. cit.

16. Mark Starowicz, op. cit.

17. Alan Hustak, "Shaw Engineered Expo 67's Success," *The Gazette* (Montreal), March 24/01, p. A4.

18. Andrew Kniewasser, op. cit.

19. "The Man Who Built Expo 67 Is Dead," *The Gazette* (Montreal), April 21/78, p. 3.

20. Author telephone interview with Moshe Safdie, Jan. 26/10.

21. Sandra Martin, "Visionary Urbanist Rescued Old Montreal from the Clutches of Freeway Enthusiast," *The Globe and Mail,* July 23/09, p. S8.

22. Pierre de Bellefeuille, op. cit.

23. "Success Succeeded by Success," *The Montreal Star*, May 25/67, p. 14.

24. Patricia Morrisroe, "The Death and Life of Perry Ellis," *New York Magazine,* Aug. 11/86, pp. 26–39.

25. John Gray, "No Cost Too High for Being a Canadian," *The Montreal Star*, Oct. 27/67, p. 1. The final deficit was reported as $210,664,811, representing the difference between costs of $431,904,683 and revenues of $221,239,872 (Exhibitions Information (1931–2005), "Previous Exhibitions," Bureau International des Expositions, *Expo 67—Wikipedia Encyclopedia,* retrieved 2007/06/04). In a note, Dec. 20/11, Steven Staples has costs of $418,014,300 and revenues of $216,315,100, and the final deficit as $201,699,200.

26. Philippe de Gaspé Beaubien, Oct. 27/09.

27. Rod Robbie, op. cit.

28. Andrew Hoffman, op. cit.

29. Bill Bantey, op. cit.

30. Philippe de Gaspé Beaubien, phone interview, Sept. 4/08.

31. Barrie McKenna, "Expo Bill Still Dogs Montreal," *The Globe and Mail,* Nov. 17/92, p. A1.

32. William Thorsell, op. cit.

33. Jack Rabinovitch, op. cit.

34. Bill Bantey, op. cit.

35. Moshe Safdie, Jan. 26/10.
36. Author telephone interview with Moshe Safdie, Dec. 3/09.
37. Author telephone interview with Moshe Safdie, Jan. 26/10.
38. Ibid.
39. Adam Gopnik, "The Return of the Native," *The New Yorker*, Sept. 7/09, p. 29.
40. Charles Pachter, op. cit.
41. Robert Fulford, *This Was Expo*, p. 30.
42. Gretta Chambers, "The Sixties in Print: Remembering Quebec's Quiet Revolution," in Dimitry Anastakis (Ed.), *The Sixties*, pp. 20–21.
43. Bill Bantey, op. cit.
44. Harry Malcolmson, Jan. 28/09.
45. Author telephone interview with Moshe Safdie, Dec. 3/09.

SELECT BIBLIOGRAPHY

BOOKS

Aykroyd, Peter H. *The Anniversary Compulsion: Canada's Centennial Celebrations, A Model Mega-Anniversary.* Toronto: Dundurn Press Limited, 1992.

Allwood, John. *The Great Exhibitions.* London: Cassel & Collier Macmillan Publishers, 1977.

Anastakis, Dimitry (Ed.). *The Sixties: Passion, Politics, and Style.* Montreal and Kingston: McGill-Queen's University Press, 2008.

Azzi, Stephen. *Walter Gordon and the Rise of Canadian Nationalism.* Montreal and Kingston: McGill-Queen's University Press, 1999.

Bantey, Bill. *Bill Bantey's Expo 67.* Montreal: The Gazette Printing Company, 1967.

Bébout, Rick. *Promiscuous Affections: A Life in the Bar, 1969–2000,* from http://rbebout.com, Toronto, 1999 (last revised June 2003; note added May 2008)

Berton, Pierre. *1967: Canada's Turning Point, A Chronicle of Canada's Centennial Year.* Toronto: Seal Books, 1998.

Bothwell, Robert. *Alliance and Illusion: Canada and the World, 1945–1984.* Vancouver: UBC Press, 2007.

———. *The Penguin History of Canada.* Toronto: The Penguin Group (Canada), 2006.

Canadian Corporation for the 1967 World Exhibition. *General Report on the 1967 World Exhibition* (multiple volumes). Ottawa: Queen's Printer, 1969.

———. *Terre des Hommes—Man and His World.* Ottawa: Canadian Corporation for the 1967 World Exhibition, 1967.

Canadian Annual Review. John Saywell (Ed.). Toronto: University of Toronto Press, 1967.

Cardinal, Jacqueline, and Laurent Lapierre. *Noblesse oblige: l'histoire d'un couple en affaires Philippe de Gaspé Beaubien et Nan-b de Gaspé Beaubien.* Montreal: Les Éditions Logiques, 2006.

Chevrier, Bernard. *Lionel Chevrier—un homme de combat.* Montreal: Éditions L'Interligne, 1997.

Cohen, Andrew. *The Unfinished Canadian: The People We Are.* Toronto: McClelland & Stewart Emblem, 2008.

———. *Lester B. Pearson* (Extraordinary Canadians Series). Toronto: The Penguin Group (Canada), 2008.

Cook, Ramsay. *The Maple Leaf Forever: Essays on Nationalism and Politics in Canada.* Toronto: Macmillan of Canada, 1971.

Davies, Helen. *The Politics of Participation: Learning from Canada's Centennial Year.* Toronto: MASS LBP, 2010.

DeGroot, Gerard J. *The Sixties Unplugged: A Kaleidoscopic History of a Disorderly Decade.* Boston, MA: Harvard University Press, 2008.

Dickinson, John (and Brian Young). *A Short History of Quebec*, Third Edition. Montreal and Kingston: McGill-Queen's University Press, 2003.

Dozois, Guy. *Terre des Hommes/Man and His World.* Ottawa: Canadian Corporation for the 1967 World Exhibition, 1967.

Dupuy, Pierre. *L'Expo 67 ou la découverte de la fierté.* Montreal: Éditions La Presse, 1972.

English, John. *The Worldly Years: The Life of Lester Pearson, Volume II: 1949–1972*, Toronto: Alfred A. Knopf Canada, 1992.

De Lorimier, Jean-Louis (Ed.). *Expo 67: The Memorial Album of the first category universal and international Exhibition held in Montreal from the twenty-seventh of April to the twenty-ninth of October nineteen hundred and sixty-seven.* Toronto: Thomas Nelson and Sons (Canada) Limited, 1968.

Expo 67: Official Guide. Toronto: Maclean-Hunter Publishing Company, 1967.

Friend, Charles, et al. (Eds.) (Expo Public Relations Department, October 1967). *The Expo 67 Story*, Volumes I and II. Compiled by PR team at Expo 67, 1967 (courtesy Yves Jasmin).

Ferguson, Jeremy. *Photography at Expo 67*, Kodak, 1967.

Findling, John E. (Ed.), Kimberly D. Pelle (Asst. Ed.). *Historical Dictionary of World's Fairs and Expositions, 1851–1988.* New York: Greenwood Press, 1990.

Fraser, Graham. *René Lévesque and the Parti Québécois in Power.* Toronto: Macmillan of Canada, 1984.

———. *Sorry, I Don't Speak French: Confronting the Canadian Crisis That Won't Go Away.* Toronto: McClelland & Stewart, 2007.

Freedman, Adele. *Sight Lines: Looking at Architecture and Design in Canada.* Toronto: Oxford University Press Canada, 1990.

Fulford, Robert. *This Was Expo.* Toronto: McClelland & Stewart, 1968.

———. *Remember Expo: A Pictorial Record.* Photographed by John de Visser, Harold Whyte, Peter Varley. Toronto: McClelland & Stewart, 1968.

Godin, Pierre. *Daniel Johnson: 1964–1968, la difficile recherche de l'égalité.* Montreal: Les Éditions de l'Homme, 1980.

Gold, John, and Margaret Gold. *Cities of Culture, Staging International Festivals and the Urban Agenda 1851–2005*. London: Ashgate, 2005.

Goodman, Donna. *A History of the Future*. New York: The Monacelli Press, 2008.

Granatstein, J. L. *Canada 1957–1967: The Years of Uncertainty and Innovation*. Toronto: McClelland & Stewart, 1986.

Grant, George. *Lament For a Nation: The Defeat of Canadian Nationalism* (Carleton Library Series 205). Montreal and Kingston: McGill-Queen's University Press, 2007.

Grenier, Raymond. *Inside Expo 67*. Translated by Patrick Gossage. Montreal: Les Éditions de l'Homme, 1965.

Gwyn, Richard. *Nationalism Without Walls: The Unbearable Lightness of Being Canadian*. Toronto: McClelland & Stewart, 1995.

Harris, Mark. *Pictures at a Revolution: Five Movies and the Birth of the New Hollywood*. New York: The Penguin Press, 2008.

Heller, Alfred. *World's Fairs and the End of Progress: An Insider's View*. Corte Madera, CA: World's Fair, Inc., 1999.

Hofsess, John. *Inner Views: Ten Canadian Film-Makers*. Toronto: McGraw-Hill Ryerson Limited, 1975.

Hood, Hugh. *Around the Mountain: Scenes from Montreal Life, The Collected Stories IV*. Erin, ON: The Porcupine's Quill, 1994.

Horrall, Andrew. *Bringing Art to Life: A Biography of Alan Jarvis*. Montreal and Kingston: McGill-Queen's University Press, 2009.

Jasmin, Yves. *La petite histoire d'Expo 67: l'Exposition Universelle et Internationale de Montréal comme vous ne l'avez jamais vue*. Editions Quebec/Amerique 1997.

Kael, Pauline. *Kiss Kiss Bang Bang*. Bantam Books: New York, 1969.

Kalman, Harold. *A Concise History of Canadian Architecture*. Toronto: Oxford University Press Canada, 2000.

Kenneally, Rhona Richman, and Johanne Sloan (Eds.). *Expo 67: Not Just a Souvenir*. Toronto: University of Toronto Press, 2010.

Kuffert, L. B. *A Great Duty: Canadian Responses to Modern Life and Mass Culture 1939–1967*. Montreal and Kingston: McGill-Queen's University Press, 2003.

LaMarsh, Judy. *Memoirs of a Bird in a Gilded Cage*. Toronto: McClelland & Stewart, 1969.

Larson, Erik. *The Devil in the White City*. New York: Vintage Books, 2004.

Lévesque, René. *Memoirs*. Translated by Philip Stratford. Toronto: McClelland & Stewart, 1986.

Loiselle, André. *Cinema as History: Michel Brault and Modern Quebec*. Toronto: Toronto International Film Festival Group, 2007.

Lortie, André (Ed.). *The 60s: Montreal Thinks Big*. Canadian Centre for Architecture, Montreal/Douglas & McIntyre, Vancouver and Toronto, 2004.

McKenna, Brian, and Susan Purcell. *Drapeau*. Clarke, Irwin & Company Limited, 1980.

Miedema, Gary R. *For Canada's Sake: Public Religion, Centennial Celebrations, and the Re-making of Canada in the 1960s.* Montreal and Kingston: McGill-Queen's University Press, 2006.

Newman, Peter C. *The Distemper of Our Times.* McClelland & Stewart, 1968.

Owram, Doug. *Born at the Right Time: A History of the Baby Boom Generation.* Toronto: University of Toronto Press, 1996.

Palmer, Bryan D. *Canada's 1960s: The Ironies of Identity in a Rebellious Era.* Toronto: University of Toronto Press, 2009.

Pearson, Lester B. *Mike: The Memoirs of the Rt. Hon. Lester B. Pearson, Volume 3: 1957–1968.* Toronto: University of Toronto Press, 1975.

Pearlstein, Rick. *Nixonland: The Rise of a President and the Fracturing of America.* New York: Scribner, 2008.

Pevere, Geoff, and Greig Dymond. *Mondo Canuck: A Canadian Pop Culture Odyssey.* Toronto: Prentice-Hall, 1996.

Poliquin, Daniel. *In The Name of the Father: An Essay on Quebec Nationalism.* Translated by Don Winkler. Vancouver/Toronto: Douglas & McIntyre, 2001.

———. *René Lévesque* (Extraordinary Canadians Series). Toronto: The Penguin Group (Canada), 2009.

Prévost, Robert. *Montreal: A History.* Translated by Elizabeth Mueller and Robert Chodos. Toronto: McClelland & Stewart, 1993.

Ricard, François. *La génération lyrique: essai sur la vie and l'oeuvre des premiers-nés du baby-boom.* Montreal: Boreal, 1992.

Ritchie, Charles. *The Siren Years: A Canadian Diplomat Abroad 1937–1945.* McClelland & Stewart, 2001.

———. *Diplomatic Passport: More Undiplomatic Diaries 1946–1962.* McClelland & Stewart, 2001.

———. *Storm Signals: More Undiplomatic Diaries 1962–1971.* McClelland & Stewart, 2001.

Rydell, Robert W. *World of Fairs: The Century of Progress Expositions.* Chicago: University of Chicago Press, 1993.

Safdie, Moshe. *Beyond Habitat by 20 Years*, Special Anniversary Edition. Montreal: Tundra Books, 1987.

Schachter, Larry. *A Park Avenue Odyssey.* Self-published, 2008.

Simmins, Geoffrey (Ed.). *Documents in Canadian Architecture.* Peterborough: Broadview Press Ltd, 1992.

Stursberg, Peter. *Diefenbaker: Leadership Lost 1962–67.* Toronto: University of Toronto Press, 1976.

———. *Roland Michener: The Last Viceroy.* Toronto: McGraw-Hill Ryerson Limited, 1989.

Taylor, Charles. *Six Journeys: A Canadian Pattern.* Toronto: House of Anansi, 1977.

———. *Radical Tories: The Conservative Tradition in Canada.* House of Anansi, 2006.

Tremblay, Michel. *The Red Notebook.* Translated by Sheila Fischman. Vancouver: Talonbooks, 2004.

Vance, Jonathan F. *A History of Canadian Culture: From Petroglyphs to Product, Circuses to the CBC...* Toronto: Oxford University Press, 2009.

Watson, Patrick. *This Hour Has Seven Decades.* Toronto: McArthur & Company, 2004.

MAGAZINES, HISTORICAL PERIODICALS, THESES AND LECTURES

Anderson, David, and Viviane Gosselin. "Private and Public Memories of Expo 67: A Case Study of Recollections of Montreal's World's Fair, 40 Years After the Event." *Museum and Society*, March 2008. http://www2.le.ac.uk/departments/museum-studies/museumsociety/documents/volumes/andersongosselin.pdf

Anderson, Virginia. "Locating the Map: Jasper Johns, Buckminister Fuller, and the 1967 Expo Lecture." *Mapping and Locative Practices* (Northwestern University), April 29, 2006.

————. "The Making of Modern Montreal: From the Iroquois to Expo." Lecture, Harvard University Art Museums, January 30, 2008.

artscanada magazine, various months, 1967.

Bédard, Claude. *How the Expo 67 Site Rose from the Waters of the St. Lawrence: A Fascinating Voyage into a Forgotten Piece of History.* Monograph; translated into English; courtesy Yves Jasmin.

Charbonneau, Annie-France (project manager). *Dernière Heure, Édition Spéciale: Hommage à Jean Drapeau 1916–1999*, 2000.

Delaney, Marshall (Robert Fulford). "Expo controls design: should our cities do the same?" *Saturday Night*, May 1967.

Dumas, Michel. *Public Relations at Montreal's Expo 67 as Seen in the Light of a Model of Quality for World Exhibitions.* Master's thesis, Boston University, Boston, 1972.

Heintzman, Ralph. "Political Space and Economic Space: Quebec and the Empire of the St. Lawrence." *Journal of Canadian Studies*, vol. 29, no. 2, October 1994.

Kahn, Jr., E. J. "Our Far-Flung Correspondents: Expo." *The New Yorker*, June 10, 1967.

Kappler, Frank, and Yael Joel. "Film Revolution at Expo 67." *Life*, vol. 63, no. 2, July 14, 1967, pp. 20–28b.

Kauffman, Mark, and Michael Rougier. "Tomorrow Soars in at Expo 67." *Life*, vol. 62, no. 17, April 28, 1967, pp. 32–41.

Kröller, Eva-Marie. "Expo 67: Canada's Camelot?" *Canadian Literature*, Spring-Summer 1997. http://faculty.arts.ubc.ca/emkroller/PAPERS/CAMELOT.PDF

Michener, Wendy. "Where's it all happening this year? In film, Baby." *Maclean's*, June 1967.

Miller, Jerry. "Expo 67: Search for Order." *Canadian Architect*, vol. 12, May 1967.

Monière, Denis, and Robert Comeau (Eds.). *L'Expo 67, 40 ans plus tard*, special issue of *Bulletin d'histoire politique*, vol. 17, no. 1, Autumn 2008.

Morgenstern, Joe. "Expo: The Point Is Pictures." *Newsweek*, July 17, 1967.

Morrisroe, Patricia. "The Death and Life of Perry Ellis." *New York Magazine*, August 11, 1986.

Richler, Mordecai. "Notes on Expo." *The New York Review of Books*, vol. 9, no. 4, September 14, 1967.

Robert, Mario. *La bataille de l'Île Notre-Dame, 1963*. Monograph; in French; courtesy Yves Jasmin, no date.

Rogers, Randal Arthur. *Man and His World: An Indian, a Secretary and a Queer Child. Expo 67 and the Nation in Canada*. Master's thesis, Concordia University, Montreal, August 1999, http://spectrum.library.concordia.ca/923/1/MQ43681.pdf.

Shatnoff, Judith. "Expo 67: A Multiple Vision," *Film Quarterly*, Autumn 1967.

Stenson, Bruno Paul. *(A) Man and His (Expanding) World: Jean Drapeau's Evolving Enthusiasm for Expo 67*. Master's thesis, Concordia University, Montreal, April 2003.

van Ginkel, Blanche Lemco. "International Universal Exhibition: 'A Concept,'" January 1963; courtesy of Blanche Lemco van Ginkel.

NEWSPAPERS

The Gazette (Montreal)
The Globe and Mail
The Montreal Star
The New York Times
The Toronto Daily Star

FILM

A Filmed Introduction to the Critical Path Method: How Man Built His World in 34 Months. Jean-Claude Huot producer, 1967. (Videotape; courtesy of Jean-Claude Huot).

Expo 67: Back to the Future. F. M. Morrison, director; Olenka Demianchuk, producer. CBC Home Video, 2004. (DVD)

The Champions. Donald Brittain, writer-director-producer. National Film Board of Canada, 1986. (DVD)

WEBSITES

Library and Archives Canada. "Cabinet Conclusions," www.collectionscanada.gc.ca/databases/conclusions/index-e_html.

Library and Archives Canada. "Man and His World ... A Vitual Experience," www. collectionscanada.gc.ca/expo/053302_e.html.

Stanton, Jeffrey. "Expo 67—Montreal World's Fair," www.westland.net/expo67 (updated November 11, 2006).

WHO'S WHO

Philippe de Gaspé Beaubien, director of operations, Expo 67; "the mayor of Expo"

Pierre de Bellefeuille, director of exhibitions, Expo 67

Paul Bienvenu, Expo 67's first commissioner general, a short-lived appointment

Cecil Carsley, Expo 67's first deputy commissioner general, another short-lived appointment

Gretta Chambers, Montreal journalist and commentator

Lionel Chevrier, former Liberal minister who was the official greeter for state visitors to Expo 67

Colonel Edward Churchill, director of installations, Expo 67

Jean Cournoyer, Expo 67 labour troubleshooter

Jean-Claude Delorme, legal counsel and secretary

Jean Drapeau, mayor of Montreal

John Diefenbaker, Conservative prime minister of Canada, 1957–63; his government started the Expo ball rolling

Mark Drouin, Conservative senator who first publicly articulated Canada's desire to host Expo

Pierre Dupuy, veteran diplomat who became Expo's commissioner general

Graeme Ferguson, Canadian filmmaker whose work was represented at Expo

Édouard Fiset, chief architect at Expo 67

Krystyne (Romer) Griffin, *maîtresse de maison* at the Pavillon d'Honneur, where the visiting dignitaries were wined and dined

Abbé Lionel Groulx, Drapeau mentor and the godfather of French-Canadian nationalism

Yves Jasmin, director of information, advertising and public relations, Expo 67

Daniel Johnson, premier of Quebec, 1966–68

Judy LaMarsh, secretary of state and in charge of the Centennial Commission; not a big fan of Expo management

Réne Lévesque, former provincial Liberal minister and broadcaster, soon to become leader of the separatist Parti Québécois

Diana Thébaud Nicholson, held jobs in protocol and operations at Expo 67

Lester B. Pearson, Liberal prime minister of Canada, 1963–68; his government inherited the Expo file and presided at its triumph

G. Gale Rediker, director of finance and administration

Claude Robillard, city planner of Montreal who was named Expo's first chief planner

Moshe Safdie, architect who was part of the early planning and design group at Expo; the visionary behind Habitat 67, one of Expo's signature buildings

Corinne Sévigny, widow of Pierre Sévigny, who worked hard to ensure her husband received proper recognition for his early role in the formulation of Expo 67

Pierre Sévigny, Diefenbaker lieutenant in Quebec and Conservative minister; in at the origins of the Montreal bid for Expo 67

Robert Shaw, business executive who became Expo's deputy commissioner general

Michael Snow, multimedia artist whose work was represented at Expo 67

Steven Staples, urban planner who became the chief planner for Expo 67 in autumn 1963 after the departure of Daniel "Sandy" van Ginkel

Blanche Lemco van Ginkel, wife and professional partner of Daniel "Sandy" van Ginkel

Daniel "Sandy" van Ginkel, urban planner who became chief planner of Expo for a brief moment after Claude Robillard relinquished the position; a visionary who helped save Old Montreal

Pierre Elliott Trudeau, minister of justice in the Liberal government at the time of Expo 67, became leader of the Liberal Party and then prime minister of Canada in 1968; many felt that the mood of confidence and optimism engendered by Expo 67 contributed to the Trudeau momentum

Robert Winters, minister of trade and commerce in the Pearson government, with responsibility for the Expo 67 portfolio; he lost a leadership bid to Trudeau at a hard-fought convention

ACKNOWLEDGMENTS

There are many people to thank for their help in the writing of this book, and at the top of the list are my supervising editors, and the people who picked me for the job, Professors Margaret MacMillan and Robert Bothwell. They offered pointed comments as well as encouragement along the way, and I am enormously grateful to them both for handing me this challenge. The team at Penguin/Allen Lane Canada have been especially supportive, and I must single out publishing director Diane Turbide, editorial assistant Justin Stoller, line and copy editor Tara Tovell, and senior production editor Sandra Tooze.

Another invaluable person on both the editorial and personal sides is my friend Julie Rekai Rickerd. Julie followed the progress of the manuscript from beginning stages to the end and never faltered in her enthusiasm and attentiveness to detail. She became a very necessary part of the process, and I mean it when I say I don't think I could have gotten through it without her.

Each of my interview subjects offered generously of their time and interest, but I have to mention a few individuals whose generosity was truly exceptional. Yves Jasmin, who headed public relations, information and marketing at Expo 67 and who today is a prominent Expo archivist, wrote a delightful history of Expo entitled *La petite histoire de l'Expo 67: l'Exposition Universelle et Internationale de Montréal comme vous ne l'avez jamais vue*, which proved an invaluable guide to many of the triumphs, as well as some trials and tribulations, of Expo. But there was no greater guide than the person of Yves, himself, who took me under his wing at the beginning of the process and peppered me with hints, and introductions, and documentation I likely would never have discovered under my own steam. Philippe de Gaspé Beaubien, Andrew Kniewasser and Pierre de Bellefeuille, three other surviving lions of Expo management, gave of their time and insights as well. Steven Staples, who stepped into the role of Expo's chief planner, has offered sage editorial advice and enthusiasm, not to mention his own voluminous collection of Expo-related data. Steven also read a later iteration of the manuscript, for which I am deeply grateful, but I add, as a necessity, that any errors of commission or omission remain mine and mine alone. The Montreal journalist Alan Hustak was also admirably kind and full of tips. Not to forget two *grandes dames* of the Expo family, both candid and fun and altogether helpful, Krystyne Griffin and Diana Thébaud Nicholson, as well as another *grande dame* who persevered mightily so that her late husband would be properly recognized as part of that Expo family— Corinne Sévigny.

I must extend my gratitude to Blanche Lemco van Ginkel, for her interest in the project and the information she provided, and for allowing me to visit her and Sandy van Ginkel in what turned out to be his final months. And I must mention a dear friend and editor, Charles Oberdorf, who bore a dreadful disease stoically but was always giving of both joy and knowledge. Other interview subjects who gave me their valuable insights but have since died include Lester Pearson's policy advisor Tom Kent; Montreal journalist Bill Bantey; and Toronto architects Rod Robbie and Peter Hamilton.

Special thanks to Bruno Paul Stenson and Michel Dumas for allowing me to read their Masters' theses (and to Bruno, as well, for some timely advice) and to Professor Virginia Anderson for sending me her lecture on the U.S.A. Pavilion. I must also thank my research assistants: Gareth

Newfield in Ottawa; Liron Taub in Toronto; Steven Serels in Montreal; and Alex Comber in Ottawa. Likewise praise and gratitude to Elsie Del Bianco at the Trinity College Library, University of Toronto; Jane Lynch and Anne-Marie Crotty at the Robarts Library, University of Toronto; Lynn Lafontaine and Janet Murray at the Special Collections branch of the Library and Archives Canada (LAC-BAC); Mike Hamilton, Don Skiepowich, Media Commons, John P. Robarts Library, University of Toronto; and Robert D. Hamilton, archivist, The Woodbridge Company Limited.

On the long list of those who aided in so many ways, and to whom I will be indebted always are: Peter Aykroyd; The Hon. Louise Arbour; Greg Baeker; Richard P. Barham; Nan-b de Gaspé Beaubien; Gloria Bishop; John Bishop; Roger Blais; Margaret Break; Jane Pequegnat Burns; Paul Chamberlain; Gretta Chambers; Alastair Cheng; Bernard Chevrier; The Rt. Hon. Adrienne Clarkson; Ramsay Cook; Gail Corbett; Jean Cournoyer; Ramsay Derry; Patricia Desjardins; Prudence Emery; Peter Erlendson; Mark Erwin; Cathy Fauquier; Graeme Ferguson; Jeremy Ferguson; George Fetherling; Graham Fraser; Bev Hargraft; V. Tony Hauser; Ralph Heintzman; John Hillier; Norman Hillmer; Andrew Hoffman; Jean-Claude Huot; Mary Jolliffe; Bruce Kidd; Matthew Koyounian; Roger D. Landry; Fred Langan; Laurier LaPierre; Portia Leggat; Pierre LePage; Barry Lord; Ann Lukits; Gar MacInnis; Ann and Harry Malcolmson; John McGreevy; Deirdre McIlwraith; Marianne McKenna; Lee MacLaren; Bruce McNiven; Heather and Peter Meltzer; Donna Mergler; Jerry Miller; Fraser Mills; Charles Pachter; Helga Plumb; John Polanyi; Michael Porritt; Steve Quinlan; Jack Rabinovitch; Arlene Perly Rae; James Ramsay; David Rayside; Judy Rebick; Dennis Reid; Larry Wayne Richards; Christopher Rickerd; Jean Thérèse Riley; Tony Robinow; Ron Rosenes; Jean-Louis Roux; Moshe Safdie; Errol Saldanha; Matthias Samuel; Johanna Schneller; Monique Simard; Michael Snow; Soft Comp (Edward, Wan and Wei); Cara Spittal; Mark Starowicz; Helga Stephenson; Susan Swan; Ashley

Symons; William Thorsell; Stephen Traviss; The Rt. Hon. John Turner; John Uren; Patrick Watson; Jill Wykes; Moses Znaimer; and John E. Zucchi.

To everyone, many thanks. And to those who visited Expo 67, may this book bring back happy memories.

March 2012

INDEX